THEATER CRITICISMS

By Stanley Kauffmann

Novels

The Hidden Hero
The Tightrope
A Change of Climate
Man of the World

Criticism

THEATER

Persons of the Drama
Theater Criticisms

FILM

A World on Film
Figures of Light
Living Images
Before My Eyes

Editor

(With Bruce Henstell)
American Film Criticism: From the Beginnings to *Citizen Kane*

Memoirs

Albums of Early Life

Stanley Kauffmann

THEATER CRITICISMS

Performing Arts Journal Publications
New York

Library of Congress Cataloging in Publication Data
Theater Criticisms
Library of Congress Catalog Card No.: 83-62617
ISBN: 0-933826-57-5 (cloth)
ISBN: 0-933826-58-3 (paper)

Graphic Design: Gautam Dasgupta

Printed in the United States of America

Publication of this book has been made possible in part by grants received from the National Endowment for the Arts, Washington, D.C., a federal agency, and the New York State Council on the Arts.

To Giles and Ann Playfair

Contents

Preface

This book contains theater reviews and essays that were written between 1975—when *Persons of the Drama*, my first collection of theater criticism, was published—and 1983. As before, I have chosen material that, because of subject or comment or both, may have continuing interest.

For ten years, until September 1979, I was both the theater and film critic of *The New Republic*. Then, while continuing there as film critic, I became theater critic of *Saturday Review*. Of the pieces following, those not otherwise identified first appeared in *The New Republic* (except for three reviews written in July and August 1982 when *Saturday Review* was in abeyance, which have not before been published). Within the three sections of the book, the order is chronological, though there are a few self-explanatory exceptions. Footnotes and postscripts have been added where needed.

Since 1966, I have also published four collections of film criticism, mostly taken from *The New Republic*, and have been told by readers that, among other uses, the books serve as guides to films that are "revived" in theaters or on television. Collections of theater criticism have no precisely parallel use; when one of the plays discussed is revived, the new production must in some way alter it. For this very reason, collections of theater criticism have, I think, a special importance that more than compensates for their lack of "utility." In a sense, one part of the past would not exist without them.

Of course such books are not primarily chronicles. Other kinds of books chronicle theater events more completely and objectively. Collections of performance criticism are books of witness. Surely they have some use as reference; and, like any other critics, performance critics can help to illuminate works, can test and revise and extend criteria. But the unique reward of performance criticism is in its immediacy and the distillation of that immediacy, in the salvaging of pertinences.

To say this is not to assume that I fulfill all these expectations, only to acknowledge that I have engaged them. But I can't see much point in being a critic and engaging less.

For much help, thanks go to Martin Peretz and his associates at *The New Republic*; to Carll Tucker, Henry Weil, and Joshua Gilder, formerly of *Saturday Review*; to Carl Brandt, agent and friend; to Bonnie Marranca and Gautam Dasgupta, publishers extraordinary. Thanks always to L.C.K.

S.K.

New York
September 1983

Productions

Travesties

(November 22, 1975)

John Wood is a scintillating actor, epitomizing an English tradition that includes Rex Harrison and Robert Flemyng and that goes back through Granville Barker at least to David Garrick. This is an acting tradition that masters
high comedy and then moves *through* it, not past it, to serious drama, even tragedy, exploring the dark places with keen, anti-sententious, poignant sensibility. (Although Garrick is probably remembered chiefly as a tragedian because of
the *Hamlet* episode in *Tom Jones*, in fact he played comedy much more often
than tragedy.) Wood, with Roman profile, with lean grace and with converse
charming awkwardness when he wants it, enters like the best news of a centu-
ries-old culture, overwhelming us with carefully controlled carelessness, announcing that from the locus of his talent and tradition he will proceed to
shape the world on stage. He does what all fine actors do: he makes us feel confident and apprehensive—confident that he will never falter in command, apprehensive that he will detonate explosions outside the range of our usual lives.
    His electric body cuts the shapes of his character's feelings. He uses language
the way Baryshnikov uses space. The voice itself is unique. A good deal of the
time it is chordal: we can hear *simultaneously* a higher and a lower register.
Then, as he chooses, Wood uses the light or the lower, returning eventually to
the double middle. At first we suspect that something may be wrong. Is the
doubleness a hoarseness of the tenor? No, it is his whole voice, unstrained,
which showers us with the pleasures of musical meaning right through to the
end.
    In Tom Stoppard's new play Wood is Henry Carr, the member of the British
consular staff in Zurich, 1917, who figured in James Joyce's life (thus in Richard
Ellmann's biography). Stoppard's story, fantasizing on fact, presents Carr first
as an old codger reminiscing about the great days in Zurich. After a brief first
scene with others in the Zurich Public Library, Wood bursts out on to the
forestage in dressing gown, slippers and hat, freighted with crankiness and
venom and glee, lights a cigarette (he smokes incessantly, dropping matches

and ashes in his pocket), shuffles rapidly to a piano at the side, whams it a bit, then comes back to the forestage and goes into a monologue—four and a half pages in the published script. I wish it had been forty: not only because Wood is wonderful but because the play starts to go downhill as soon as he finishes. Then he sheds his robe and hat, pulls the slipper-covers off his shoes, and in elegant 1917 dress steps out of the figurative chimney-corner from which the old crock has been surveying the past into a manner—English, dandified, serene—that is itself a code of ethics. Through the play Wood moves back and forth from 1917 to old age, but that is the least of his varieties; *within* each of those ages he discriminates spectrums of pathos and wit that are almost physically pleasurable.

But when are we going to see Wood in a good play? All he has done previously in the U.S. are an earlier Stoppard play, the fleetingly clever *Rosencrantz and Guildenstern Are Dead*, and Gillette's *Sherlock Holmes*. Glittering as I thought him in both, I would have an inadequate idea of Wood's resources if I hadn't seen him in the Royal Shakespeare Company production of Gorky's *Enemies* in London, 1971, turning the drunken Yakov into a character of Chekhovian depth. In 1970 he had played Richard Rowan in the Royal Shakespeare Company production of Joyce's *Exiles*, directed by Harold Pinter, and if I could have afforded it, I'd have flown over to see the play. Wood's career has included much Shakespeare of course. And Stoppard writes for him, which is understandable on Stoppard's part but circumscribing for us.

Because Stoppard is still only a bright, juvenile sprinter. His brightness includes an eye for striking situations and an ear for witty diction at a level slightly higher than that of general English articulateness. He is juvenile because, although he seems to be dealing with such matters as fate (*R & G*), moral philosophy (*Jumpers*), and art *v.* politics (*Travesties*), he is merely using his subjects as trampolines for undergraduate acrobatics: getting credit for penetrating these subjects when he is only bouncing off them. He is a sprinter because he starts fast and finishes quickly: he plunges into promising situations and then breaks their promises, too shortwinded to fulfill them artistically and intellectually.

He was bright enough, for instance, to note that Joyce and Lenin and Tristan Tzara, father of Dada, were all in Zurich at the same time; and to imagine that they were all acquainted (which they were not); and to choose as his focal point this Henry Carr who was in a Zurich production of *The Importance of Being Earnest* for which Joyce was business manager and who got involved with Joyce in furious quarrels and lawsuits over trifles.

Stoppard's method has been figuratively to let Wilde's comedy and *Ulysses*, which was being written at the time, soak into one another in a purée of parody and cross-reference, laced with some volatile Wildean imitations of his own. (Carr's manservant informs him that social revolution has broken out in Russia, and Carr assumes that, for past grievances, the masters have taken up arms against the servants.) When I read *Travesties* some months ago the first thirty pages or so seemed to bubble in my hand, whizzing with vaudeville and caprice; but it soon became clear that the play had nothing to do *but* bubble, that it wasn't heading anywhere, and the bubbles flattened. By the second of the two acts Stoppard began to realize that he had to find some place to go in order to justify the first act, so he whipped up a feeble undergraduate controversy about the validity of art in the presence of political urgencies, and he spun it around a bit to fill out the structure. Here are old Carr's last words, the last of the play:

> I learned three things in Zurich during the war. I wrote them down. Firstly, you're either a revolutionary or you're not, and if you're not you might as well be an artist as anything else. Secondly, if you can't be an artist, you might as well be a revolutionary . . . I forget the third thing.

That is bankruptcy trying to put a brave face on it.

Matters are worsened in proof because of the casting in this RSC production. Peter Wood (no relation, I think, to his leading actor) who directed the first Ionesco and Pinter in London some twenty years ago, has deftness in the staging of this free-wheeling kind of play, but he has done the same thing here that he did with his American reproduction of Stoppard's *Jumpers* last year: he has cast it inadequately. The best we get from them is passable dullness—Harry Towb (Lenin), Frances Cuka (Mrs. Lenin), John Bennett (Carr's servant). But Beth Morris (a librarian), Tim Curry (Tzara), James Booth (Joyce) and Meg Wynn Owen (Carr's sister) are painfully bad. (And Owen gets to murder a whole Shakespeare sonnet.) The long scenes when John Wood is offstage seem interminable—wet prankishness—and when he is on with the others, their incompetence is even more clear. The evening is like Beverly Sills in flashy minor Donizetti with a scratch supporting cast.

And, speaking of music, I don't understand the anachronisms of the incidental score. Care has been taken with period costumes, but one of the songs played in 1917 is "Louise" from Maurice Chevalier's *Innocents of Paris* made in 1929.

The title *Travesties* is, I suppose, meant to be descriptive of the method of the play and the vanity of human wishes. But Stoppard's script is only a travesty of the travesties that might have been there. On the evidence so far John Wood is a much more important artist than the author to whom he is devoted.

Pacific Overtures

(February 7, 1976)

Pacific Overtures is one of the most exquisite textile exhibitions I've ever seen. The setting is Japan, and the costume shapes are what we would expect from prints and films, but the textiles chosen by or woven for Florence Klotz are beautiful, ravishing in design and texture. Klotz has often done costumes for Harold Prince, who produced and directed this show, but has never done better.

Boris Aronson, now unquestionably the oldest scenic designer at work in the American theater and a master, has done almost as well.* In most of his work, which has ranged widely in style, Aronson has been able to pick a mode—the romanticism of *Fiddler on the Roof* or the constructivism of *Company*—and then fly. I feel that the canons of Japanese design have constricted him just a little. Nonetheless he has come up with such ideas as a permanent sky backdrop made of immense screens, instead of a seamless cloth, with white clouds on a light beige sky. Exhilarating.

Obviously if a review begins with comment on costume and scenery, the show itself lacks something. *Pacific Overtures* lacks so much that I want to emphasize its virtues which also include some spruce lyrics by Stephen Sondheim and a few adequate tunes by Sondheim delicately orchestrated by Jonathan Tunick. The opening number ("In the middle of the sea / We float"), which sets the quality of Japan before Commodore Perry's arrival, is lovely, well staged by Prince and well choreographed by Patricia Birch. A sparkling show ought to follow that number.

But it doesn't. What we get is a desultory account of the transformation of Japan following Perry's visit in 1853, historically questionable and theatrically flabby, painfully straining to patch in various Japanese authenticities at the same time that it painfully strains for Broadway "numbers." In between the Kabuki snippets there are such items as a duet for two men walking through the woods and composing verses alternately or a duet for an old man and himself as a boy recalling a conversation he heard between Perry and Japanese officials. Both songs are cute and deadly.

Thematically the show has no base. Is it supposed to be telling us that the West ravished Japan? That Japan would still be a tranquil little (murderous) state if it weren't for the U.S.? Hardly credible. Then is it just telling us about the changes of the last century? Pretty commonplace stuff—in Japan or Carpathia. Anyway, there is no protagonist of interest to follow, there is no drama other than hoked-up intensifications of inevitabilities. And since the women are played by men, in Kabuki tradition, there isn't even any sex appeal—particularly since all these men are homely! An excellent score could make us forgive a lot, but most of the songs, which ought to be the stars, are only serviceable background music.

The show gave employment to, I'd guess, half of the Japanese-American actors in existence. Only one of them is remarkable—Mako, the shaven-headed man who is the narrator and plays several roles. Not the least of his contribu-

---

*Boris Aronson died on March 16, 1980, aged seventy-nine.

tions is that he kept Yul Brynner out of the part.

In the career of Harold Prince *Pacific Overtures* is an unsuccessful episode but a concentric one. During that career, which has mostly been concerned with Broadway musicals, he has increasingly tried to bend big musicals to some kind of contemporary pertinence while still trying to make them hits. I'm not urging philanthropy. *Pacific Overtures* must have cost close to a million dollars. Some people had to put it up and naturally would like their money back, plus. I'm simply pointing out that, in recent years, social urges have been grafted on to organisms designed to make money, by college-educated Broadway and film and TV producers who want to feel culturally good at the same time that they knock out successes.

Prince, often with Sondheim, has produced shows derived from Ingmar Bergman and Kazantzakis and Sholom Aleichem and Plautus, has tried to deal with contemporary moralities and cultural shifts (*Company* and *Follies*), has drawn on avant-garde theater to resuscitate a previous failure (*Candide*). Sometimes he has tremendous hits, and who would wish him anything else? But he has become an epitome of the man who swims with one foot on shore and who, in our culture, sometimes gets swimming medals.

The Good Woman of Setzuan

(March 13, 1976)

Andrei Serban is the greatly gifted young Romanian director who was brought to New York by Ellen Stewart of La Mama Theater and who developed a repertory company at that theater. In 1974 that company presented *Trilogy*, splendid productions of Serban's versions of three Greek plays. Serban and his company have since traveled through Europe with these plays, even daring to take them to Athens. (Athenians to whom I spoke last month were as enthusiastic about the productions as I had been.) Serban's company returned to La Mama this winter with two of the three Greek plays, slightly altered but still very fine. When I asked him why he had dropped the third play, *Medea*, he said he had been doing it for five years, had no fresh ideas with which to keep working on it, and didn't want to carry a mere staple item.

Last year the company gave a few public dress rehearsals of their new production, Brecht's *Good Woman of Setzuan*. They use Eric Bentley's familiar translation with new and vigorous music by Elizabeth Swados and a good setting by Jun Maeda—an alterable two-tiered facade across the back of the large playing space. The show was called a "work in progress" and that's exactly what I thought it: an interesting, internally consistent proposal for handling the play. Now it is "fully" presented, and I'm sorry to report that it's pretty much still the "work in progress" more confidently done. It's as if the notes for a production had been rendered more legibly without being fully realized.

Of course I have a disadvantage with the play itself. For me *The Good Woman of Setzuan* is lesser Brecht. His best plays crystallize some aspects of the modern consciousness in new dramatic modes; his lesser ones are explicit, didactic, linear and relatively unresonant. Set in Brecht's imaginary China, *The Good Woman* tells the story of a good-hearted prostitute who is the one person in her city to be hospitable to three gods who arrive incognito. They reward her with money, with which she buys a tobacco shop, and her new prosperity brings leeches. To protect herself she has to adopt a male alter ego, tough and ruthless. Her lover makes her pregnant, and that (one may say) blows up her disguise. At the end the gods permit her to be tough just once a month to protect herself; and Brecht coyly leaves it up to the audience to decide whether the world or human nature must be changed in order for good people to be wholly good.

The play is engaging for about ten times the time it takes to read the above précis: the rest is increasingly wearisome working-out. Serban has faced the thinness of the play (why he chose to face it is another question) and has rendered it as a super child's story. The irony of the mortals' relationship to the gods, which is the only locus of possible depth, is absorbed into Serban's almost dainty allegorical mode. All the roles are played with conscious, sometimes charming "pantomime" chinoiserie. But nothing really affects us deeply because all we get is a pleasant pattern, not a dramatic experience. Add to this that many of the lyrics are incomprehensibly sung, and it removes the performance further into balletic abstraction.

Serban's best theatrical idea was the use of rods that progressively form a pattern on the stage floor during the performance. From time to time, one or another character lays a six-foot wooden rod on the floor in relation to other rods, the whole gradually becoming a maze through which the actors have to move. At the very end the heroine gathers up all these rods, thus symbolically clearing away the ethical maze that the people have created and shouldering those ethical burdens herself. In another play the device might have seemed intrusive: here at least it provides some texture.

The rewards of the performance were accessible, I think, only to those who had seen *Trilogy*: the pleasure of perceiving these performers' range. This is especially true of Priscilla Smith who is the company's Electra and Andromache and was the Medea—full-throated and primal—and who plays the prostitute with dancer-like lightness and the other self with Chaplinesque villainy.

Mrs. Warren's Profession

(March 20, 1976)

One of Bernard Shaw's *Unpleasant Plays* provides a pleasant surprise. Joseph Papp's production of *Mrs. Warren's Profession* is very unevenly cast but is nonetheless something of a treat.

The author tells us that the play, written in 1894, was intended to force home the truth that prostitution is caused by capitalist abuse of working women, "not by female depravity and male licentiousness." Everyone knows that the play was a scandal when first produced and is utterly unscandalous today, but the play is in fact helped by the fading of the scandal, even of the thesis. (Conditions for working women, for all workers, are now paradise compared with what they were then.) *Mrs. Warren's Profession* now stands on its own, so to speak, as a work of some art and continuing life.

This in spite of the casting of Ruth Gordon in the title role. Gordon, born in 1896, a theater star since the 1920s (best-known in films as the witch in *Rosemary's Baby*), would never have been right for Mrs. Warren even when she was young enough to play this woman "between forty and fifty." She never had the requisite sexual aura. More, she has never really been an authentic actress, only an increasingly accomplished trickster. But given that Papp has his (imperceptible) reasons for casting her in the part, give Gordon too some credit for her tricks. Her mannerisms are as annoying as ever—the sidewise hitching, the drawling blend of Massachusetts and Manhattan accents—but she knows how to get and keep attention. See the way she tosses a biscuit in the air with the last line of Act One; hear the way she drops her voice at key moments to make you listen harder. It's the George Arliss school, alive and fairly flourishing.

The production is righted because the leading role is Vivie, her daughter, and Lynn Redgrave is fine. Her accent is too coarse for the education she is said to have received, but she plays with clarity and strength. Edward Herrmann is delightful as the affectionate idler, Frank Gardner. From his film appearances, even such a good one as the homespun mechanic in *The Great Waldo Pepper*, I would never have expected this high-comedy finish. Ron Randell is most appealing as the kindly old esthete Praed. The likable Philip Bosco has a hard time making the libertine Crofts as urbanely detestable as he should be. Milo O'Shea is much too Irish and broad for Frank's father, the social-climbing clergyman.

Yet the strengths of this spotty cast have been enough for the director, Gerald Freedman. I haven't been a devotee of his, but here he has at least had the sense to (in a way) simply stand aside and release the Shavian dynamics, the Mozartian energy that drives not only through the structure of scene and act and play but of every line. Freedman shows some response to the process by which, in Shaw, electrons make atoms that make cells that make the body.

Some of the dramaturgy, the sheer traffic management, is much less adroit than in later Shaw; and Mrs. Warren herself thins out a bit at the end into a mere Mom instead of a Force-Who-Is-Also-a-Mom. But in intellectual terms it's wonderful to see how Shaw, as against his later and more complex plays, makes a full work of one theme by ringing all the possible harmonics in it. And that fact connects with this play's continuing vitality as an artwork; it gives us a set of late-Victorian attitudes around a central issue, but each of those attitudes is embodied in a person of at least some interest. Today the play centers on the tensions between them as human beings; the once-topical issue is now simply the catalyst for continuingly relevant relations in interesting people.

For a chief instance of Shaw's art here, look at Vivie. One of the lesser theatrical tractarians of the time might have made her a "normal," romantically inclined girl who is hardened by the discovery that her mother has been and is a successful madam. Shaw *begins* Vivie as a vigorous H.G. Wellsian New Woman. She feels only sympathy and admiration when she discovers what her mother has done; but she steels herself against her mother when she learns that the brothel-keeping still goes on. The difference between these two reactions implies some hypocrisy in Vivie (everything would have been all right if the whoring were over) which deepens her humanness; and her resolve for independence at the end shows her, in her own way, to be her mother's daughter. Her moment of recognition makes her more clear-sightedly what she was at the start, instead of converting her into something else—a mode of dramatic daring that Shaw learned, and learned well, from Ibsen.

About the settings: David Mitchell designed four good realistic ones, as he did earlier this season for *Trelawny of the 'Wells'*. This made me realize that there is now only one theater in New York doing plays that require four full sets, the subsidized Beaumont.

Knock Knock

(March 20, 1976)

I went to Jules Feiffer's new comedy *Knock Knock* Off-Broadway some weeks ago and, for the first time at a Feiffer work, was pretty thoroughly bored. It got rave reviews, hailing it for what it claims to do rather than what it does. Now the same production has moved uptown where I saw it again and where the added glare of Broadway shines behind it to show the seemingly delicate fabric as the merest cheesecloth.

Two middle-aged Jewish men live in a house in the woods—an Odd Couple gone pastoral. One is a philosophical materialist, the other a romantic. By rubbing a lamp they've had around the house, one of them gets three wishes—and gets the genie with it, who appears in various guises. One of the results—I think it's a result—is the arrival of Joan of Arc, complete with (comic) voices and armor and banner and sword. She wants the men to accompany her on a mission to the "emperor." Eventually there is a predictable switch in the viewpoints of the two men, with Joan stripped of her Joan-ness and made a household drudge.

All this is sustained, which is not the right word, by a lot of stage business and mechanical devices: much cooking and eating, cascades of steam to cover magical appearances and breakaway walls and the levitation of Joan at the end.

This stuff is used instead of imagination and wit, just as Feiffer quotes old jokes when his flabby gags and word-play falter. (At both performances that I saw, the biggest laughs came from the old jokes.) Two moments were funny: a parody of a movie-tough-guy card game and a stream of platitudes from Joan as she rises at the end.

There isn't any genuine point; there is just a series of *ad hoc* points, of excuses. There aren't even the true high spirits to make it a consistently entertaining improvisation (in effect). A few years ago Feiffer published a mild sketch called *Cohn of Arc* in the *Partisan Review*. Its mode was incongruency. Here he has just pumped and strained to make the incongruencies go on long enough to pad the sketch into an evening. It's the currently successful Mel Brooks-Woody Allen method of grab-bag comedy: absolutely anything goes if you think it will get some laughs and if the budget will permit it. Feiffer used only four actors and one set; with another $100,000 his play could have been twice as long or anyway twice as complicated.

What I got of any consequence from the play was probably unintentional. It seemed to me that the author of *Little Murders* and *Carnal Knowledge*, sick of urban stew and sexual fray, had fantasized about living cozily off in the woods with an old crony, visited asexually by an asexual girl.

Neil Flanagan, as one of the pair, imitates one sort of Jewish inflection quite well. The other three actors are not adequate. Marshall W. Mason of the Circle Repertory Company, which originated the production, has directed with unfailing awkwardness and small feeling for pace. Comically cluttered sets are always easy for designers, still John Lee Beatty did this one well.

(July 3 & 10, 1976)

When my time comes, I expect to go straight to heaven, no questions asked. I've earned it by seeing Jules Feiffer's poor play *Knock Knock* three times. First, Off-Broadway. I didn't write about it. Then it moved to Broadway, and in a sense, became unavoidable: in order to write about it (which I did, see above) I had to see it again to check on any changes. Now, unprecedently, the producers have changed all four actors and the director. Since I complained about four of these five people, I felt duty-bound to see it again to find out whether it is now any different. It is. It's differently bad.

José Quintero, the new director, has better control of tempo, phrase, and composition than his predecessor. All of the new actors except the drooly John Heffernan are improvements. Ironically, now *both* of the old Jews are played by Irishmen (only one was Irish before); Charles Durning, though unbelievable as a man named Cohn, at least has skill. But the basic trouble with the new cast is that their very professional skills only reveal the threadbareness of the play even further. Lynn Redgrave in particular keeps looking for something to *act* as Joan of Arc. The dumb incompetence of the first Joan didn't expose the inconsequence of the part as mercilessly as Redgrave's competence.

The Lady from the Sea

(April 10, 1976)

Vanessa Redgrave, lovely, a light upon the stage as she is on the screen, joins her sister in the New York theater season. Four weeks ago I wrote of Lynn Redgrave's sturdy performance in *Mrs. Warren's Profession* which (principally) made the production a pleasant surprise. Now Vanessa R.'s lyric performance of Ellida in Ibsen's *The Lady from the Sea* is that production's only stay against disaster.

I admit that I went to this play with considerable fear. Quite apart from its intrinsic quality (of which more later) I've always thought it so allusive and rarefied as to be virtually unactable. (This is even more true, I think, of Ibsen's much superior *When We Dead Awaken*.) I knew something of the stage history of the piece, including Duse's success. But Duse's very success confirmed my feelings. If one can rely on theatrical history at all, then she was an actress who specialized in Soul and Beauty, both spelled with capitals, and she performed for a society that spelled them the same way. I found it hard to imagine how, for a contemporary audience, one could authenticate—with real, physically present people—this drama of a woman who is in the thrall of a mystic marriage to the sea. Despite Redgrave's gifts, and even speculating about improvements in other roles, I still can't imagine it.

Ellida is the young second wife of Dr. Wangel, a gentle middle-aged physician who has two teen-age daughters. (The younger one, Hilde, reappears in *The Master Builder*.) Before she met Wangel, Ellida, herself the daughter of a lighthouse-keeper, had a romance with a mysterious sailor, and they "wed" each other by throwing rings into the sea. He disappeared; eventually she allowed herself to become Mrs. Wangel and came to live in this house above the fjord, still near the sea, still "belonging" to the sailor. She had one child, who she thinks had the sailor's eyes (though the man had been gone for years). Since the child's death she has had no marital relations with Wangel, feeling that she has betrayed the sailor. The sailor suddenly appears one day, claims Ellida as his own, and says he will return next day to take her away. Wangel refuses to "release" Ellida, for her own good. But when the sailor reappears, Wangel does "release" her so that she can choose freely between him and the sailor. With the choice now entirely hers, she chooses her husband (a foretaste of *Candida* here), and the sailor disappears forever.

The central idea—a woman enslaved by her past who is freed to remain as she is by being given freedom of choice—is a blank symbol which can be colored any hue that the reader-spectator brings with him. Many distinguished critics have commented on *The Lady from the Sea* and have found in it everything from analogies with Dante to prescience about Freud. (It was written in 1888.) I have no special quarrel with any of the analyses I know and will even offer the lame tribute that their variety is a compliment to Ibsen. My difference with them is in value judgment, not in analysis. Just because the play is varyingly analyzable; just because many interpretations of Ellida's enslavement and release are possible; just because there is a contrast in the play between a safe pool in which carp live and the wild sea in which people drown; just because the sailor killed his captain long ago and would say only that it was the right thing to do (which Ibsen never clarifies even as metaphor); just because there's a parallel between Ellida and her older stepdaughter who accepts the proposal of an older man; just because many other patterns can be winkled out—it doesn't necessarily follow from all these "becauses" that *The Lady from the Sea* is a good play. One affliction of serious criticism is the belief that if a work can sustain analysis, it's good.

Esthetic experience is something else. The evaluative truth, for me, is that this play is tenuous, strained, and even arbitrarily cobbled in places. A young would-be sculptor, now wooing a Wangel daughter, just happens to have been on a ship with the mysterious sailor and just happens to have heard him make a revealing remark which he now just happens to remember, a device (like others in other realistic Ibsen plays) right out of the nineteenth-century theater of carpentry where the author had labored for eleven years. Tenuousness and strain dominate the subplots of *The Lady*. It's patent that they are meant analogically to the central story, but they are simply not very engaging in themselves; they are mere padding to bulk out a full-length play. As for that central story, Ellida spends most of the first three acts remembering something that happened long ago. This is a very different theatrical conception from *Hedda Gabler*; she too is in the thrall of her past, doomed by it, but with the very start of the play, that doom begins to be dramatically articulated.

Another point—a criticism that Strindberg might have made in the vein of his criticism of *A Doll's House*. It seems to me that the crucial action of the play is Wangel's, not Ellida's. It is he who goes through the greatest transformation, a conventional and deeply loving husband who is moved to grant his wife her freedom so that she may make a free choice between him and another man. True, it is she who then has to make that choice; but she has been shown as a person of greater imaginative reach, so the making of that choice is little temperamental wrench for her, even though it's an emotional one. The real character enlargement is Wangel's, not hers; the whole play can be seen as a drama of his belated maturation—possibly it should be called *The Husband of the Lady from the Sea*. The reason that *A Doll's House* and *Hedda Gabler* end so much less happily than this play is that the husbands in those two plays are incapable of growth.

Agree with my estimate of *The Lady* or not, still you would likely agree that any performance of it runs a constant risk of slipping into the unbearably precious. That, at least, does not happen: because of Vanessa Redgrave's purity, concentration, grace. It's not possible to believe in Ellida any more than one can believe in a character in *Everyman* or *The Faerie Queene*. Redgrave's job is harder than it would be (figuratively) in those works because Ibsen has surrounded her abstraction with detailed realistic characterization. Redgrave seems to realize this and seems to abstract *herself* without any touch of posing. She speaks quietly and moves gently, *confiding* her story to Wangel rather than displaying her delicacy. (She never really raises her voice until the last act.) Redgrave is a large woman with immediate stage command; I've rarely seen that command used so easily for intimacy and sensitivity.

But then there is Pat Hingle, the Wangel—pedestrian and trite, just another slice of Dear Old Dad in any domestic American play. One of the problems in using an English actress in America is how to surround her with accents that don't make her sound alien; in this regard Hingle was an especially poor choice. The others in the cast range from the bearable—George Ede as the jack-of-all-arts Ballested, Kimberly Farr as the older daughter—to the utterly unbearable—Richard Lynch as the Stranger (the sailor). It's a hellishly difficult part: he has to walk in and immediately justify everything poetical that has been said about him. Christopher Walken at his best might be able to do it, if he would accept such a small part. Lynch simply hasn't any of the requisite powers.

And Tony Richardson, the director, has handled him especially badly by plunking him into the middle of that wretched Circle in the Square playing oval. Earlier, Richardson has staged the first act at the far end, an effect something like watching a tea party at the distant end of a small race-track. When he comes to an actor who *should* be kept distant, Richardson whams him at us, pores and all. To put it kindly, Richardson is one more director beaten by that theater, which should be razed and rebuilt.

Michael Meyer's translation leaves some flexibility to be desired. When Ellida says at the end that she was blind to Wangel's love, he says: "Your thoughts were directed elsewhere." Couldn't Meyer at least have left out "directed"?

Henry V

(May 15, 1976)

For the past several years the Royal Shakespeare Company of London has been visiting the Brooklyn Academy of Music with new productions. The ones that I've seen have impressed others far more than me. What I saw looked like a few of the better RSC actors surrounded by a kind of second team, directed indifferently (Gorky's *Summer Folk*) or trickily (*Richard II*). Now the RSC has brought *Henry V*, part of a trilogy they have done with both parts of *Henry IV* to celebrate the centenary of their company. This *Henry V* is by far the best production of theirs I've seen in Brooklyn: in some ways it's stunning. But it's a mixed bag—very mixed and decidedly baggy.

The troubles began, I would say, with the choice of this play. In recent years some commentators have tried to show that *Henry V* is not a drama of militaristic patriotism, of war as a country's highest calling and finest test. They have failed, I think. The director of this production, Terry Hands, would like to have it two ways. In his program notes he says that *Henry V* was chosen, in a time of the RSC's and of Britain's troubled circumstances, because it is "upbeat," it is about unity and brotherhood. Then, perhaps, embarrassed by a rah-rah tone, he hastily adds that "the play is full of doubt," as if the presence of doubt would prove modernity. What demonstrates this "doubt"? The fact, says Hands, that the Chorus begins with an apology for the limitations of the theater in dealing with this vast chronicle. But this argument is specious. One might as well argue that Handel was apologizing for his own music when he wrote "O had I Jubal's lyre." That opening Chorus of *Henry V* is Shakespeare's tribute to the way the theater triumphs imaginatively over its merely physical limitations. Hands's insistence on viewing it negatively is a prime instance of his schism about the play, a schism that starts with the program notes and runs through his whole production.

Still that schism is understandable in a present-day director. It's understandable that he would feel compelled, in the post Hitler, post Stalin, post Vietnam age, to have one or both of two views about *Henry V*: either to treat the war in it as a metaphor of non-martial national unification or to bring to the pervasive militarism some anachronistic humane regard. The RSC, says Hands, selected it out of the first motive; and he has obviously directed it out of both motives.

But they don't really blend. No matter how one plumps for a metaphoric view of the war in the play, the ringing language—glorious in itself—is the best statement in English of ideals that many of us have come to loathe. And the humane considerations, which have to be inserted by a director, remain blatant inserts. For instance, after Agincourt when Henry reads the rolls of the nobles killed on the French and English sides, Hands makes the king break off in tacit horror at the numbers and identities of the dead men. This is a raw 1976 intrusion completely unsupported by the text. Henry's sole comment is that he sees God's hand in the fact that more French than English nobles were killed.

This schism in the director affects every aspect of the show. Take the visual aspect. The performance begins with patronizing hip cheapness. The curtain is up when we arrive, showing a big raked stage and plain walls on the two sides, each of which has a high gallery with a "chaser" spotlight on it. (Later electricians come out and maneuver those lights; musicians, also in modern dress, appear there from time to time.) Before the play begins, actors drift out on to the stage in informal modern dress, lounge about, chat with members of the audience, and otherwise put one off. When the show starts, Henry himself appears in similar dress. Then, suddenly and contradictorily, the French ambassador enters in period costume, the first of the lovely costumes in which everyone but the Chorus is dressed beginning with the second scene. (Costumes and setting were designed by Farrah—that's his whole name.) What was the point of the glib "Off-Broadway" beginning? To "shoehorn" us into the past? To assure us that Shakespeare and his characters are not really remote and dusty? Thanks a lot, Hands.

But *truly* thanks—in further contradiction—for the excellence of the stage movement and compositions, among the finest I can remember in a Shakespeare production. Hands has an eye for sweep and pageant, tempered with the astringency of modern painting (another contradiction!). All his "pictures," particularly those involving the comic characters, are striking without being static.

He has worked some wonders with Farrah's ingenious yet simple scenic design. Two great canvas canopies, one for each act, are hung by multiple cables. The first is bunched upstage in the air at the start, like a furled umbrella, and as the English gird for France, the huge tent unfurls out over the stage to parallel the surges of music and rhetoric. The canopy is even lowered flat on the floor at one point: the bunchy canvas with the cables hooked to it suggests rough ground with underbrush. Before Harfleur, the back half of the raked stage swings up toward us on hinges, ladders and ropes hanging from it to suggest battlements, and the English clamber over. Henry is on the ladders and the ropes as he exhorts them once more unto the breach. Then when the town is taken, the back half lowers again, revealing Princess Katharine standing behind it, waiting for her English lesson. All these things are excellent.

The handling of the text is as mixed a matter as the visual elements. "Once more unto the breach" and "How yet resolves the governor of the town" are handled traditionally, in the mode of "Di quella pira" from *Il Trovatore*. But the St. Crispin's Day speech, surely intended to be an equal rouser, is fragmented and "internalized."

The casting, too, is mixed. All the comic characters are superb—weathered and true. Richard Moore, the Pistol, is even scurvier than Robert Newton in Olivier's film. Trevor Peacock, the Fluellen, is robust and winning. Carolle Rousseau, the Katharine, is pleasant. But Clement McCallin, the French King, is dullness incarnate, and Emrys James, the Chorus, is a limp, pudgy leprechaun.

Then there's Henry himself, and himself a mixed matter. Alan Howard is a greatly skilled actor. (I've seen him in London in Gorky's *Enemies*, in New York as Theseus/Oberon in Brook's production of *Midsummer Night's Dream*, and on TV.) Howard begins here with a basic handicap. The essence of Henry is the ephebe, the wild youth entering responsible manhood. Howard, now around 40, looking and sounding every minute of it, suggests a mature rake, jaded with sin, who has decided to try virtue for a change. He looks like a cross between Robert Redford and a witch. His voice is more nasal than ever—though, within that timbre, it's marvelously strong and capable. In stamina (Henry is a gargantuan role), in intelligence, in absolutely precise control, Howard is splendid. Sometimes he slips into the José Ferrer syndrome, showing how well he enunciates by adding a tiny syllable after a closing word. ("Soul-uh." "Hand-uh.") But he can cope with the heroic when he needs to: he gives us "God for Harry, England, and Saint George" like a trumpet call, instead of Olivier's cop-out scream. On the other hand, he doesn't have Olivier's charm. He doesn't have anyone's, not even his own. He isn't temperamentally suited to sympathetic characters, and he has to work like blazes when he's in one, as here. This is not to derogate the admirable Howard, only to place him, and to underscore that the contradictions in the production also mark his performance.

Hands is clearly one of the inheritors of Granville Barker's pre-World War I revolution in Shakespearean directing: the insistence on what Barker believed to be Elizabethan pace, simplicity of setting, use of tradition without slavery to it. But *Henry V* is a very difficult play to produce in the third quarter of this century. My guess is that it's even more difficult (*another* contradiction!) in Britain than in the U.S. because Britain has suffered more in twentieth-century wars, let alone the fact that they still have a monarch. Hands's production, beautiful in some ways, is split by embarrassment, by apology.

The Threepenny Opera

(May 22, 1976)

For the first eight or ten minutes I thought this production was going to be brilliant. The setting, visible when we arrive because there is no curtain, suggests a great empty warehouse. Two arched windows high in the back are touched with gray light at the start. Iron stairways are lowered. Sections of iron railing are deployed on stage as dividers throughout the play. The apron is cut up into warrens and areaways. The song titles are announced (which Brecht wished) by being flashed on a sort of beam, lowered when needed, flanked by two iron factory wheels that pull back a small curtain. This grim, soulless environment was designed by Douglas W. Schmidt, but its insistence on sheer depth—as well as the two strings stretched across the front of the stage just above the actors' heads—shows the hand of the director, Richard Foreman, founder of the Ontological-Hysteric Theater. (So does the use of a p.a. system for the announcement of the scene titles.) Foreman was nominated for this job by Brecht's son Stefan because of the O-H Theater's work and because of the Off-Off-Broadway musicals that Foreman has done with Stanley Silverman, who is the music director for this production.

And brilliantly it begins. As the music starts, out of the cavernous dark at the back emerges a threatening line of Victorian beggars and whores stretched right across the wide Beaumont stage, moving forward, forward. They are met by more human flotsam seemingly floating up from the pits in the front. A fat ballad singer is pushed up from below who then gives us the opening song, "Mack the Knife." (Lotte Lenya, Kurt Weill's widow, who was in the original production, writes that this now-famous song was *added* to the score by Brecht and her husband during rehearsals to please the actor who first played Macheath and who wanted the opening number to be about his character.) The setting and the choric beginnings combine to suggest Mayhew's agonized nineteenth-century London, wriggling into ominous view. Some of the chorus are even treated in the abstracted, physically stuttering style made familiar by a Brecht devotee, Peter Brook, in his *Marat/Sade* production.

Now this tonality—this grim, cold ghastliness—accords with what can be call-ed Brecht's second view of *The Threepenny Opera*. The first production in 1928 was apparently done in a bitterly high-spirited way, a gallows-humor, let's-at-least-have-some-fun-out-of-this-lousy-world way; and since Lotte Lenya, of that production, was also in the 1954 revival in New York and advised on it, presu-mably that revival aimed for the tone of the original. Brecht had transposed John Gay's eighteenth-century *Beggar's Opera* to nineteenth-century London in order to make a comment on twentiety-century Germany, which turned out to be a comment on the twentieth-century world. With Weill's marvelous score, full of eccentric rhythms and soaring lyric lines and fine classic parody, the show faced (in its view) the ethical hopelessness of capitalist society—and kicked its heels and snapped its skinny fingers.

But Brecht later changed his mind, as Eric Bentley reminds us that he often did about his works. Later Brecht wanted the piece played more darkly, less sa-tirically, more as a dour cautionary tale. This is the way (I'm told) that the Berliner Ensemble now plays it. This is the way it was done in an Italian pro-duction that Brecht saw in February 1956, not long before he died, and highly approved—directed by Giorgio Strehler at his Piccolo Teatro in Milan. Strehler soon afterward brought his *Threepenny* to Rome where I saw it. I remember that this intricately detailed production had very much more of the feeling of *The Lower Depths* than of the wry, glinting production that Carmen Capalbo had directed in New York.

There seems to me nothing arbitrarily better or worse about Approach No. 2: it simply needs to be realized. This is what Foreman has not done. All the *ideas* of his production are good, even the clearly derivative ones like the wall with many doors out of Meyerhold's *Government Inspector* production. But Foreman's casting and his directing of actors are generally poor. The spherical C.K. Alexander has several kinds of weight as Peachum, the head of the Lon-don beggars' consortium. All the other principals are either flavorless or mis-cast or incompetent.

The Macheath is Raul Julia, who can't sing. By Brecht's own standards that may not be a handicap, but Julia also can't act very well, is dim in personality, and has little power. Even if Macheath is not conceived as a dashing daredevil brigand, he must be credible as a sexual magnet and magnate; Julia isn't. To hamper him further Foreman has imposed on him a sole-first, soft-footed walk which had previously been imposed on the protagonist of Foreman's musical *Hotel for Criminals*. Perhaps that walk, like those silly strings across the stage, exemplifies some theory in Foreman's manifesto-burdened mind, but in proof it's pointless and harmful.

Elizabeth Wilson is a good actress, but as Mrs. Peachum she is only a healthy Midwestern lady pretending to European depravity. David Sabin, as the crooked police chief Tiger Brown, is without oil or guile, simply a younger Santa Claus. Ellen Greene, as Jenny the prostitute who undoes Macheath, looks and sounds like a starved Bronx runaway dragged from a SoHo drug pad. The "second" heroine, Lucy Brown, daughter of Tiger, is played by a competent redhead, Blair Brown, whose extraordinary good looks throw the casting out of whack. Partly this is because the "first" heroine, Polly Peachum, is played by Caroline Kava, a zero.

(If you want some idea of the original flavor of *The Threepenny Opera*, you can get it from Pabst's dubious film, made in 1931. Possibly you can get even more of it from Sternberg's *The Blue Angel*, made a year earlier. Kurt Gerron, who plays the head of Marlene Dietrich's troupe, was the first Tiger Brown and also doubled as the ballad singer. Rosa Valletti, who plays his wife in the Sternberg film, was the first Mrs. Peachum. Evidently Sternberg was trading on their *Threepenny Opera* flavors and reputations when he chose them.)

The music is very well played under Stanley Silverman's direction. (The musicians are snuggled into a remote corner upstage left.) In an interesting interview (*Performing Arts Journal*, Spring 1976) Silverman said that he was trying to get Weill's own orchestration which had not previously been used in the U.S. I'm not competent to say whether this is what's actually used here, but it all sounds good, not the least for Silverman's own playing of the banjo and several added guitars. He's a gifted theater musician.

Theoni V. Aldredge's costumes are up to her usual high level, particularly the beggars' rags, which really look about a century old. Pat Collins's lighting underscores Foreman's humorless approach. The translation is new, by Ralph Manheim and John Willett, and is in the series of new Brecht translations edited by Manheim and Willett that Pantheon is publishing. This translation is a lot less singable than Marc Blitzstein's for the 1954 revival, still, as the producer Joseph Papp points out in a program note, it does contain the word "shit" and some references to race prejudice that were missing in Blitzstein. On the other hand, the Manheim-Willett words are hard to follow when the music goes faster than *andante*, so much of the new fidelity is wasted—in the theater, at any rate.

The paradox of *The Threepenny Opera* is that, although Brecht's view of human behavior is unremittingly harsh, the work is exciting, when well played, because of the cut of Brecht's lash and the excellence of Weill's score. When well played. It isn't Approach No. 2 that stymies this production, it's Foreman's bungling of it. In his own theater pieces he has shown fertility and inconclusiveness. I had hoped that one of this century's best theater works would supply the form to make the most of his gifts. Again he shows certain kinds of fertility, but—through mishandling of his actors—the result is inconclusive again, and failed.

Streamers

(June 12, 1976)

The American theater may be short on lots of things, but one gift it's loaded with—the ability to make mountains out of molehills. A current playwriting molehill is David Rabe. Now that he has written a play that is not as artily imitative in form, not as rankly jejune and shallow as were, in varying degree, *The Basic Training of Pavlo Hummel, Sticks and Bones, The Orphan* and *In the Boom Boom Room*, he is hailed as near-Olympian and garlanded further with prizes. *Streamers* is called his best play and the best American play of the season. Both of those statements may in fact be true; but they strike me as mournful.

Rabe has some ability to write dialogue (although it wavers: see below). He has some instinct for dramatic action and for the revelation of character through contest. But that's like saying of a painter that he understands perspective and can turn form with color. *Then* what? To begin with Rabe's fundamental lack, which would govern even if he were technically and stylistically more accomplished, he has no insights deeper than those of his audience. And his artistic gifts are insufficient to turn his commonplace percepts into strong dramatic emblems for us so that, even if he didn't enlighten, he could at least fix memorably what we've seen for ourselves. Rabe asks for our attention to tell us what we already know about ourselves and our society, and he puts what he has to say in very earnest but rickety form.

In *Streamers* he has at least abjured second-hand expressionism, bloated neo-classicism, melodramatic physical images. It's a linear play in realistic mode. Of course this doesn't preclude symbolism, of an internal "literary" kind, and Rabe hurries to exercise this option, beginning with the title. "Streamers" are paratroopers whose parachutes don't open. This play is set in an Army barracks in 1965, but it's not about paratroopers. So, you see—you quickly see—the title is symbolic.

The play opens with a young soldier who has cut his wrists and is hustled out. As it gradually becomes clear that he's not going to be seen again, we realize that he's been laid on us to prefigure something. This is symptomatic of Rabe's techni⌐   ⌐ over and over we can see him portentously making deposits for future check-writing.

The three regular occupants of the barracks room on stage are a black man, submissive to routine, and two whites, one of whom is campy, the other "straight." All are being trained for Vietnam. These three are often visited by another black who is menacing, rebellious, unhappy. Under the pressures of alienation from normal life, three of the men alter. The campy one is revealed as truly homosexual. He insists that the "straight" is fighting the latent homosexuality that's in him, and the "straight" begins to be frightened. The maverick black, desperate for pleasure as a narcotic, tries to have sex with the homosexual in the barracks room before the others. When the "straight" interferes, terrible knife violence follows. This is followed by a long, stagily quiet coda whose materials have been heavily planted earlier.

The key incidents have the smell of matters that Rabe himself saw or heard of in the army, that greatly disturbed him, and that he wanted to make some statement about. But he has merely pushed some accidents into a sack. (Whether they are based on his experience or not, they are just accidents of occurrence.) He wants us to think of the purposeless horror of Vietnam hanging over the heads of these men, but the matters he describes could have happened—surely did happen—in the barracks of such a different conflict as World War II. He wants us to feel how the ripping of young life into the disequilibriums of the Army results in havoc: but what we see could have happened in the merchant marine. The incidents in the play remain accidents. The two stories—of homosexual tension, of black disquiet—are arbitrarily pushed together, as if there were some real relation between psychosexual drama and racial bitterness; and the two are hurriedly married at the end by a sheerly insane violent act, unfounded in character, only prefigured by the playwright *outside* these characters (that opening touch of blood).

Outstanding amidst the gimmicks banked for later reference is "Beautiful Streamers," a paratroopers' song given to us early by two drunken old professional-army sergeants. (The tune is Foster's "Beautiful Dreamer.") We get it early, so that we can get it late—in that painful coda—a big windy metaphor which we are supposed to accept as Poetry without question. But what does it symbolize? What does the symbol of an unopened parachute mean to anything we have seen? Alternatively, what would an "opened parachute" have been in any of the lives we have seen tangled?

Rabe's dialogue is equally unsteady. Much of the time it's limber, sometimes quite breezy in a barracks-chat way; but he can't resist Poetry here either. One of the old boozers, describing a jump, talks about "an unexpected and terrible wind," about a chute that "opened like a tulip." As for clichés, you can actually hear the phrase "mad as a hatter" in this play.

Dorian Harewood gives a fair copy of what can by now be called a stock "dangerous black" performance. Peter Evans camps with some felicity as the gradually revealed homosexual. Paul Rudd is all right as the bewildered "straight." Rudd is himself an example of possible molehill-elevation. He made some success as the chauffeur in the late TV series "Beacon Hill," then in the

New York season he did passably in *Ah, Wilderness*, unpassably in *The Glass Menagerie*. Now he is scheduled to play Henry V in Central Park this summer and Romeo in the fall. Next spring perhaps Oedipus and Lear? I wish him well, but, hoping that I'm wrong, I don't so far perceive the reasons for his advancement, let alone the rush about it.

Streamers was directed by Mike Nichols, first at the Long Wharf in New Haven, then (with a cast change) at Joseph Papp's Newhouse in New York. I have never seen the thrust stage used more adroitly. But though Nichols grows no less deft, he does grow less interesting, in his choices, in his shrinking compass.

The Architect and the Emperor of Assyria

(June 26, 1976)

The Annex of the La Mama Theater, a few doors down from their headquarters in the East Village, is a large rectangular space that has been used by Andrei Serban in quite different ways for his productions of *Trilogy* and *The Good Woman of Setzuan*. Now Tom O'Horgan uses it quite differently again for his production of Arrabal's *The Architect and the Emperor of Assyria*. The audience files into two narrow tiers of seats, one above the other, that hug three of the walls. The entire floor space is filled with Bill Stabile's set, an irregular series of brown platforms of slightly different heights, the spaces between them filled with undulated "trampolines" of brown burlap. The immediate, correct impression is of footholds of rock in the sea, one barely distinguishable from the other.

The play, set on a desert island, has two characters, a native and a new arrival who is the sole survivor of a plane crash. This Crusoe-Friday relation is used for two long acts of symbolic sequences, including impersonations, maskings, transvestism, and eventual reversal of roles. It ends with the opening scene, except that the actor who played the native now plays the new arrival and vice versa.

Apart from the substance of the play, its methods are perfectly suited to the perfervid O'Horgan. I first saw his work in a bill of La Mama short plays in 1966 and was immediately struck by a theatrical talent—explicitly, a talent for theatricality. Soon afterward he did Rochelle Owens's *Futz*, about the love of a farmer for his sow, and handled it with just the right outrageous lyric wildness. His film of *Futz* was the first sign that the outrageousness was beginning to overgrow, and by the time he did the Broadway production of *Jesus Christ Superstar* he had become America's most daringly chic theatrical window-dresser. But with *Superstar*, admittedly, he had to manufacture a dramatic occasion where none really existed. Now in *The Architect* he has at least found a work intended to live as a play and, what's even happier for him, a play that plumbs the fruitiest reaches of O'Horgan's rank, jungle-growth temperament;

and that revels in the scatology and campy naughtiness he loves.

The opening moment is sensational. Loud airplane crash noises frighten the native, and as he cowers, the Emperor arrives through a hole evidently made specially for this purpose in the Annex ceiling, floating down with an umbrella and a carpet-bag, wearing a stained white double-breasted suit and no shoes, while dozens of tiny lights twinkle under the far-flung burlap. From then on, the extravagances never falter. With the aid of good lighting (Cheryl Thacker) and costumes (Joseph Aulisi) and masks (Barbara Sexton) O'Horgan gloats over every chance for visual explosion, inventing chances—especially ribald ones—even where they don't exist. But plenty exist. Visually it's all florid and entertaining. I had the feeling that, instead of a director finding exactly the right play for him to serve (as with Peter Brook and *Marat/Sade*), a director had found exactly the right play to serve him. The substance and intent don't particularly worry O'Horgan: there are just enough of both to serve as scaffolding for him. Style is damned well going to be all, he implies.

But is that all that Arrabal wanted? *The Architect* is certainly concerned with the *way* it exists, but it exists for a reason. It's one more symbolic play that tries to encapsulate the history of man and/or a conspectus of the contemporary human condition, like Frisch's *The Chinese Wall*, Wilder's *The Skin of Our Teeth*, Barry's *Here Come the Clowns*, and Stoppard's *Jumpers*. The ambition to write such a play helps in itself to define its author; but O'Horgan, infatuated with glitz and his considerable power to produce it, manages to subordinate Arrabal's ambition to his own.

Nevertheless, hazily, some of Arrabal's design, more grandiose than grand, comes through. The native is called the Architect: choose your own symbolic resonance. The newcomer calls himself the Emperor of Assyria, and cows the Architect with stories of past glories, as long as the other man remains gullible. Early on we get the absolutely breathtaking idea that these two men are differing aspects of the human psyche, that we are seeing a parable of what civilization does to simplicity, but Arrabal is too fancy to leave it at that. Both characters go through series of impersonations, trumped-up crises, switches. At last the Emperor stands trial, not for imperial crimes but for ordinary bourgeois life, is guilty, sentenced, to death, and asks only that the Architect eat him after his death. Which is done. Then it ends with the mirror-image of the opening scene.

Of course one doesn't look for external consistencies in a work propelled by flights of fancy, but one does hope for some central vision, at least some compelling hunger for a vision. If a lot of intricate symbolic equipment is rolled out onto the runway, it had better take off. Not here. What is approximately central here is the stalest of disgusts; what is *really* central is the author's smugness, a conviction that the true test of your spirit will be your appreciation of his poetic play, that to ask any questions of its theme or its symbols is to betray your dullness. This is one of the con games of the avant-garde hack—not of the genuine avant-garde artist—and Arrabal lolls in the middle of it.

As if to certify his avant-garde status, he soars and he dares. His soaring consists of ecstatic passages (in this translation by Everard d'Harnoncourt and Adele Shank) that occasionally reach the Creative Writing 401 level of purpled rhapsody. His daring is even more puerile—small-boy bravery with a wooden sword and a paper cocked hat. Imagine a writer whose idea of iconoclasm is to write a parody of the *Dies Irae* that ends "Shit on God." (A line Arrabal has in fact used elsewhere.) Or whose idea of exposing our sexual inhibitions and dishonesty is to talk about a mother fellating her son. (On a level with the fellation of Jesus in his later play *And They Put Handcuffs on the Flowers*.)

Arrabal—he has only lately been using his first name, Fernando—is a Spaniard, born in 1932, who has been living in France since 1954, who wrote in French for many years, and has recently gone back to writing in Spanish. (*The Architect* was first produced in Paris in 1967 and was published here in 1969.) His themes have been political, clerical, and sexual, usually combined: he is against fascism, particularly Spanish; he is against churchly imposition; he is against puritanism. He seems to think that these stands in themselves make him extraordinarily adventurous. The work of his that I know shows him to be a baby Buñuel, a vapid Valle-Inclan. (His new film *Guernica*, based on an earlier play, is ludicrous: trite artiness; *El Topo* gone anti-fascist and much less visually ingenious.) One need only think of Genet—*The Maids* as against *The Architect*, *The Screens* as against *Guernica*—to see the difference between a genius of the Other Side and a frittering little symbolist-absurdist fop.

Two pairs of actors are alternating in performances of *The Architect*. I saw Lazaro Perez and, as the Emperor, Ronald Perlman. Perez is pallid. Perlman is the best reward of the evening. I had been seeing him for a couple of years with the CSC, a repertory company of unsteady ability in the Village, where he had been consistently vital and impressive. Last year Perlman played the leading role in the CSC production of Büchner's *Woyzeck* and was quietly gripping—oafish yet vulnerable. Here he absolutely fills the bill—a vaudeville as much as an acting bill, but he fills it. He is tall, solid, frizzy-headed, with rather coarse but strong features: he is funny, moving, dynamic, flexible. The show he puts on here further convinces me that he is an actor of potentialities.

The Prince of Homburg

(November 20, 1976)

Obscured by German political behavior in the last hundred years is an astonishing fact of Western cultural history. There is a line of radical German-speaking dramatists, radical in their views of the theater and of society, stretching from the eighteenth century to the present, virtually unbroken except for the twelve years from 1933 to 1945. One of the towering plays in that line is

Heinrich von Kleist's *The Prince of Homburg*, and now, 165 years after it was written, it has its American professional première.

Two weeks ago *The Marquise of O . . .* arrived, Eric Rohmer's lovely film of Kleist's novella. *The Prince of Homburg* was written six years after the novella, in 1811, not long before the author committed suicide (at thirty-four). The play carries forward many of the themes of the novella, enriches them because it's a more substantial work, and embraces still more themes.

Apparently *The Prince of Homburg* grew out of two quite different factors in Kleist's life: his seven years' service in the Prussian army, between the ages of fifteen and twenty-two, and the subsequent impact on his mind of Kant, especially the Kantian thesis that our perceptions of objective reality depend on subjective concepts of reality. The Prince in this play is a military hero seen under the aspect of dream. The basic conflict is between the idea "There is a beauty in duty" and the question "Am I really here?" It's something like a blend of Sophocles's *Antigone* and Calderon's *Life Is a Dream* taken into private precincts.

The year is 1675. Brandenburg is fighting the Swedish invaders. The young Prince is the Elector of Brandenburg's chief general of cavalry, has won some victories and is now given an important part in the plans for the battle of Fehrbellin, with strict orders about how he is to proceed. He disobeys the orders impetuously and wins the battle, but the Elector nevertheless sentences him to death for insubordination. The law is the law. Under pressure the Elector agrees to spare him if the Prince will say he has been sentenced unjustly. The Prince cannot say so. We can call this the *Antigone* element.

But the Prince's life is eventually spared because of matters arising from the dream segment of the play. The very first time we see him he is awake but dreaming, and all through the play—in a wonderful manner too complex to detail here—this waking-sleep element is interwoven. (The director here emphasizes it with a striking touch at the very end.) This "Calderon" element consists of the compulsion to step back from the moment, to see one's self *in it*, and therefore the inability to believe that the moment one has been seeing is the whole of reality. It's the quality that Büchner was to fix in his Danton twenty-four years later—a man in the midst of violent action who suddenly pulls back to *see* himself in the midst of that action.

As with *The Marquise of O . . .* Kleist builds his dynamics on the conflict of opposites: reality/dream, heroism/cowardice, loyalty/treason, sternness/mercy, and more. (He uses again here, as in *The Marquise*, a report of a death in battle that turns out to be false, so we get grief/joy.) This dialectic of opposites keeps moving toward a synthesis, but this synthesis is not really a resolution, it's a perception about "pure" states, about the impossibility of absolutes, including of course good or evil. *The Prince of Homburg* is one of the plays that have made it difficult for succeeding dramatists to write villains.

One can view this play as a theological parable with the Elector as God and the Prince as Man, with God insisting that Man take awareness of sin on himself, instead of relying on Daddy for everything, including punishment. It's also easy to view the play as a pre-Freud Freudian analogue, roaming through two levels of consciousness, dominated by a father figure whom the protagonist wants both to revere and to best. And it can also be taken as a cultural-historical statement: the Prussian Kleist trying to accommodate the values of "Prussianism" with an increasing awareness of ambiguities.

Robert Kalfin of the Chelsea Theater Center views the play as a means of questioning the very idea of reality. Kalfin, who is the artistic director of CTC, is presumably responsible for the generally excellent choices of plays in their eleven-year existence and is certainly responsible for some of its poorly directed productions. This is his best work I've seen. He adapted the James Kirkup translation. He "saw" the play, he also saw how to deal with this large-scale drama in the small space at his disposal. He commissioned from Christopher Thomas a raked-stage setting with three panels on which light-projections set the place and mood, he has good lighting by Marc B. Weiss and helpful music by Mel Marvin. The costumes by Ruth Morley are Napoleonic and contradict the historical references (as some Shakespearean productions do), but possibly Kalfin wanted to aid Kleist's blow against Schiller-like classicism by bringing the look of the production as close as is credible.

Kalfin has permitted some gaucherie in his actors—especially George Morfogen, the overdoing Hohenzollern—but most of them are adequate. Frank Langella is the dreaming, fiery Prince. Langella pops his eyes a bit to indicate amazed dream-states, but he gets much of the Hamlet-like quandary, the *aristocracy* of quandary, that the part needs. The Elector is K. Lype O'Dell, and he is perfect. O'Dell has authority without pomp, and he gives this key role exactly the magisterial-humane quality that helps the play to function.

No Man's Land

(December 11, 1976)

Thoughts While Watching Harold Pinter's New Play:

Pinter can't get over his good luck at having been born English. How he enjoys the proudly articulated architecture of British utterance, the knowledge that this utterance is both his own and part of a community's, the protocols of various British strata. I can imagine a French Pinter (Pan-tay) but not an American or German one. He needs his characters' faith in language itself and the insolence of whatever class they happen to be, whether they are the two servants in this play or the two writers.

The social line in Pinter's work has been mobile upward. A few of his early one-act plays dealt with middle-middle or upper-middle people, but most went lower. His long plays began at the bottom of the social scale (*The Birthday Party*,

The Caretaker), moved up to working-class that at least produced a university professor (*The Homecoming*), through middle-middle people not much interested in class (*Old Times*), to upper-middle people who, by their bearing in several senses, are much interested in class (*No Man's Land*). Cyril Connolly once said—of British writers—that one of the perquisites of an author's success was his entry into societies that might not otherwise be open to him. Pinter has long had that entry, but it has only lately been much reflected in his work.

Because, in result of this, Pinter has lately been using high-comedy dialogue as one element in his mix, he has been accused—fallaciously, I think—of becoming like Noel Coward. This is to confuse one writer's conscious use of the flossy with another writer's desperate clinging to flossy-as-all. (And before we try to sink Coward without a trace, let's remember that T. E. Lawrence compared his prose to Congreve's.) In *No Man's Land* Hirst tells Spooner how, years before, he seduced Spooner's wife: "Proposed that she betray you. Admitted you were a damn fine chap, but pointed out that I would be taking nothing that belonged to you, simply that portion of herself all women keep in reserve, for a rainy day." Only superficially is this passage like Coward. The wit serves an observation, instead of vice versa. (Besides there is a counterpoint of four-letter profanities through the play to put the elegance in harshened context.)

Ralph Richardson is Hirst, a successful man of letters. John Gielgud is Spooner, a scruffy, erudite poet. (Londoners tell me that Spooner is virtually a portrait of a local figure—not conceivably Auden, as one New York report said.) The two have just met in a pub, and Richardson has brought Gielgud home for more drink. At least that's the first version that we see. To watch these two actors together, and it's much truer here than in Storey's unrewarding *Home*, is an immensely moving experience: not because the play is moving—it stays well within the limits of the comic-menacing—but because we know we are witnessing the vintage years of two greatly gifted artists.

A long-time observer of these two men can note how they have grown. Gielgud, when I first saw him in the early 1930s in *The Good Companions* and *Hamlet*, was a nervous, strong, rather too chic actor with an adenoidal timbre to his voice. The maturing of his artistic intelligence and the development of his voice comprise one of the fine, intrinsically theatrical achievements of our time. Richardson in his earlier days was only a clever trickster, with a way of reading lines off kilter that was meant to draw attention to itself. His Falstaff in 1946 was merely nasty. Under the mannerisms a mine of humanity has been opened, enveloping and consuming the tricks. For me the change was finally clear in his Peter Teazle in 1962.

Both of these now-wonderful men have at their command deep resources in every kind of role, but what gives their performances here a special beauty is their classical experience. Take the opening lines. Both men are discovered on stage in Richardson's living room. The host is pouring a whiskey for his guest and in his first line he asks whether Gielgud wants it straight. "As it is?" A banal colloquial line, and only an actor of classical command could read it as Richardson does, putting his vocal "hand" firmly on the audience, determinedly *beginning* the play with three separate utterances. "As. It. Is?" Gielgud replies, "As it is, yes please, absolutely as it is," with a deliberately outsize fervor on the word "absolutely" that is comic mastery. These very first lines register so deeply that they work retroactively when we later see that nothing in the play *is* "absolutely as it is." It's not impossible, Pinter being the writer he is, that this reverberation was intentional. But it's also not impossible that, hardly for the first time in theater history, two actors have enriched a play.

This is a production of the National Theater of Great Britain, directed by Peter Hall, the new head of that theater. Hall has treated the play like the conductor-choreographer he proved himself in *The Homecoming*. John Bury, Pinter's customary designer, has done a setting that is at once *luxe* and supportive of the title.

Thoughts After The Play:

By now it's the received wisdom about *No Man's Land* that it is lesser Pinter, well-written but meaningless, that its only apparent point is to describe one man's realization (Hirst's) that he has reached No Man's Land (spiritual desolation) and the other man's attempts to befriend him for personal advantage. The last seems to me to be true so far as a point can be isolated. I agree, too, that the play is lesser Pinter so long as the phrase is kept strictly relative; and that the play is meaningless—in the conventional sense of meaning.

There are four distinct, unconnected states of relationship between the two men. The first is as described above; the others, which contradict it and each other, it isn't necessary to detail. The shifts are arbitrary, from one to the next. For me it's the expansion of an approach that Pinter began in *Old Times*: superimposing, one on the other, different ways in which relationships between the same people can be imagined or extrapolated. It's a kind of dramaturgic cubism, combining "simultaneously"—as far as the serial time of the theater permits—different views of the same objects, to intensify our response to them. I kept thinking of the Resnais-Robbe-Grillet film *Last Year at Marienbad*, or at least of the impulses behind it. We enter a room (the curtain rises) and see two people: quickly their relationship is defined, one way or another. But it *could* have been defined quite differently. A could have been B's brother, instead of his cousin, if the author had said so: B could have been a dentist instead of a textile converter, and so on. To play with these possibilities is to try to make reverie real, to enclose on stage a territory of imagination, to substitute for logical development a texture of mystery.

Hirst's two ominous servants are a sounding-board, resonating the mystery, compounding the comedy of contradictions with shadowy overtones.

This play is lesser in Pinter's work because No Man's Land is only described, never realized (as the dark immanent dragons of threatening sexuality were realized in *Old Times*). But *No Man's Land* is meaningless only by a canon that denies much of twentieth-century art.

Nightclub Cantata

(February 5, 1977)

Anyone in New York or elsewhere who saw Andrei Serban's productions of three Greek plays, called *Trilogy*, has heard the music of Elizabeth Swados. It was wonderful. It ranged from primally exciting percussions to the lyric swell of a desolate chorus. *The Trojan Women* was subtitled "An Epic Opera," and if opera means music and theatre united to approximate Athenian tragedy—which is why opera was invented—then the name was not misapplied.

Swados is now all of twenty-five. (Some will wonder about her relation to the late Harvey Swados: second cousin.) After other work with Serban on Brecht's *Good Woman of Setzuan*—and she had worked with Peter Brook before Serban—she has now made a production of her own. It's unique, lovely and endearing.

And very hard to describe. Description, we've been told, is the bedrock of criticism. Well, *Nightclub Cantata* can be described: as a collection of twenty numbers. The term "cantata" is a loose one anyway, but Swados's work is even looser—in convention. The twenty pieces, not one with a really memorable tune, are performed in a cabaret by eight people (herself included), a pianist and a percussionist, in ensemble, solos, and differing combinations. But then I must describe the disparity of the songs. Five of them have words by Swados. Others have words by a number of poets including the noted Turk, Nazim Hikmet. Some lines of a few songs are in Hebrew. Two numbers, "Bird Chorus" and "Bird Lament" are non-verbal, only sounds. Swados does the latter as a solo. It's an enchanting piece: not whistlings but throated warblings, flutings, trillings, and owl cries, arranged in stanzaic form. It's extremely difficult to perform, I should think, quarter tones being the easiest part of it, and marvelous to hear.

And *then* I must describe the unity of this same seeming ragbag of pieces. Style is the key. Swados staged the production herself and has made the best possible use of an eccentric space: a small platform with an alcove behind it, snuggled into the angle of an L, which is how this cabaret is shaped. She also moves her people through the audience as far as is helpful. Speech of joyous clarity and fine emotional candor are what lift these songs and pieces to a plane of intense *address*—a style that would be impossible for most singers but not for actors who can sing. Often the group bites out words in unison: sometimes a pair reply to each other with almost demonic vigor. The inspiration behind the sound of this cantata is the work that Serban (presumably with Swados's help) accomplished with his actors: the sensation that a flood of sound is pouring forth from the innards and is being shaped into precise language: to put it emblematically, a combination of heart and head. The beauty of the diction is part of the beauty of the song. It's not elocutionary, it's sculptural.

The exception to the multifarious unity of the evening is the one funny number, at which I laughed but which I nevertheless wish had been omitted. "The Pastrami Brothers," done by the four men in old-style costumes, is a parody of an acrobatic act in which there is a lot of springing into position and "Hup!" and bracing, with a ludicrous payoff to each portentous preparation. Parody is not the point of the evening, even in the affectionately mocking rock number "Indecision," and the fact that this acrobat number is not musical makes it even more egregious.

Cabaret shows in our culture have come to mean, usually, either political satire or various forms of sexual confession. This show has none of the former and little of the latter. There is no one theme: the songs range from the wry, subtly dense despair of Delmore Schwartz ("In Dreams Begin Responsibilities") to the pleasant flutings of Frank O'Hara ("To the Harbormaster"). Binding all together is the sheer relish of Feeling: exultation in response to the stimuli of the world, darker or brighter stimuli, pride in being a human who can have this range of response.

Yet *Nightclub Cantata* is spheres away from "commune" soppiness. If you saw Alain Tanner's recent film *Jonah Who Will Be 25 in the Year 2000*, you will recognize how opposed this show is. Tanner's picture, skillfully made, is drenched in fellow-feeling-as-politics, the implicit dictum that "we deserve to inherit the world because we eat health foods and screw freely." Swados believes in discipline: in fellow-feeling as the impulse and end of intelligence and dignity. No lolling communard could do those bird calls, could inspire a group to the precision reached here. Feeling starts it, as it does all art, but goes through an arduous process before it comes out as good feeling again. There is an ethics in this production.

Other than Swados, I knew only two of the performers. Diminutive Shelley Plimpton, who was the permanent waif in *Hair*, curlicues affectingly here again. JoAnna Peled, who was excellent in *Trilogy* in Helen of Troy and other roles, is excellent again. Her song and dance "The Gypsy" takes the familiar Carmen sex-as-banner rubric and makes it fresh. All the others are good. William Milhizer is a deft percussionist (which, with Swados, means more than drums), and Judith Flejsher is the exceptionally sensitive pianist. (Fleisher, says the program, is a resident psychologist at the Bronx Psychiatric Center.)

"Cantata" is an inadequate tag for this work, except in the literal meaning of "a sung piece." Through the 1960s, Al Carmines of the Judson Church in New York did shows called cantatas or oratorios, that were collections of musical numbers meant to hold an audience through their theatrical effect as much as their musical appeal. A Carmines highpoint was his setting of quotations from Chairman Mao's Little Red Book for various combinations of voices—music that had vaudeville, jazz, ragtime as its sources. Swados's music is, rather more than less, *sui generis*. She too has made a collection of musical numbers into a vital theatre piece.

Ashes

(February 19, 1977)

Ashes is a love song, sung in the language of PC tests, ovulation charts, and sperm counts. Colin and Anne are in their late twenties, live somewhere in the English Midlands, and are trying very hard to have a child. The sex is fervent: before we actually see them, we hear them pumping away, and they keep pumping, merrily and even less merrily when they "have to," at doctors' orders. But pregnancy doesn't happen, so from their privacy, they move into the helpful but cold humiliations of laboratories and examining tables. The details are clinical, but we soon feel that what is propelling and sustaining them through these ordeals, like a prosy Tamino and Pamina, is the strength of their love and their great wish for that love to produce a child.

Of course this process, with its bathing of the balls in cold water, its screwing at the thermometer's behest in the doctor's prescribed position, has its ludicrous aspects; and Colin and Anne know that, in some regards, they have become comedians of coupling. But through the frigid indignities of science and the funny ones of directed sex, there burns a romance. It's helped by the flexible structure of this play: a swift series of short scenes, moving (by suggestion) through many places, with occasional addresses to the audience and with conscious attempts to correlate experience to some understanding of fate and purpose. These latter reflections are not notable for depth but, together with the pulse of the play's movement and the emotional truth of the biological agon, they create an appealing gravity.

That gravity is enhanced by the couple's acceptance of each other, her acceptance of his homoerotic component, their mutual acceptance of their "settling." He had wanted to be a playwright, she an actress; now it's schoolteaching and planting spuds and the hope to be fertile. Then at last the egg weds, the fetus begins. Then, after much (explicit) travail, the fetus is lost. Then there are complications and Anne's womb is removed. Then they decide to adopt a child. Then they are turned down.

So the play is a progress of sheddings: they shed their first hopes for careers, their hopes for a child of their own, for any child. Against this story runs a counterpoint of minor frustrated births: their cat kills a nesting goldfinch; one morning there's even a breakfast egg with a rotted chick in it. The drama is in the commonplace but exacting series of cruelties that make Colin and Anne stand clearer and dearer to each other—through severances.

David Rudkin, the author, has said that there is a great deal in the play that is autobiographical. This and its desperate humor reminded me of Peter .

Nichols's *A Day in the Death of Joe Egg*, but *Ashes* has a better (though imperfect) structure. Rudkin is forty, has written radio and TV plays, worked on the script of Truffaut's *Fahrenheit 451*, and has written about a half dozen plays. I saw his first play *Afore Night Come* at the Royal Shakespeare in 1962 and was much struck with its conviction of primitiveness persisting today. An itinerant Irishman becomes a fruitpicker in the Midlands, and his sheer strangeness leads to his murder by his co-workers. (Out of the huddled mob at the end came an arm bearing Patrick Magee's head aloft!) Rudkin is half Irish and spent some childhood years in Ireland, and this early play was rooted in a sense of xenophobia.

It continues in *Ashes*. Colin is Irish, a Protestant from Belfast, and is very conscious that he lives (what is for him) abroad. Near the end of the play, after Anne's operation, he goes back to Belfast for the funeral of an uncle who has been killed by a terrorist bomb. When he returns, while Anne drives him home from the airport, he has a long speech in which he describes the pieces of people he saw scattered at a bus stop after a bomb ("atrocious anagrams of people going home") and how his cousins refused to let him help carry his uncle's coffin because they said he was a runaway, not a true Ulsterman. So Colin has had another loss: his country.

After this scene comes a soliloquy for Anne in which she recounts a symbolic nightmare of sterility. Then Colin brings in the letter from the county adoption agency telling them they have been turned down. And there they are at the end, alone, together. Both words have weight; and have meaning even for those of us who haven't suffered precisely the same severances and losses.

But those two concluding monologues are appendages that connect to the body of the play only with some effort on Rudkin's part and some (earned) good will on ours. Patently he wanted to move to a thematic conclusion, but he might have had more reliance on what he had already accomplished: most of what is (thematically) in those two last speeches has already been engraved. Anne's last speech, particularly, is somewhat redundant—included mostly to balance Colin's last speech. Anne throughout is a less complex and surprising character than Colin.

Not by design, surely, the production compensates with a somewhat better performance of Anne than of Colin. Roberta Maxwell is one of the younger actresses who give a glow to our theater these days. (Pamela Payton-Wright, Tovah Feldshuh, Priscilla Smith, Kathryn Walker and Meryl Streep are others.) Small, with bright dark quick eyes, a wide but fine mouth, an upcurved nose, Maxwell radiates a feeling of intelligence, a touching apprehension, before she speaks. Her sensitivity has charm as well as emotional effect. Her voice could use some extension and enriching, but she uses it truly. A few years ago at the Long Wharf in New Haven she gave the best performance of Strindberg's *Miss Julie* that I have seen. I've seen *Ashes* twice: and the second time, even though I knew the moment was coming when she had to "do" this or that, she made it happen, freshly, without platitude.

The English actor Brian Murray, who looks like a slightly doughy young William Holden, is Colin, and he works a bit less close to the bone. He's generally effective, but we can sometimes see him summoning up what he needs for a moment or shifting gears for a transition. A special word for John Tillinger who plays several doctors well and is moving as the kind but stern adoption chief. The last of the four-person cast, Penelope Allen, is OK as several nurses and a friend.

Ashes had its first U.S. production last year at the Mark Taper in Los Angeles. Its first New York production was a few months ago at the Manhattan Theater Club, that hive of theaters on the upper East Side run by Lynne Meadow, who directed this production. It's by far the best work of hers that I've seen, lean and succinct yet feeling (barring Murray's occasional bulges). John Lee Beatty did an astringent setting. After a good press Joseph Papp moved the play to one of his downtown theaters, where I saw it again and where everything was nicely adjusted from the needs of a proscenium stage to a thrust stage.

The Cherry Orchard

(March 26, 1977)

Andrei Serban's production of this Chekhov play is a battleground—and of some importance as such. Serban is the young Romanian director whose productions of Greek plays with his own company, done at La Mama in New York and throughout the U.S. and Europe, have rightly earned him a high reputation. Though clearly influenced by Grotowski and Brook, those productions were thrillingly successful achievements in themselves. Then Serban did a production of Brecht's *Good Woman of Setzuan* that had some illumination in it but showed a basic discomfort with the very idea of "doing a play"—that is, fulfilling an author's design instead of making a new work derived (or not derived) from the author's script.

Now the trouble has increased. Serban's success with his own company has slid him out of that environment, out of the methods he developed with and for a permanent group, into a theater of jobbing actors operating under different perspectives. Of the local invitations he got to work elsewhere, Serban accepted Joseph Papp's. (So his experience repeats, at a higher level, what happened to Richard Foreman when he left his own theater to direct *Threepenny Opera* for Papp.) Serban's production of *The Cherry Orchard* at the cavernous Beaumont has so little to do with what Chekhov put on paper, so little to do with what we expect in a performance of this play—with what, in my view, we have every vital esthetic right to expect—that it crystallizes the conflict of strong forces in the theater of this century.

Start with two stipulations. Serban is greatly talented, and he is not irrational. To note the bizarre materials in this production is not like noting the flabbiness in such traditional productions as Lee Strasberg's *Three Sisters* or Mike Nichols's *Uncle Vanya*; nor is it to cite perverseness, irrationality. A gifted and thoughtful man made some decisions. It's *that* fact that's disturbing: anything else would be trivial.

The prime decision was about the physical design. Serban decided not to supply the (requested) three realistic settings on the Ranevskaya estate: he and his designer Santo Loquasto decided instead to provide three impressions of creeping desuetude. The first act is a light-colored stage and backdrop—no walls—with some pieces of furniture under light-colored dust covers; and the motif is amplified in the fourth act when the same room is seen with no furniture at all, just that light backdrop and an immense light-colored cloth that is thrown forward over the floor as if the entire estate were being put under dust covers. So, from the start, Serban chose to abandon Chekhov's realism for a style of abstraction.

But then he contradicts this choice with two other styles: with literal devices, like the cherry orchard itself made visible through a scrim at the back, or Ranevskaya's dead son seen wandering between the trees when she speaks of him, or peasants hauling a heavy plow; and with sheer symbolism, like a rear projection of a gigantic modern factory predicting the future, or a little girl in a white gown who comes in at the very end carrying a sprig of cherry blossoms and kneels behind the dying old servant Firs.

Still the production holds generally to the keynote of abstraction. Two ideas seem to have been uppermost in Serban's mind. First, he remembers that Chekhov called the play a comedy and repeated it over and over again in correspondence. But, as Simon Karlinsky points out, this was a strategy against "the slow and mournful tempo he knew Stanislavsky would try to achieve," and at any rate what "Chekhov clearly had in mind was a high, serious comedy" like *Measure for Measure*. Second, Serban is apparently working out of the Meyerhold tradition in which the actor is an anti-naturalistic *performer* with at least as much relation to the circus as to psychology. But Meyerhold was a particularized genius working with a highly trained ensemble against a dominant tradition exemplified—exalted—by the Moscow Art Theater. Serban is working with a group of actors hired for a few months with no Moscow Art reference point in sight.

So, on the one hand, there is a masterwork of poetic realism using character insight and emotional nuance to fix a crisis in Western civilization, and on the other hand there is a production that attacks the work with physicality, horseplay, and improvisation on the text rather than an attempt to embody the text.

The center of the play is the young merchant Lopakhin, the son of peasants who now can buy the estate where his parents labored but who does so with as much awe as triumph: an estate whose bankrupt owners, a middle-aged brother and sister, are unable to save it because they are incompetent, unwilling to face facts as being unworthy of their breeding, and whose troubles entangle the lives of a lot of people bound to them by blood and circumstance. Under Serban, the reticent, much-moved Lopakhin is transformed into a kind of simian who celebrates his purchase of the estate by leaping up and swinging round the columns of a dance pavilion. (No need to quote Chekhov's somewhat different stage directions.)

Shyness, in the clerk Yepikhdov and the maid Dunyasha, is cartooned into constant furniture-bumping by one and drawers-dropping by the other. Madame Ranevskaya (Irene Worth, utterly wasted here), in the moment before she leaves forever, runs three or four times in a circle around the huge stage. I suppose this was intended to externalize her impulse to "gather up" as many of her memories as she could, but it only made me think of a circus horse, thus underscoring the circus element in the Meyerhold legacy.

Well, that's enough. Hardly a moment in the performance is intended to fulfill what is specified or implied in the text. Now no one knows this better than Serban. So his production becomes a battleground—for two conflicts, in fact. The first is by now a familiar one in this century: the idea of the directorial concept versus the text of the play. Part of the turbulence of the modern era has centered on the presumed necessity to break with the past in the production of old plays. Changes of period or place were only one such strategy. (Occasionally a change succeeded: A. J. Antoon's *Much Ado about Nothing*, set in the U.S. c. 1900, really heightened the play's immediacy.) Changes in the text and deliberately inapposite performance styles have also been used.

Often these productions reflected one or more of various motives: Fear (My God, we've got to make today's audience care about this play); egotism (The author, never having read Freud—or Marx or Artaud—didn't really know what he'd written here); incompetence (Since I have no command of classical style, I will derogate it and will substitute something else); vogue-slavishness (How dare I *not* have a concept these days when all my competitors have them?). But radical interpretation, as proof of vitality, is beginning to look terribly conformist and willed. Most of Serban's innovations here have an air of heavy breathing.

The second conflict connects with that. There was no vestige of laboriousness in Serban's Greek productions. He was working with a trained, relatively singleminded company on the creation of new theater pieces. The plays were not realistic to begin with, and in any case there was no intent to "do" them. The intent was to find and project their primal lines of force, their mythic antecedents. Here he doesn't have his company. (Only two came with him. One is in a bit part, the other, Priscilla Smith, is Ranevskaya's adopted daughter, Varya. Further proof of disaster is the way that Smith, so brilliant in the Greek plays, is flattened here.) Here he *is* working with a realistic play which he has constantly to contradict if he's going to be himself at all. The result is not a production, it's a collision.

Serban is next scheduled to direct *Agamemnon* at the Beaumont. Naturally I hope it's better than the Chekhov. But I hope even more strongly that he will soon go back to his own company, take Smith with him, and make more theater pieces congenial to his talents.

Waiting for Godot

(April 23, 1977)

Twice in my life I've had the chance to see a masterpiece of drama as directed by its author, and, by coincidence, both plays were in German. The first was *Mother Courage* done in London in 1956 by the Berliner Ensemble fresh from the hand of the lately deceased Bertolt Brecht. (Subsequently I've seen other Berliner Ensemble Brecht but not so fresh from his hand.) Now I've seen *Waiting for Godot* played in German by the Schiller Theater of Berlin and directed by Samuel Beckett. Brecht was a professional director: some who knew him say that, as time went on, he became primarily a director who wrote pieces to direct. What's lost sight of about Beckett, who is not a professional like Brecht, is that nonetheless he has done a very considerable amount of directing, of his own plays, since 1966: in theaters of France and Germany (his German is said to be flawless) and on television. And Alan Schneider, credited as director of Beckett's one screenplay *Film*, says generously that Beckett, who was present throughout the shooting in New York, was "its real director."

This is not only the best production of a Beckett play that I have seen, it is among the best productions of anything I have seen. Many authors cannot, or should not, direct their own plays just as many composers cannot conduct their own scores. But if the author *can* direct, then it's possible—not inevitable— that he will give the work its best imaginable production. I have admired some previous productions of Beckett plays (not of *Godot* particularly), but I've seen nothing quite like this. From the first moment I felt I was being made privy to confidences that had only been hinted at in prior productions, that a texture was being initiated surely and easily. From the first moment I knew I was being given a clear vision of the play, not so much of its center as of its whole.

One of the actors, Carl Raddatz, is familiar from films: he's the hawk-faced Pozzo, tyrannical in Act I yet haunted by a prediction of his fate in Act II. Horst Bollmann, the Estragon, is a fine example of that staple of German stage and screen, the short, *gemutlich*, wryly humorous comedian, like Max Adalbert and Heinz Rühmann. Stefan Wigger, the Vladimir, long and lean, is plainly an actor of the first rank, using here only a part of his vocal and physical range and finding range within that narrowed range. His walk, with thighs pressed together and feet flapping, his hands like those of a protesting scarecrow, do not fit the physical concept of Vladimir that I have had but, especially as harmonized with this Estragon, Wigger soon replaces my preconceptions. The Boy is Torsten Sense, who is more youth than boy. Klaus Herm, who reveals a sort of white fright-wig when he takes off his hat, is Lucky and does the great tirade in a manner unlike any I have heard. The very first Lucky, Jean Martin, in the production directed by Roger Blin, is reported to have played the speech with an extreme nervous tic. Alvin Epstein in New York exploded in an unforgettable frenzy. Herm does it in a relatively calm, carefully structured manner.

This speech of Lucky's was where Beckett began his rehearsals. There's an invaluable journal by Walter D. Asmus, Beckett's assistant in the rehearsal period from late December 1974 to early March 1975, that was published in *Theatre Quarterly* (London), September-November 1975. (The production has been kept in the Schiller repertory, has played in various European cities, and now goes to Ireland and Israel.) Beckett opened by explaining the three-part structure of the monologue. I won't take space here to repeat divisions and comments, but future productions of *Godot* must at least agree to disagree with them.

The predominant quality of the whole performance is, again, one that I haven't seen and hadn't imagined: delicacy. Everything, including the buffoonery and physicality and grossness, seems to be touched lightly, sustained with light fingers. And it all seems to flow, like the best kind of dream: movement flows into movement, speech into pause, pause into speech, movement into stasis and vice versa. The core of the staging procedure is rhythm: everything has been thought of in terms of tempo and fit. Everything has been measured, but, as in good dance and good singing, the rightness and preciseness of the measuring make the measuring disappear. The flow is seamless.

These tempos are not arbitrary, they grow out of the scene (as well as the scenes on either side of it), out of the moments within the scene. I won't attempt to describe (if I could remember) the color and pace and movement of each scene, I'll note only that the director's aim, through the delicacy and flow, was to keep it all a clown show, two tramps perambulating around a great invisible question mark. Once in a while Beckett underscored the clown-show idea by having them do something together, next to each other, like a chorus line—a move, a turn, a gesture. What a lovely rubric for a play about the fate of Western man.

Theatrically, *Godot* is deceptive. First, it deceives you into thinking that it's easy to perform; then it deceives you into thinking that (again: theatrically speaking) it's a bit tedious. The test of any production is the opening of Act II. The first act has taken us from near-stasis with the two tramps up through an arc that includes a long scene with two newcomers back to the two tramps alone in complete stasis. Then the next act begins in the same barren place (a few leaves added to the gaunt tree) with the same two tramps in the same mood. No matter how much we like the play, at that moment there's a slight apprehension as to whether the actors have sufficient variety to keep us interested for another comparable act. Wigger and Bollmann, under Beckett's hand, seem consciously to face this initial obstacle; they work variations in color, beginning with Vladimir's opening song, that promise us facets within this paradoxically constrained but universal play, facets we haven't yet seen.

As many have pointed out, the original French title of the play *En Attendant Godot* translates more literally as *While Waiting for Godot*. We can't fault the translator in this case: it's Beckett himself, of course, who opted for a phrase as easy for the English tongue as the original is for the French. (He didn't do the German translation—it was made by Elmar Tophoven.) But the French title puts more exactly the play's central agon: the passage of time. As Hamlet strives to fulfill his father's mission, as Oedipus strives to help his stricken city, so these two tramps struggle merely to pass the time of their lives. E. M. Cioran once said that the essence of Beckett is not despair but mysticism: as if earthly life were an interruption of a perfect state, an interruption somehow to be endured. Whether that is one's own view or not, this great play certainly puts the enduring of life—the sense of passage through it—under the aspect of eternity. And this delicate, delicately modulated production by the author is a subtle theatrical articulation of these two hours in relation to all of time.

As with lots of good things that come along, I now can hardly believe that this production really happened, although much of it is and will be vivid in my head. The dream on stage is like the realization of something I might have wanted to dream. And I can't see the production again because the company stayed for only seven performances. Still, to commemorate it, here is one small way to certify it and to share it.

There's a better way. Asmus reports that Beckett prepared a *Regiebuch* for this production, a sort of heavily annotated promptbook, and shows a sample. At least one other such *Regiebuch* exists, for Beckett's production of *Happy Days* at the Schiller in 1971. These books should be published: not as law for all future productions but as testaments of how a theater genius saw his work—at least at one point in his life—in the theater.

Agamemnon

(June 11, 1977)

At last the stage of the Beaumont, that notorious white elephant, has been put to good use: the audience sits on it. The first things we note when we come in are two big sections of bleachers on the stage, full of people facing us. In front of them, between that portion of the audience and ourselves, many rows of seats have been ripped out to make the Beaumont a theater-in-the-round. But that's not all: in that center is a large triangular metal grating, as a platform, with two ramps leading up to it from the bowels of the building. (Of course the space under the grating is visible, and is later used.) And *that's* not all: those two bleacher sections are mobile. Thus chunks of the audience are swung aside and moved back and forth during the action, so that portions of what was formerly the stage can be added to or subtracted from the center.

This first view, before the play begins, announces that the director Andrei Serban, who was so galvanically ill-at-ease with Chekhov's realism in *The Cherry Orchard*, is back in a mode where his imagination can work fruitfully. The play is billed as Aeschylus's *Agamemnon* "using fragments of the original Greek and Edith Hamilton's translation." The statement about fragments is true, but this is not Aeschylus's play. That fact makes for real shortcomings, but the faults do not obscure some high theatrical magnificence.

In the monumental productions of Greek plays that Serban did at La Mama and at other places around the world, he worked only in foreign languages—Greek and Latin, mostly—and he condensed greatly, crystallizing à la Grotowski. Here he has worked in Greek and English, roughly half and half, and has expanded. Since Serban changed his method only when he moved to a large uptown theater that aims at a wide audience, I dare to infer that the changes were made for (let's call them) ecumenical reasons.

It's risky to argue against plays being performed (at least partially) in the only language I understand, but the experiential truth remains that, in those earlier productions, the strangeness of the language, telling a familiar story, and the compactness of the action made for power. Strict comprehensibility and customary characterization were abandoned in order to create archetypal figures obeying primal dark dynamics. What's more, those productions made a case—incomplete but undismissible—that *in the theater* the Greek tragedies are more effective these days if treated mythically rather than as plays whose every nuance of character and reference is pertinent. (How many people, intelligent and cultivated, recognize the name Leda in *Agamemnon* and know that she was the mother of both Clytemnestra and Helen?) Serban's grasp of those tragedies' perennial essentials, in great *sound* of words interwoven with fine music, was very strong.

But now Serban has tampered with his own purity by, paradoxically, putting much of this play in English. Even to the end of clarity it's not wholly successful, especially when one section of the chorus is singing a line of notes while another section is speaking. (Wonderfully striking when you're not expected to understand the words!)

And Serban has added explication. Evidently he has little faith that the audience will read the synopsis in the program or understand it if they do. The performance begins with a dumbshow, like the one before the play-within-a-play in *Hamlet*, synopsizing the action: Agamemnon sacrifices his daughter Iphigenia, then his wife Clytemnestra slays him in revenge, then her son Orestes slays her in revenge. And then, during the play, we get full-scale enactments of these matters, although they are only referred to in Aeschylus and although Orestes doesn't even appear until the next play (of this one surviving Greek trilogy).

Now these insertions, and others, tamper with something more than scholastic chastity. Possibly the best-known fact about Greek tragedy is that, though bodies were sometimes displayed after death, killings were never shown. The Greeks were not interested in the details of violence, essentially indistinguishable between *The Oresteia* and *The Godfather*, they were interested in causes and effects. And they used the theater, not to present fact but to infuse imagination and spirit. This purpose, despite the particularity of his La Mama productions, Serban once enhanced. Now, up in the Big Time, he fiddles with it. The excuse presumably is that this counter-distillation, this expansion, makes things clearer for those who don't know the story and won't read the synopsis. I would insist, unabashedly, that one of the best aspects of Serban's earlier productions was that they were done for those who did know or at least would read. If that is elitist—that meager distinction—then we're very hard up for elitism these days.

The result here tends toward the lurid and therefore banal, even though these insertions, like every moment in the production, are beautifully designed in themselves. This tragedy is not about killing, it's about justice: and the gods' view of man's view of it.

Serban then contradicts his "modernization" by having two actors play two roles each, in early Aeschylean manner. Priscilla Smith performs Clytemnestra titanically, with open-throated Doric force; but she also has to play the captive Cassandra and, in that role, has to spend much of her energy merely in differentiating her second performance from her first. Why? Valois Mickens, who did Cassandra so well in Serban's *Trojan Women*, is in the chorus here—and is understudying Cassandra! Why not have Mickens play it? Jamil Zakkai, well equipped for the title role, must also deal with the role of his enemy Aegisthus. Why?

Some other defects. George Voskovec is miscast as the chorus leader. That moving-about of the bleachers is a poor substitute for having the audience literally follow the action as they did at La Mama. (In Athens a few years ago the audience followed Serban's productions through the streets to the top of Mount Lycabettus.) This bleacher shuffling is the "uptown" comfy version. The lighting by Jennifer Tipton, fine most of the time, becomes as blandly white as that of a basketball court in the scene of Agamemnon's return from Troy.

At the second performance after the official opening, the production seemed under-rehearsed. (The Serban company at La Mama had worked together for years.) Even though some of the chorus had been with Serban previously, the movements of this group lacked the tensile quality of his former chorus; here they sometimes seemed to stroll from one position to another. And Zakkai, who—thanks to Apollo!—replaced the actor originally in his roles, needs more work on his readings and his movement. He uses his arms and hands with modern casualness, which wasn't true of his Jason in Serban's first *Medea*. This constrasts weakly with Smith's graphic formalities of gesture, derived from Greek friezes and vase-paintings. I'm planning to see *Agamemnon* again in a few weeks to see whether Serban has tightened the production.

But because of all my reservations, which I think are serious, I must shout even louder my praise, my joy. Serban has a gift for elemental theater—the most difficult kind—that stuns and thrills. I haven't seen the work of Ariane Mnouchkine in Paris or of Peter Stein in West Berlin, directors different from Serban yet who, by report, work in comparably large, large-spirited ways. Possibly excepting them but certainly including Peter Brook, Serban is peerless in his sense of theater space: how to reveal it, mine it, exalt it. With the flow of individuals and groups, with the exploitation of every bit of his environment, with torches and darkness, with simple huge props—the famous purple cloth for the king's return, the net to trap him in, the car in which Apollo descends to ravish Cassandra with a long spear—Serban moves in marvels to create a tragic line. The shape of this production is a work of vigorous imagination, fertile and confident.

And so is the sound. The production was conceived, says the program, "by Andrei Serban and Elizabeth Swados." Her music is not accompaniment, it's integral. Serban directed the speaking, I'm told, Swados the singing, all of which is performed by the same people. The barbaric-gentle quarter-tones, the dramatically used instruments (especially flutes and drums), the overlay of august song are inseparable from the whole. Does Swados write Attic music? No one on earth knows. But if the Theater of Dionysus didn't have music as good as this, the Athenians were deprived.

It's wonderful to see Serban's talents turned again to congenial material. It's troubling to see the hemming and stitching of (presumable) concessions. I offer him deep admiration: and some worry.

(July 9 & 16, 1977)

I've seen Serban's *Agamemnon* again at the Beaumont. The second time, four weeks after my first visit, I sat on the stage, in one of the two bleacher sections that were moved about. I enjoyed it more than I thought I would: it was a fairly good approximation of following Serban's *Trojan Women* on foot, which I had done four times. At one point the bleachers were shoved far upstage, and I could see all the stage mechanisms behind the proscenium arch as I watched the Argive world in the center. This, paradoxically, helped. I got an added sense of immediate imaginative creation, rather than pretended actuality, as I watched Apollo descend and ascend in his cart and also saw the stagehands over against the wall tugging at Apollo's ropes.

What I had disliked in the production the first time, I disliked more intensely the second time—like the miming of the Trojan war and the bathtub murder of the king. The clean line of Aeschylus's play was certainly zigzagged by Serban. But the individual zigs and zags were well composed. And the (many) elements I had liked the first time, I liked even more.

As I had hoped, Jamil Zakkai, Agamemnon/Aegisthus, had firmed his grip on both roles. Some of Serban's best touches were even more thrilling the second time: *e.g.*, the Watchman, who has spent years on the palace roof waiting for the signal of Troy's fall, beginning his speech in an immense stage whisper, then gradually finding his voice; the doubling of the Herald who tells the story of the victory—the role is done by two actors, one behind the Chorus Leader, one facing him, speaking in unison.

And, which I had praised but not enough, Priscilla Smith's Clytemnestra. (I regret even more deeply that she also plays Cassandra: the point of this completely eludes me.) The sheer size of Smith as the Queen, the size of the imagination and self and technique implied in her performance, soars. Soars. She made me think of Flagstad in the first act of *Tristan und Isolde*, in the passage that ends "*Rache! Tod! Tod—uns Beiden!*" Smith's Clytemnestra went through to the end in that vein—"the avenger, ancient in anger." I'll never forget it.

The Gin Game

(November 12, 1977)

In 1895 Henry Irving did a short play by Conan Doyle called *A Story of Waterloo* in which he played an ancient veteran of the battle and was hailed for his masterly portrayal of age. Bernard Shaw, reviewing the performance, dissected it in terms of its familiar set-ups and derivations, then concluded:

> Every old actor into whose hands this article falls will understand perfectly from my description how the whole thing is done and will wish that he could get such Press notices for a little hobbling and piping, and a few bits of mechanical business with a pipe, a carbine, and two chairs. The whole performance does not involve one gesture, one line, one thought outside the commonest routine of automatic stage illusion.

This is not entirely true of Hume Cronyn's performance in *The Gin Game*: there are flashes of authenticity, moments when he doesn't come up with quite the anticipated gesture or inflection. But I ascribe—unjustly?—those moments to Mike Nichols, the director. Nichols's ambition continues to shrink but his skill is undiminished, and I assume, on past experience, that it was he who occasionally brought Cronyn past his usual mechanics to some touches of truth.

In the main, however, the crusty old man whom Cronyn plays is "created" for us: a) before the play begins by the photographs and reviews and by yum-yum anticipations of a two-character "character" play; b) after a few minutes, by the old-folks-home setting, the unkempt white hair, the creakiness of the joints, the arthritic turns of the head. How can he miss being hailed for his artistry? But then how could any competent actor miss? Ten minutes into the play, Cronyn is on a secure, time-tested toboggan slide, coasting home.

His co-star Jessica Tandy (Mrs. Cronyn) is a somewhat different case. She has always been better skilled, less self-conscious and quasi-apologetic, and she does have some natural warmth (unlike her husband). Also she is benefiting from the passage of time. Some actors grow, through the years, into the much-needed aging of their faces and the right use of them. With Tandy, it's happening with the voice. Her voice has always had a breaking, unbased, fluttery quality, which was distracting even in her best work when she was younger. It's more appropriate to the characters she can do now.

The play, in a few facts, is about two lone people who meet in a home. He, who was there first, plays a lot of solitaire and—let's hear that heartwarming chuckle, folks—cheats. When she comes along, he enlists her as a partner for gin rummy, a game she doesn't know. He teaches her. They play. She wins. They play many times through the two acts. She always wins. At the beginning this makes him amusingly irate, at the end it fills him with blind fury. The gin games are presumably meant as double symbols: first, as a geriatric substitute for courtship-and-sex, in which she is unwelcomely, even unwillingly, dominant; second, as an x-ray exposure of their characters, revealing darknesses in both, beneath the cozy old-folks exteriors.

The only really noteworthy aspect of this play is that there's another play lurking within it. The author, D. L. Coburn, whose first play this is, may be delighted with this production for all I know, but it occurred to me while watching it that the very same text could be legitimately used to less conventional ends. *The Gin Game* is now being done in (let's call it) the Paddy Chayefsky-Neil Simon vein: "We are ruthless modern truthtellers who scrape a whole millimeter below the Norman Rockwell surface, and we prove our *bona fides* by not giving you the hand-in-hand sunset-trail ending you expected." But this script could, I think, be played so that the ending is not a surprise, is inevitable, so that the intent is not to put a stinger at the end of a bittersweet piece of candy but to strip away some of the sentimental prerogatives of old age. If these two old people exploited their age, as stupid or vicious or spoiled elderly people often do, knowing even with each other that they were claiming wisdom and respect the way one claims a pension, just because one has reached the right age; if it were the intent to show that age, not patriotism, is the last refuge of scoundrels, this might have been a moderately scathing play.

But it wouldn't have been a hit. So we get a "realistic" play instead of a real one.

Tartuffe

(November 12, 1977)

I still hope that some day, somewhere, I'm going to see this play performed as written. *Tartuffe* is by no means my favorite Molière, but it's a better play than—and *different* from—any production of it I've seen.

I'm not talking about failures of "style," that terminological rabbit-punch by the critic who doesn't like a revival of an old play and doesn't really know why. Stephen Porter's directon here seems more fitted to *Charley's Aunt* than to Molière, as do the performances of some of the cast, notably Tammy Grimes; still the worst trouble is not the matter of "proper" style. I've seen the Comédie-Française, the House of Molière, in several of his plays, and even they don't use a consistent style. (Old story: when someone complained to Louis Jouvet that one of his Molière productions was not in the Molière style, Jouvet said: "How do you know? Do you have his telephone number?")

I'm talking about the text. Anyone who reads this play with eyes unfogged by past productions must see that the title no more specifies the protagonist than does the title of *Cymbeline* or *Julius Caesar*. A protagonist—and this is an empirical theatrical definition, not an academic one—is the chief bearer of the agon, the one to whom most happens, the one who is most changed by the action of the play. And in this play that person is not (repeat: *not*) Tartuffe. He remains absolutely unchanged from beginning to end. The character who changes is Orgon, the husband who brings Tartuffe into his house and is so far deceived by him that he almost ruins self and family. Orgon is finally undeceived by that family who, undeceived from the beginning, have not changed. The experience of the play is Orgon's.

One other character changes, from utter belief in Tartuffe to shocked disbelief: Madame Pernelle, Orgon's mother, who appears only at the beginning and the end. This seems to confirm that Orgon is the center by helping to delineate his character. He's a middle-aged man dominated by a religious nut of a mother, a man who is remarried to a younger woman, who presumably has the panic of middle age in relation to a younger wife, who needs a reason to reject worldliness (read "sex"), and who is encouraged by mom to believe in the religiosity of a swindler. When Orgon's wife proves Tartuffe's lechery, she is really proving her love for her husband and is erasing his doubts about his maleness. It's not a play about religious hypocrisy: Tartuffe could be, has been, another kind of swindler. Tartuffe saw what would work best in this case, and Orgon is the case. And it's all right there in the text.

Porter, never an inspired director, heads straight for the old wrong-headed interpretation, puts a dull and inadequate actor in Orgon, and gets an excellent actor, John Wood, for Tartuffe. Porter then proceeds to encourage or permit Wood to construct a rococo superstructure on this falsely elevated part. Wood was brought over from England to be a virtuoso, and does he ever deliver! If there was ever an example of virtuosity distinct from real acting, this is it. What a bouquet of florid inflections and exaggerated serpentine movements.

The production uses Richard Wilbur's verse translation, the best I know, but the rhymed couplets that imitate Molière are finally uncongenial to English. The chief pleasure in the production comes from Zack Brown's setting which does a good deal to mitigate the wretchedness of that Circle in the Square playing space.

Saint Joan

(January 7, 1978)

Watching even this sorry production, one sees again a truth about Shaw that is often scanted. Many of the plays of this man celebrated for comic sparkle and dialectical thrust are centered on passion. Underneath diamonds lavished by the handful along the way, there is fire.

Think of them: Marchbanks in *Candida*, the poet who harrows through love to the heights of lonely exultation; John Tanner in *Man and Superman*, slashing at the world of acceptances; Father Keegan in *John Bull's Other Island*, still another religionist who loved his religion not wisely but too well; Major Barbara, a votary searching for a temple in a materialist age; Dubedat in *The Doctor's Dilemma*, the painter who doesn't mind consuming everything and everyone, including himself, in his hunger for art; and the figure at the height of the flame's leap, Joan herself. Among the many misconceptions about Shaw—and no genius of the drama has been heaped with more—is the attribution of coldness. This lie was best caricatured by Shaw himself (of course) in the epilogue to *Fanny's First Play*. Two critics are discussing him, and one says: "I've repeatedly proved that Shaw is physiologically incapable of the note of passion," and the other responds, "Yes, I know. Intellect without emotion . . . A giant brain, if you ask me; but no heart."

Even in this production, the first scene made me cry. After that, the action and direction grimly wrestled the script to the ground; and it's not even a fair fight because the text has been cut here and there. For instance, in the epilogue Stogumber, the crazed old English cleric, says that the burning of Joan twenty-five years earlier made him understand horror in a way that paintings of the Crucifixion never had done; and old Bishop Cauchon says, "Must then a Christ perish in torment in every age to save those that have no imagination?" Some of us think that this is a key line in the play. Not this theater: they cut it.

Lynn Redgrave's performance of the title role is a betrayal from first moment to last. Joan bursts into the play on a great wave of health, a country girl who is as sure of her mission as she is of the ground under her feet. Redgrave comes in to flirt coyly and simperingly with the Squire whom she wants to send her to the Dauphin. From then on she yowls and moans, she keens and attitudinizes vocally, she makes a lot of what can only be called goofy faces that I found hard to relate even as mechanical face-making to what she was supposed to be thinking or feeling at the moment. And since in most of this play she appears in male dress, it's appropriate to note that she is knock-kneed and splay-footed, a fact that is less apparent in skirts and that hardly makes her an inspiring military leader as she galumphs about like a dromedary. Physical inadequacy aside, I have rarely seen a performance of a major role by an allegedly serious actress that was so blatantly without a center, so blatantly a mere aggregation of attempted effects.

I blame her husband, John Clark, who directed, for at least some of this hollowness and failure. Under Gerald Freedman's direction a year and a half ago Redgrave gave a sturdy enough performance of Vivie in *Mrs. Warren's Profession* to make me hope for her Joan. Her failure, plus the other performances, points squarely at Clark. Philip Bosco, whose work has so often been appealing, plays Warwick in the top third of his good voice and employs every cliché of theatrical suavity. Robert LuPone plays the carefully drawn Dauphin like a homosexual twit. The only well realized acting comes from Nicholas Hormann as Brother Martin Ladvenu, the compassionate cleric at the trial.

As for the staging, one example will suffice. At the end of the trial scene Joan tears up the recantation she has signed under duress when she hears that, though she could escape burning by recanting, she would now be imprisoned for life. Ladvenu says: "You wicked girl: if your counsel were of God would He not deliver you?" Joan's last speech: "His ways are not your ways. He wills that I go through the fire to His bosom; for I am His child, and you are not fit that I should live among you. That is my last word to you." After that magnificently free statement of faith and final triumph, this Joan is *dragged out backwards by two guards!*

It's very difficult to refrain from cursing a director who would ask such a thing, a Joan who would agree, and a theater that would sponsor such a production.

Play and Other Plays

(January 14, 1978)

Samuel Beckett is still sending back messages. Who really knows where he is any longer?—out there in lonely splendor and splendid loneliness. The residual wryness of his career is that he keeps on writing at the same time that he writes more and more minimally. He has a physical being still, one hears that he has friends and plays tennis and corresponds, yet more and more his new writings have the effect of posthumous messages. More precisely, they are like pieces written during the very passage out of life, while crossing the border, and somehow sent back—diamond-clear, humorously unremitting. The pieces are not about death but about life seen in the longest perspective from which one can still write, and they have his Irish insistence on facing the void with a bit of a grin at its silliness in being empty.

This bill of three Beckett plays, two of them new, was first performed in 1976 at the Arena Stage in Washington where the two new pieces had their U.S. premières. They have been brought to New York by the Manhattan Theater Club with two of the three members of the first cast and the same director. It's a good set of pieces. All three of them are located near the end or just past the end of life, when the tugs and countertugs of living can still be felt but when judgments are altering.

The familiar piece, *Play*, is, as Sir Thomas Browne might have said, hydriotaphic—we see three large urns containing three dead people, their heads just visible above the tops of the jugs. (No absolute proof in the text that they're dead but what else could we be expected to assume?) The three are a man, his wife, his mistress. This is the third time I've seen the play, and if it's well-rehearsed, which includes the spotlight that keeps flying from one face to another as one or another speaks, it *must* be effective. Acting, in any full sense, is not required: acutely timed and phrased part-singing (almost) is. It's a bitterly comic canon on human vanity—specifically the vanity of sensuality and of the deceits necessary to accommodate it in our world.

I alway feel that it's Beckett himself flicking that spotlight from one head to another. The explicit directions for the lighting call for a single spot, and add: "The method consisting in assigning to each face a separate fixed spot is un-satisfactory in that it is less expressive of a unique inquisitor than the single mobile spot." And who, finally, is that inquisitor other than the author?

That Time, one of the new plays, is another essentially musical piece. All we see is an old man's head, eyes closed most of the time, and see it as if from above, with the white hair streaming. The face does almost nothing throughout, except that it breathes and we hear the breathing. Mostly we hear three separate recordings of the man's voice "coming to him from both sides and above. They modulate back and forth without any break in general flow except where silence is indicated." The piece might be called *Three More of Krapp's Last Tapes*, for tapes they are, from a place of further finality, three streams of memory pouring shards of sensory treasures on the man—trifles in themselves, some of them, but treasures because they happened and in memory still happen. We hear childhood memories and much later ones—the feel of stone, of sunlight on a particular day, of a love, of a last departure—the small and the great now equally important because they all *happened*, back there in lovely life. The tone is generally tristful, but at the last, after the voices cease, the eyes in the face open and the old man smiles.

Footfalls is a dialogue between a middle-aged woman and her unseen ancient mother, as the woman moves in dim light back and forth on a stipulated line on the stage floor. This brief play is in two parts. The first part, mostly one long speech by the unseen mother, centers on a remark that the daughter made when she was a child walking on a deep-carpeted floor: "Mother, this is not enough . . . I must hear the feet, however faint they fall . . . The motion alone is not enough." In the "sequel," so called, the mother is presumably dead, and the daughter transforms her memories into a passage from a novel. ("Old Mrs. Winter, whom the reader will remember. . . .") The woman's childhood insistence on hearing the steps that she took is counterpointed with her "footfalls" here; and with the memory of an Evensong service that she attended with her mother once, where the motions alone were not enough.

No admirer of Beckett will maintain that these two new pieces rank in the forefront of his work; neither could they have been written by anyone lesser. What stand out in them are the elements that have always been present in his plays but that have grown in dominance as his plays have grown shorter: the central feature of a Beckett play is its *image* and next in importance is the very sound of the voices. All else follows from and through those considerations. Increasingly Beckett has been using the theater as a medium to make painting and music bloom into drama and philosophy. I don't imply that what is said in these new plays is in itself of no consequence, only that the sound precedes the meaning in consequence: not just in sequence, in consequence. It's worth noting, too, that the style of the writing in these recent plays is closer to that of Beckett's novels than that of *Waiting for Godot* or *Endgame*.

The time has come, inevitably, for reaction against Beckett. An instance is in the Winter 1977/78 issue of the *American Scholar* where John Romano writes a critical reassessment that concludes: "In the end [Beckett] offers the best example of a paradoxical tendency in contemporary literature, whereby, under the guise of experiments in form and language, we are actually being reconciled to our social and spiritual givens, confirmed in our complacency and stasis." If I understand at all the words "guise" and "reconciled" and "complacency," then Romano is calling Beckett a con man, in which case Beckett must be the most successful con man in literary history. It wasn't, after all, an austere new art forged to face stark moral and spiritual truths, it was only a counterfeit, a semblance. And why was the semblance fabricated? To lull us. His esthetic sleight-of-hand was designed to make us think he was facing perceptions so vast and lonely that it wasn't even worth our trouble to go as far as he had gone: we might as well stay at home because there was nothing out there. And he has done all that careful writing of novels and plays and poems just to deceive us. What gulls we are to think Beckett not only a great writer but a moral hero moving us closer to negative capability.

Reassessment of Beckett will doubtless continue, but I hope it will smack less of Oliver Edwards's familiar remark to Samuel Johnson: "You are a philosopher, Dr. Johnson. I have tried too in my time to be a philosopher; but, I don't know how, cheerfulness was always breaking in."

Meanwhile, thanks to the Manhattan Theater Club for bringing us this bill.

The actors are Suzanne Costallos (her professional debut), Donald Davis, and Sloane Shelton, all of whom do well. So does Alan Schneider, an old Beckett hand, though it must be said that directing these three plays well consists in some measure of obeying Beckett's explicit instructions. The designs by Zack Brown and the lighting by William Mintzer convert nowhere into a place.

A Touch of the Poet

(January 28, 1978)

When Eugene O'Neill was awarded the Nobel prize in 1936, congratulations poured in from around the world, "but," says Louis Sheaffer in his biography, "what particularly pleased O'Neill . . . was that the Irish ambassador in Washington praised him on behalf of the Irish Free State 'as adding . . . to the credit of old Ireland.' " Said O'Neill to a friend: "What could be more perfect?"

We forget, in our view of O'Neill as the best American dramatist, how Irish he thought himself and how important his Irishness was to his best work. In fact a rough rule of thumb could distinguish between his (many) lesser plays and his (few) towering ones by that very Irishness: it doesn't figure in the former and it does in the latter. (Even Hickey in The Iceman Cometh, though his origins are unspecified, always seems Irish-American.) Obviously O'Neill was American but not single-mindedly: it's the conflict of cultures, Irish-Catholic versus American Protestant or American godless, that lies at the base of his best dramas.

This conflict ground to the forefront of his mind as his life went on. Between 1935 and 1941, when he was at his creative peak, he planned a cycle of seven long plays to be called A Tale of Possessors Self-Dispossessed and said that he was " going on the theory that the United States, instead of being the most successful country in the world, is the greatest failure. It's the greatest failure because it was given everything, more than any other country." At the core of that statement is the voice of the disappointed immigrant, the unrequited lover.

Only two plays of the cycle exist—O'Neill burned some manuscripts. More Stately Mansions, which was to be the second in the series, was not revised or polished: posthumously, it was adapted and produced and published. (I saw it, or some of it, in Germany with Elizabeth Bergner.) The first play is A Touch of the Poet.

The day is July 27, 1828, the place Melody's tavern, a few miles from Boston. Con Melody is Irish-born—high-born, he insists—a former major in Wellington's Spanish campaigns. Come to America with his wife and daughter, he lets them do the work in the place while he boozes with his cronies and lords it over them with his past grandeur. Today is the anniversary of the Battle of Talavera in which Con won glory, and on every anniversary he puts on his uniform.

Convalescing upstairs in the inn (we never see him) is a young "Yankee," Simon Harford, the poet of the title, who had been living a Walden-like existence nearby, fell ill, and is being nursed back to health by Con's daughter, Sara. The central action involves a possible marriage between the two and Con's terrible degradation when he attempts to avenge his and his daughter's honor for an insult from Simon's father. At the end Con, his uniform torn, his face bruised, his illusions broken, shoots the thoroughbred mare that was his token of gentility and goes to join his cronies in the bar. The gentleman in exile has been replaced by the commoner at home—in a new home.

One of the play's several interests is formal: to see how close it is in tone and in dramaturgy to the nineteenth-century popular theater and to see how this links O'Neill with other great writers. Ibsen's realistic period, beginning with *Pillars of Society*, shows the effects of the "well-made" plays with which he had dealt in his six years' practical work in the Bergen theater. Martin Meisel has written an excellent book on *Shaw and the Nineteenth-Century Theater*. The paradox of O'Neill is that, because he was sickened by his actor-father's career in such vehicles as *The Count of Monte Cristo*, he began his writing in the "new" realist-symbolist vein, yet in his maturity came back in certain aspects to his father's theater. Talking about the role of Con Melody, he said: "What that one needs is an actor like Maurice Barrymore [John's father] or James O'Neill, my old man. One of those big-chested, chiseled-mug, romantic old boys . . . Most actors in these times lack an air." And because he could not find such an actor, he would not let the play be performed in his lifetime.

The link with the theater's past is not only in such conventions as the innocent lower-class maiden and the visiting upper-class poet: in the protagonist who is both dashing and devilish, like Robert Macaire: in the construction with its onstage action that is almost naively designed to cover lapses of time while things happen off-stage. It's in O'Neill's reliance on the actor of Melody, as the quotation above proves, to complete the play, in a way that his other good plays do not so absolutely require. *A Touch of the Poet* is not on the scale of *Long Day's Journey into Night*, but it does have tragic dimension—the fracture of European romance on American reality—if it has the right actor to give us both sides of the catastrophe.

In the last twenty minutes or so of the play, Jason Robards is fine as Melody, on the other side of the catastrophe in which Con is degraded. When the role comes to Robards, when he can once again do the one character he can do well—the ironic, self-loathing drunk, the Jamie of *Long Day's Journey* and *A Moon for the Misbegotten*—he fulfills it. But in the major part of the role (pun intended), he is, frankly, appalling.

I could hardly believe what I was seeing and hearing. Instead of a Byron-quoting ex-officer, a fallen emperor with a ragged retinue, we get mugging and caricature. For just one instance: when the elegant Mrs. Harford, Simon's mother, enters unannounced, Robards turns from his mirror and discovers her. Then he does a full unabashed "take" from her face to the audience, like a baggy-pants comic when a pretty girl comes in. Throughout, until the very end, he kept reminding me of Harvey Korman of "The Carol Burnett Show" playing a lord. Then I realized what was happening. Robards (and his director) took the "elevated" portion of the role as impersonation, a kind of W. C. Fields act of grandeur. Nothing could be falser or more destructive of the play. Either the grand Con is *not* "acting" or there is no tragedy. The two actors I've seen previously in the part, Eric Portman and Denholm Elliott, had their shortcomings, but both of them understood that basic truth. Without it, without Con's belief in himself as a gentleman, all we get is the exposure of a self-conscious faker, which is trivial.

Kathryn Walker, who plays Sara, is a beautiful and greatly gifted actress, but if you remember her as the team owner in the film *Slapshot*, you will understand that she is too mature for the part. That lovely contralto of hers is not the voice in which to rhapsodize about a first kiss. Milo O'Shea, as a former fellow-campaigner of Con's, is pedestrian as ever; he is evidently making a career of being an Irish actor in America. Betty Miller gives an adequate but trite genteel performance as Simon's mother. The treasure of the evening is Geraldine Fitzgerald as Nora, Con's patient, devoted wife. Beginning with her Mary in *Long Day's Journey* in 1971, Fitzgerald has shown how an actress of middle years can grow. Her Nora is rich, peasant-wise, enduring and endearing.

This is Ben Edwards's second design for the play: he did the setting for the first New York production in 1958 which I saw. Refreshing myself from a drawing, I prefer that early setting. Most of the entrances are now squinched on one side, and Edwards has built a staircase so steep and ill-placed that it gives us the most ungainly view possible of descending actors.

I've seen most of José Quintero's direction of O'Neill plays since *The Iceman Cometh* in 1956, and I think he has declined badly. His *Anna Christie* last year was clumsy: this production is even clumsier. In addition to the character-misinterpretation and the faulty acting he permits, his use of the stage is either cluttered or frenetic—from the stagy opening scene between O'Shea and the barkeep, uneasy and phonily played, to the last act when Quintero has the barefoot Walker race back and forth across the stage like a Paul Taylor dancer.

And Quintero has nibbled at the text. Indeed, the very last line is missing.

Blvd de Paris (I've Got the Shakes)

(February 25, 1978)

Blvd de Paris (I've Got the Shakes) is the latest production of Richard Foreman's Ontological-Hysteric Theater. Close students of Foreman—and there are a sizeable number—have written almost as much about his work as has Foreman himself. I'm neither a close student nor an unqualified admirer and haven't written about him since February 8, 1975, except for his direction of *Threepenny Opera* at the Beaumont, which was not with his own company; but I've seen all of his New York productions since 1975. The exegetes make much of the fact that, in a recent show, sitting at his usual desk in front of the audience, controlling sound cues and tapes, and shouting "Cue!" to conclude scenes, he had a sword suspended over his head. Imagine the flutter caused by this latest show in which someone else sits at that desk working the controls—no sword, no shouts of "Cue!" We're now told that Foreman is objectifying his work more than before.

From the name of his theater to the titles of his pieces (the title of his latest one is abbreviated above), Foreman's work is easy to ridicule. This is stupid. He is a highly intelligent, completely serious man of, to me, very limited gifts, and those gifts are more pictorial than theatrical. His theater on lower Broadway, where his group plays when not working in Paris, is long, and it narrows like the inside of a camera, with the (small) audience on bleachers at the wide end. The stage design, by Foreman, uses rapidly converging perspectives with curtains and screens and mobile pieces (a railway compartment in this latest work) that are ingenious. *Blvd de Paris* is done in black and white, except for one red roll of carpet, and it's visually delightful.

Foreman's pieces—he calls them plays—are meant as suprisers and rearrangers of perception. Last winter I was in a symposium about the O-H Theater, along with the amiable Foreman himself, where it developed that one of the books that have influenced him is Anton Ehrenzweig's *The Hidden Order of Art*. Ehrenzweig explicitly is "not advocating a cult of spontaneity at the expense of intellectual control," but the concept of "unconscious scanning" is central to him. To speak reductively of a complex theory, Ehrenzweig sees creation in three stages: the first stage projects fragmented parts of the self into the work; the second initiates unconscious scanning that integrates the substructure; the third takes the "hidden substructure . . . back into the artist's ego on the higher mental level." This all may sound classic rather than innovative, but Ehrenzweig puts heavy emphasis on the psychological aspects of the three stages and on the determinant power of that unconscious scanning. My own difference with Foreman is all in stage three. What I see in his finished work is almost entirely his unconscious scanning; but he insists that he has brought it all up to stage three—intellectual control and esthetic organism. He sees his works as complete; I see them as enacted notebooks.

I'm not going to detail, even if it were possible, the contents of *Blvd de Paris* except to say that this time the medium for Foreman's perception-shatterings is *fin de siècle* Paris. But I can use, as an example of our difference, the work of his leading performer Kate Manheim, who appears again in the recurring star "role" of Rhoda. To Foreman and to his admirers, Manheim has grown increasingly expressive, has become an excellent agent for his work. To me she is only an increasingly confident amateur about whom the word "talent" is irrelevant, who is now less doggedly unashamed of being on stage at all—let alone naked, as she has often been—whose movement is now a bit less patent obedience to a director's orders, and who can now make three or four faces more than she used to be able to make. I do not mock her or Foreman: I simply cite her work as prime instance of my difference with Foreman about "stage three" of his theater pieces.

On the Twentieth Century

(March 18, 1978)

Almost every Broadway musical that I've seen in the last dozen years could have served as the subject of an article called: Whatever Became of the Broadway Musical? On the Twentieth Century, which has just puffed in, is no exception. It's chockfull of the desperate bustle of the very weary and the imaginatively bankrupt. It was written and directed by Big Names, but they are Big Old Names, which in this case means tired.

Like marathon runners who don't know that they've passed the finish line, they just keep jog-jog-jogging along. This has been going on for some time. Betty Comden and Adolph Green, who wrote the book and lyrics, and Harold Prince, the director, have done such dismal musicals in the last dozen years, that this new show is not a falling off, it's simply a non-falling-down as they keep jogging. Cy Coleman, the composer, responsible for (at his best) the dull score of Sweet Charity and (at his worst) I Love My Wife, of which I will never hear the second half, has tried to write a florid score here to match the florid comedy of the show. I'm afraid it does. But the whole febrile exhaustion is worth some inquiry.

The book began life as an unproduced play, Napoleon on Broadway by Charles Bruce Milholland. It was rewritten by Ben Hecht and Charles MacArthur, retitled Twentieth Century, and produced in 1933 with Moffat Johnston as a theatrical producer modeled on David Belasco and with Eugenie Leontovich as a film star who had begun as his theater star.

She had been a shopgirl; he had made her, in several senses. Then after some years of stress, they had quarreled, she had left his bed and boards and had gone to Hollywood. Now several years after that, the producer is returning from Chicago to New York on board the crack Twentieth Century Limited, broke after the latest of a series of flops. She is on the same train. His only chance for survival is to get her name on a contract before the train reaches New York, with which signed contract he can raise money and revive his career. Out of all this, lots of comedy—swashing and buckling and theatrical alley-cat yowling and scratching.

Hecht and MacArthur adapted the play for the screen, mostly by tacking on to the beginning a long opening section that comically dramatized what had happened in the years before the play begins. The result was immortalized—the word is calmly chosen—in Howard Hawks's film (1934). Hawks's direction is brisk and witty, Walter Connolly as the producer's aide is unforgettable, Carole Lombard gives her first really "free" comic performance, not technically secure but full of a beautiful woman's temperamental excitements; and John Barrymore plays the producer. A print of this film should be in every acting school in the country. What you get in Barrymore's performance, besides its many immediate pleasures, is a hundred years of American theatrical history. His maternal grandparents and his parents had been prominent in the nineteenth-century theater, his uncle was John Drew; he himself grew up with that style which could be (but was not restricted to) larger-than-life; and he brought that style into the modern age with surety, respect, and relish; and, in this case, a touch of spoofery. Since he was a master of it, he *could* spoof it. His electric movements and Palmer-penmanship gestures are just slightly italicized: his ability to sustain vowels and even some consonants to make effects without losing credence is just slightly *bel canto*. His personality and his emotional range are staggering every time one sees the film. The only actors I know of today on this continent who could come close to what Barrymore does in this film (now that Fredric March is dead) are George C. Scott, Christopher Plummer, and Richard Kiley. Well. . . . Robert Preston, maybe.

Now why did anyone choose to make a musical of this play without understanding that, first and last, it's a vehicle for irresistible star performers? It's not a show that can perhaps get by on its book and music (even if they were excellent) and with only an adequate cast. The producer is played by John Cullum, who has a passable operetta-baritone. That is absolutely all. He cannot act; he has no charm, sex, or color; and worst of all, considering what he's called on to do here, he has no comic sense and no ability to move. His first number, "I Rise Again," is about his determination to recoup, histrionically exaggerated by throwing himself to the floor, then struggling to his feet, etc. Cullum, unfunny, simply looks foolish or sick—possibly an advanced case of St. Vitus's dance.

The glamorous tempestuous star—and I can hardly believe that she's really in the role even as I type her name—is Madeline Kahn. She, too, has an adequate voice. All that she has besides—as you may have observed in her films, including Mel Brooks's recent disappointment *High Anxiety*—is some mincing smart-aleck, mock-sexy wit, like the cleverest girl at any Central Park West party. Imogene Coca plays the religious fanatic who figures decisively in the plot (a man in the original). Coca was once rightly popular on TV for her winsome kookiness. The day is past.

With Cullum and Kahn in the leading roles of a comedy that is supposed to dazzle us with fireworks, the best book would suffer. Comden and Green have not written that best book. The beginning: Cullum makes his entrance on the train by clinging to the outside as it leaves the station (in order to elude the marshals), then climbs through a window. This entrance helps to kill his character before Cullum finishes the job. Barrymore walked calmly past the marshals watching for him in the station; he was dressed as a stock Southern colonel, and even stopped to ask for a light. That was a theater man's ruse, not an acrobatic trick irrelevant to atmosphere and theme. The ending: Comden and Green have juggled the business of the star's signing the contract at the end—I won't detail it—so that instead of a ruse and a victory over someone really wanting to be conquered, we get mere confusion.

Even before the curtain goes up, trouble bodes. As the overture starts, steam puffs out of the orchestra pit. Immediately we worry about the lack of confidence that needs this trickery and the focus on the train itself, instead of on the action aboard the train. The latter continues, highlighted—no, lowlighted—by the opening of Act Two, four porters singing "Life Is a Train," my nomination for the most embarrassingly bad number I have seen in a Broadway musical.

Coleman's music is all shapes, no melodies. Larry Fuller's direction of the musical numbers is a string of reminiscences—of past numbers. "She's a Nut," for instance, a fast song that bounces around the stage from group to group, reminded me of "Catch Hatch" from *One Touch of Venus* (1943). Harold Prince is the *capo* director, and it can only be said that the talent whose absence he so plentifully displayed in *Zorba, Pacific Overtures, Candide* and others is still conspicuous in the same way.

Lehman Engel wrote in *The American Musical Theater* (1967):

> . . . the majority of our newest musicals . . . though enormously successful, seem to me to have little more than empty interiors, sometimes rather adroitly concealed behind colorful and swiftly changing facades. The material . . . tends to be perfunctory . . . What this material . . . lacks chiefly, in my estimation, is *feeling*.

Still true, and right on target here. Feeling is what we want from a musical, easy fast-flowing quick-changing showers of all kinds of feeling—nothing deeply comic or deeply moving but nothing *unmoving*, either. How could there be any feeling for *Twentieth Century* with two inadequate stars, an eviscerated story that could only barely have been made engaging with two sparkling performers to flesh it out again, and a score without one affecting phrase?

Twelve years ago I wrote that, in the world of the Broadway musical, the sound of music had been replaced by the sound of carpenters. Now I'm afraid that what they have been building are coffins. Oh, there are hits—Engel, too, concedes that—but the hits seem more the result of a Broadway-Greater New York-U.S. Chamber of Commerce imperative than spontaneous. (Can you remember one note of *Company?*) The whole Broadway area, which once was almost every theater person's goal, has grown decreasingly interesting to the best new talents in the last two decades, and anyway the incredibly greater expense has made producers of musicals less and less willing to take chances on newcomers. (*Twentieth Century* couldn't have cost much less than a million.) About the youngest person to have made an impression in the Broadway musical world is Stephen Sondheim, b. 1930. (No, I haven't forgotten Stephen Schwartz, b. 1948, composer of the forgettable *Pippin*.) So when the Broadway show-shop feels it needs a new musical, usually meaning one more conversion of previously successful material, the people hired for the job are those like these long-drained fabricators, who stir their aching bones once again.

Predictions are perilous, but at any given moment, the past, if not the future, is fixed. And on the basis of the past dozen or so years, it's possible to believe that, on its own level, the Broadway musical is in the same condition as opera. The optimum period for new works may have passed, because of economic and cultural reasons. The future of both of these theaters may lie predominantly in the revival of past good works. The new works seem to need artificial respiration, pumped by a determinedly benevolent press and by dogged producers' insistence on continuing a tradition that may have had its day.

Postscript. For a later development, see p. 81.

Curse of the Starving Class

(April 8, 1978)

Sam Shepard is phenomenal. He is the best practicing American playwright, I think, now that Tennessee Williams is doodling. Since 1964 he has written about thirty plays of differing lengths which have been produced all over the U.S. and in some other countries. He is world-famous in the theater world. (And this without ever having been produced on Broadway. One play, *Operation Sidewinder*, was done at the Beaumont in 1970 under Jules Irving's management.) Several volumes of his plays have been published. But part of the Shepard phenomenon is that, in a sorry way, he represents the course of American playwriting in the last twenty years. After all this time Shepard continues to "show talent." It's the most dazzling talent we have at the moment, but showing talent is not quite the same as making art. (As Harold Clurman once said, "America is lousy with talent.") Much of Shepard's work is unforgettable, seen or read once. Very little of it is worth another visit, which is surely one valid test of real quality.

Curse of the Starving Class is another of Shepard's heartbreakers—it contains so much, yet it finally comes to not enough. First produced in London a year ago when Shepard was living there, it deals with California sheep raisers and thus immediately strikes a distinctive Shepard note. He often deals with nonurban people, often in the West; most of our playwrights are urban in setting and feeling. There's a family of four: the father, a former Air Force pilot, now boozing most of the time; a kooky shiftless mother, scheming to sell the place and scurry off to Europe with her children; a son about twenty, easy and competent but frightened of his father; a daughter, sturdy, frightened of no one.

The play's first virtue, as in most Shepard, is that all the roles are good acting parts. No play survives in the theater without that virtue, and some survive that have no other virtue. Shepard writes dialogue that actors can *use*, in situations that have good rising motion, for characters that leave the audience finally with a high opinion of the actors even though/if the actors have concentrated on the characters.

And beyond this, which might in itself be true of a thin and silly play, Shepard stokes a simmering heat under the whole play, even under the punchy comic sections, a ruthlessness, a kind of anger that makes the essential drama seem to be not in the story but between the writer himself and the world. Once again a Shepard play testifies to the fact that he is a true man of the theater: he doesn't see life as material for drama, he sees life *as* drama.

But once again he has plunged, so to speak, into a turbulent pool simply because he knows how to swim in turbulence; and, to finish the figure, he has surfaced some time later only to head for the nearest shore without necessarily having intended to go there. *Starving Class* starts as sweaty, cartoon-character comedy—people living wildly and uncaringly in a poverty they not only don't take very seriously, they use as a medium for farcical family life. They are something like John Steinbeck's Okies seen by Donald Barthelme. In the opening section the son is cleaning up the fragments of the front door that his drunken father broke down the night before, the mother comes out in a wrapper and is unconcerned to find the refrigerator nearly empty, the daughter comes out in her 4-H uniform carrying charts she made for a demonstration she's going to give at a fair on how to cut up a frying chicken. When she finds that her chicken is missing from the fridge, she gets furious. Her brother puts her charts on the floor and pisses on them. Pretty soon the boozy father comes home, providing for his brood by bringing them a large sack of artichokes.

The opening atmosphere, which persists through a good deal of the play, is hard to reconcile with the conclusion. The play ends as a paean to agrarian values, to those who love Nature and Space and Simple Things and who are being forced off their land by exploitative commercial combines. It becomes a drama of rustic simplicity being strangled by city greed. That ending is simply not in the play's beginning: moralism has been tacked on to a work whose vitality is in its passionate rowdyism and its very oblique social comment.

Shepard is not much of a thinker: when he does think, or feels he needs to, he usually comes up with the same theme—the battle between the pure and the impure in America. And when he needs evil, he usually calls on the movies to supply it: cinematized criminal types of various kinds. This deliberate use of movie types is part of Shepard's general method: the language and music of rock, spaceman fantasies, Wild West fantasies, gangster fantasies—pop-culture forms that he uses as his building blocks, rituals of contemporary religion to heighten communion.

My discomfort with Shepard is not with this symbology, which he often exalts into pungent theater poetry, but with his careless grabbing at chunks of it to get him out of his dramatic difficulties. The best work of his that I know, *The Tooth of Crime*, which casts the rivalries of rock stars in the mode of a 1930s gangster picture and which spits along in wonderfully bitten-out language, completes what it's about through the form in which it is put. But the gangsters at the end of *Starving Class* have just been shoved on stage by the scruffs of their necks, to commit a murder that is grossly disproportionate to the reason given. To heighten the inconsistencies, just previously the son has wandered naked across the stage, put on his sobered-up father's drunk-soaked clothes, and has sat himself down in front of the now-loaded refrigerator to stuff his face—in an orgy less of starved gluttony than of rarefied symbolism.

Shepard is for me the archetypal post-Broadway American playwright: the leader of a generation dating from the early 1960s that grew up without the ambition that had dominated previous writers, serious and otherwise—the ambition toward Broadway. Even though the works of some of these newer writers eventually get to Broadway, they have rejected the constrictions and intents of the commercial theater for the freedoms of Off and Off-Off Broadway. But, as with everything else everywhere, they have paid a price.

I do not for the smallest fragment of a second suggest that Shepard would have benefited from the advice of a show-shop wizard like George Abbott, that Shepard should have rewritten this play or any of his plays in New Haven or Boston on the way to New York. I do mean that he is the leader of a group which has used its freedom in order not to grow. I know there are earlier versions of many OB and OOB plays, I know that there are summer and winter and non-seasonal theater conferences where plays are read and criticized and discussed. I also know the results. I see, for instance, that Shepard is as wonderfully gifted now as he was when he wrote *La Turista* in 1968 but is not notably more in control of his plays as organic works. If I say that one cannot discern in the post-1960 playwrights the increased technical skill discernible through the careers of, say, Robert E. Sherwood and Elmer Rice, the response will of course be that one prefers the freedom and commitment of the post-1960 people to the middle-class tailored seriousness of the former. To which *my* response would be: Why must one choose? Between art and freedom? The reaction to the strictures of Broadway has been an overreaction: *pace* all the latter-day theater conferences, the away-from-Broadway theater in New York and elsewhere has functioned more as a conduit than as a sieve. It's too broad a statement but not really untrue to say that the non-Broadway theater has pushed liberated talent at the expense of refining it, and now we have a group of playwrights on either side of forty—Shepard the best—who are not much better now than when they started. Perhaps it's time for the non-commercial theater to learn the idea of discipline—to its own ends—from that nasty old commercial theater.

This production of *Starving Class* is firmly and sympathetically directed by Robert Woodruff, who knows how to graph the action in and under the dialogue. James Gammon as the boozy father, Ebbe Roe Smith as the lean and moody son, Pamela Reed as the gutsy, sassy daughter, are excellent. *Excellent.* Of the principals only Olympia Dukakis, as the mother, seems to be artificially acting her way down to a stratum beneath her.

Runaways

(April 22, 1978)

This is the moment to praise Elizabeth Swados. Her new show is not as good as the previous one but it attests to her uniqueness just as strongly, and one feels the impulse, as one often does with admirable artists, to love her just a bit more when she takes a worthwhile chance and stumbles.

Swados's last production was *Nightclub Cantata*, a set of twenty pieces mostly written by others that she set to music—piano, percussion, and her own guitar—and staged with eight performers in a large corner of the Village Gate. It was a generally wonderful evening, composed of old-fashioned (that is, 1960s) "communal" feeling fixed with performance discipline and theater invention. *Runaways*, done on a conventional stage in Joseph Papp's building before an auditorium that has been converted into a cabaret, has nineteen performers and forty-one numbers. The cast is young since the theme is runaway children. I recognized only two performers from *Cantata*: Karen Evans, a strikingly gifted black girl, and David Schechter, strikingly ungifted but so ecstatically committed to what he's doing that he becomes touching. And there is Judith Fleisher again at the piano, Swados herself playing offstage, and four other musicians, including two devoted to that Swados necessity, complex percussion.

Runaways is less good than *Cantata* not because it's bigger: Swados has no splashy ambitions. First, most of the words are her own this time, and they are just not as good as those of the many poets she used last time. But she had to write her own words because she's dealing with one theme—runaway children —and that leads to the second defect: the narrowness of the theme. I'm obviously not talking about the social problem but about Swados's show when I say that two and a half hours about the fate of today's runaway kids, white, black, Hispanic—the street life, the drugs, the prostitution, the kinds of home problems that drove them out in the first place—simply get repetitious. At any rate Swados and her friends have not found enough different ways to deal with these subjects to keep us from wondering why the performers don't, in effect, hear themselves repeating.

This is particularly true since Swados's method of composition, as is well-known, is not with melody in any conventional sense but through a kind of theater-music that attempts to render speech in rhythms and pitch and tempi that enlarge the words with minimal concession to melody.

One wry result is that the two best pieces are spoken, not sung. Near the end (it ought to have *been* the end) Karen Evans speaks an impressive piece called "To the Dead of Family Wars." And in the first act there's another spoken piece, done by young Jon Matthews, called "Current Events"—a rushed insane litany of what's happening in the world, with the impassioned refrain, "Please don't flunk me, please don't flunk me" as if he were reciting in a high school class. Matthews pours out at breakneck speed all the madnesses in the newspapers, from the murders in the street to the terror of wars to the fact that prostitution is on the increase just outside Disneyland; and all through this frantic flood of human misery and mayhem, he keeps pleading "Please don't flunk me." I'm not expecting to forget "Current Events" very soon.

And there's a song in the second act called "Where Are Those People Who Did 'Hair'?" No comment necessary. But one irony will be lost when *Runaways* moves to Broadway, as it will next month. This present building is the very one in which *Hair* started eleven years ago. (Will there be a show eleven years from now with a song called "Where Are Those People Who Did 'Runaways'?")

But that move to Broadway will lessen a different irony. All this talk and song about starving street kids takes place before a cabaret audience at tables laden with huge salads and pita-bread sandwiches and gorgeous desserts topped with whipped cream. Talk about Brecht's "culinary theater!"

Well, Brecht himself performed in cabarets, of course, and the real trouble with *Runaways* is deeper than this irony—it's tied to the repetitiousness, to the lack of awareness about it. The show has bathos below the pathos. The show begins to think of itself as heroic. Everyone takes on a slight air of valor, as if he were engaged in a struggle instead of representing it and, like many people in trouble, they go on about it too long. (This confusion of self with subject is, again, un-Brechtian, by the way; and again is typical of the people I met who were in *Hair*.)

Nevertheless, and to my mind indisputably, Swados is a contemporary marvel. Her instinct for material is quick; her use of it is at the furthest reach from formula; her ability to summon performances—no, subscription—from her people is phenomenal; her imagination with simple scenic elements, with lights, asymmetrical movement, variations, and rhythms, produces what I can only call command. Of the audience. She supplies novelty without dealing in it. And she summons energy from her group that is completely unrelated to show-biz pizazz.

I feel once again, as I did with *Nightclub Cantata* that—without any intent to dig at Andrei Serban—Swados's contributions to Serban's monumental Greek productions must have been large. Serban himself has said so, and Swados's solo work supports it. This production of *Runaways* is not as good as it might have been with better words, with more stringency, a bit less "weeping *with* it" by Swados herself. Still her unique and fine qualities are more than visible.

Swados is a genuine artist making a real contribution to our theater. Strength to her.

Da

(May 27, 1978)

Odd about the Irish. In the first decades of this century, Irish writers, headed by Yeats and Lady Gregory, were a chief force in the theater. The impulse behind the self-styled Irish Dramatic Movement was curious (and may be uncomfortable to remember). Until that time the Irish theater generally thought of itself as part of and dependent on the English theater. Yeats, first and in particular, thought that this theater was suffering from the pallor of Ibsenite realism and that the Irish could infuse it with poetic vigor. Says Una Ellis-Fermor in her book on the subject: "It was thus left to the Irish Dramatic Movement to bring back to the English theater the poetry it had missed in [middle-period] Ibsen, presenting it, if not in terms of English society, at least in a language which Englishmen could understand . . ."

Of course it was already a standing joke that many of the leading "English" dramatists were Irish: Sheridan, Goldsmith, Farquhar, Shaw, Wilde. But here was a programmatic effort, doubtless spurred by growing Irish nationalism, and its results were epochal, especially in the works of the founders and of Synge, who was evangelized by Yeats to leave his esthete's life in Paris and go home to write of his native land.

Even after its highest days, which included the Dublin-slum dramas of Sean O'Casey, the Irish movement continued to bless the theater with plays of worth: some of the later O'Casey, Lennox Robinson, Denis Johnston, Paul Vincent Carroll, several others. (Charles Chaplin was so impressed with Carroll's *Shadow and Substance* that he bought the screen rights and wrote a screenplay. He abandoned production only because Oona O'Neill, who was to play the saintly girl, decided after their marriage that she didn't want a career.) It was a rare Broadway season between the wars that didn't bring us at least one new Irish play, even if it was only such a trifle as *Old Man Murphy* (1931), which I saw twice in one week when I was fifteen because it starred Maire O'Neill who had been Synge's beloved before his early death.

And if there was or was not a new Irish play, there might be a visit by the wondrous Abbey Theater, which then included such actors as Barry Fitzgerald, Sara Allgood (Maire O'Neill's sister), and a forgotten fine artist named Eileen Crowe. And in 1948 came the excellent Gate Theater of Dublin, with its two founders Hilton Edwards and Micheál MacLiammóir in plays of Shaw and Johnston.

But what's happened? Obviously no New Yorker, reliant on imports, can pass on the state of Irish playwriting or production, but on the basis of what is imported and of what one reads in journals, it's hard to avoid concluding that the arc of Irish theatrical inspiration has badly declined. Theater writing of consequence in every country seems to go in waves, admittedly, but the falling-off in Ireland seems especially drastic.

The best new Irish play I've seen in recent years was Brian Friel's *Philadelphia, Here I Come!*(1966), and that one I thought "amiable and appealing enough but unexciting." I missed some subsequent Friel productions, but nothing I read about them made me regret it. The Irish writer who has probably been produced most in the U.S. of late is Hugh Leonard: a pointless dramatization of Joyce's *Portrait of the Artist As a Young Man* (1966), *The Poker Session* (1967), which I didn't see, *The Au Pair Man* (1973), which unfortunately I did see, and now the flaccid *Da*, which has had productions at two resident theaters, then Off Broadway at the Hudson Guild. That production was loudly cheered and has been moved to Broadway where it was cheered again.

The title is the Irish familiar for "father," and I need hardly say more. What else *could* this be but a play about a lovable old curmudgeon? Quintessentially it's the same play as some others of the past decade—not Irish but American and English: Robert Anderson's *I Never Sang for My Father*, John Mortimer's *A Voyage Round My Father*, and Peter Nichols's *Forget-Me-Not Lane*. In Leonard's play, as in the others, a grown man has psychic-emotional ties to his father that he wants to understand and control. In Leonard's play as in (I think) two of the others, the action begins after the father's death. Most of *Da* is either flashback or quasi-fantasy with the just-buried father merrily refusing to stay in the grave, continuing to be visibly present in his son's life. In most of these plays the father is so much more interesting than the alleged protagonist that the author has to compensate by dividing the protagonist into several simultaneously present roles, at different ages. (Even Friel's *Philadelphia* divided its hero in two and its most effective scene was with the father.)

In *Da* the one notable difference is that the son was adopted, as a baby. Otherwise it's the same split hero again: the adolescent and the man, now a playwright in London who has returned for the funeral, the same sparring conversations between the split two, the same fundamental sets of relationships between the two and the father. The professed object of this play is to understand the past and lay the ghost of the father. The real object is to squeeze more sentimental ooze out of reminiscence observed by an older self, with easy *Our Town* pathos and with the audience snug in its foreknowledge that the narrator comes out all right in the end, even if bearing the proud scars of additional irony.

Da was a gardener on a large estate so we get his provincialism and sentiment and servility and stubbornness contrasted with the mod grown son. We get the adolescent's first try at sex, unwittingly frustrated by Da. We get, in short, what we deserve for going to see a play called *Da*. The one modest surprise, moderately unsuccessful, is Leonard's attempt to write the grown son's dialogue with elaborately artificial "English" wit, à la Stoppard. ("The dog was poisoned, and in my considered view, it was suicide." "Blessed are the meek, they shall inherit the dirt.") At its feeble best, Leonard's play fails to reassure us about the resurgence of the Irish Dramatic Movement.

Barnard Hughes, the Da, is an experienced actor and does all with the part that experience without charm can do. Brian Murray, who last year was good if somewhat muzzy in *Ashes* (a semi-Irish play), is much more muzzy than good as the grown son. He always chooses the most superficially effective way to say and do everything, then says or does it without clean line. The best performance is by Sylvia O'Brien, as the mother badgered into bad temper; and she's the only one in the cast with a consistent and credible Irish accent. Marjorie Kellogg's set tries to cram a lot of places into one space; cramming is what it looks like. Melvin Bernhardt's staging only emphasizes Kellogg's defeat.

The Inspector General

(October 28, 1978)

The scene is the mayor's house. On stage the mayor and a lot of town officials. The mayor says: "I have invited you here, gentlemen, in order to communicate a most unpleasant piece of news: a government inspector is coming to visit us."

We can digest that opening when we read it, perhaps feel a twitch of comedy-to-come, but what's to be done with it in the theater? A play can't begin so baldly. Any production of Gogol's *The Inspector General* that I have seen or read about has opened with some sort of pantomime. The new production at the Circle in the Square has three or four minutes of it, surely no world record. When Meyerhold produced the play in Moscow in 1926, a production that elicited more critical literature than any other in the history of the theater, the performance began with slow music and a rolling platform that bore a tableau out toward the audience. And the embellishments continued. Meyerhold's script was longer than the original, and he put in tableaux and pantomimes that made it even longer. Further, he shaped the whole production under cinematic influence: he divided the five acts into fifteen episodes, and he enjoined his actors to "remember Chaplin . . . or Keaton . . ."

All this means that Meyerhold thought the play needed *treatment* to give it theatrical life and comic effect. And this was in a country where the many word-plays in the characters' names were understood (to translate them would be unbearable) and where the national smell of the corruptions that are the play's target was right in the audience's nostrils. For us, the play as such suffers further, not because we are exactly corruption-free in government but for sheerly artistic reasons. When *The Inspector General* was first done in 1836 it was a bombshell; but it has since sired so many bombshells that a comedy of political chicanery now needs more substance and disclosure than, ironically, its very sire. We must all take off our hats before the Wright Brothers' airplane, but who wants to fly in it? After the who-knows-how-many plays and films on this subject—Kanin's *Born Yesterday* and Sturges's *The Great McGinty* come first to mind—*The Inspector General* is Kitty Hawk.

This is a theatrical judgment. Gogol's comedy, loved by so many readers, is weak on stage today. Theater expectations, conscious or not in us, are very different from reading expectations; and to watch *The Inspector General* is to watch one joke spun out. The crooked officials of a provincial town learn that a government inspector is coming who can expose and ruin them all. They mistake a penurious visiting government clerk for the inspector, and they ply him with bribes. The mayor's wife offers herself, the mayor's daughter gets engaged to him. When the clerk has gathered up a bundle of loot, he sneaks away—and the arrival of the real inspector is announced. (Victor Erlich suggests that the new man may be another impostor!) The scenes of bribery and cajolery are simply repeated over and over with insufficient intrinsic variety and no line of growth. We just wait the play out, with respect.

This comedy is not alone in declining stage life. I could easily list fifty classic comedies, powerful in the theater's past, that would have a hard time on stage today. (Why this is not equally true of serious plays, and it's not, is too complex to explore here. I'll only cite W. H. Auden, a classicist, who says that in epic or tragic or lyric art, "we see change but no progress . . . When, however, we consider comic art, it seems to us that the progress has been immense.") So for critics to complain, as some have done, that Liviu Ciulei has inserted a lot of "business" in *The Inspector General* is to miss the point. To revive this play means, as it does with many old comedies, to revise it. Only two things can give it a chance for new theatrical life: the director's invention and the cast's virtuosity.

The Circle production is weak on the first point and null on the second. Ciulei is a fifty-five-year-old Romanian, active in both theater and film (one of his pictures took a Cannes prize in 1965), who has done several American productions in recent years. He is, in Gogol or elsewhere, in comedy or tragedy, a director who believes in expropriation of the work. I saw his productions of Büchner's *Leonce and Lena* and of *Hamlet* at the Arena in Washington; the first was a boutique of avant-garde fashions, and the second was squashed, all the mysteries trodden out. I saw, too, his production of Wedekind's *Spring Awakening* at the Juilliard in New York which seemed primarily designed as a Ciulei showcase but where he at least showed some ability to release young actors.

In Gogol he has apparently followed Moscow Art Theater models. When the MAT did their production of Gogol's *Dead Souls* here in 1965, most of the characters had physical properties extended into costume: performance and dress were inseparable, as if each actor had put on a monkey suit or a rooster suit and was moving about, faceless, within it. That style has been followed here, with William Ivey Long's good costumes, and it gives each supporting actor one note to strike, but one only. Worse, the notes are struck in a limbo between realism and Meyerhold's grotesque. Three exceptions: Renee Lippin as a tongue-tied maid, Bill McIntyre as a nobody, and Bob Balaban, in white wig and whiskers, who gets off a pretty good act as an antique servant.

The two leading actors would have sunk a better production. Theodore Bikel, the mayor, tries to be bear-like but is only self-consciously noisy. Max Wright, the false inspector, is a wispy whiny poseur, a miniaturist of parlor-cutup range, with the annoying vocal trait of letting his voice run continuously through lines, so that the words come like blobs on a continuous hum.

The inadequacies of the Circle playing space can possibly be blamed for some of Ciulei's clinkers—for instance, the attempted seductions of mayor's wife and daughter both take place on the floor because there's no way to get furniture out there in that scene. But most of it is pure, or impure, Ciulei: Eastern European hand-me-down sparked by egocentricity. The latter sticks out especially in changes for change's sake. Gogol asks for a minute and a half of frozen dumb show at the very end after the real inspector is announced. Ciulei gives us the dumb show *before* the announcement. We hear a long chunk of Tchaikovsky's *1812* while most of the cast just sits there. And we sit too, while the point is missed and the tedium protracted.

The San Francisco Mime Troupe

(December 16, 1978)

The San Francisco Mime Troupe recently toured the East, including New York, with a piece called *False Promises/Nos Enganaron*. (The Spanish phrase means "We have been had." Despite the bilingual title, very little of the piece is in Spanish.) Since the end of the Vietnam war, the avant-garde theater has been greatly depoliticized. The SF Mime Troupe is an outstanding exception, along with El Teatro Campesino, which grew out of it, and the Bread and Puppet Theater, which performed in New York last January and which, in my experience of it, is as spiritual as political.

The SF Mime Troupe, founded in 1959 by Ronnie Davis, was an offshoot of the then-famous Actor's Workshop in that city. (I'm citing Arthur Sainer's *Radical Theatre Notebook*.) Says a member of the Troupe: "Very early, the group stopped doing mime as most people understand it—performing without words; as Ronnie meant it—acting with the body—we're still working with it." The work is very physical *and* verbal—and musical. The company has a theater, but in the warm weather it plays in parks in the Bay area. It's the oldest company in the area and, I think, must be one of the oldest of the post-World War Two crop, avant-garde or otherwise. The Troupe declares sympathy for the avant-garde but wants to remain outside it, as an "art and propaganda" team, working for different groups—for example, a group of Latinos who were charged with murder—as needs arise. This company is both non-profit and unsubsidized: government or foundation aid is not forthcoming. The Troupe lives by contributions and, when admission is charged, by receipts.

What they do, they do with competence and conviction. I don't know how long each member has been with the Troupe—I don't even know their names: no individual is mentioned in the program because they work as a collective—but they have real ensemble ease and flourish. There are about a dozen of them, some of them musicians who play at the side of the stage and also step into roles; all of them sing and dance. Everything flows, everything has been worked out communally by the group, and everything is borne on an assumption of community with the audience. And when I was there, in a large packed house, they were right.

Their style, they feel, is *commedia dell'arte* and since no one really knows what that style is, they may also be right about that. I'd say that their style is revue-sketch acting—cartooning, with control. It also has elements of old-time U.S. medicine-show flavor and of Brecht's presentational method. The first is the air of "We just got up on the back of this wagon to entertain you folks—we're no different from you, we just spend more time at this sort of thing." The second, Brecht's theory, asks that the actor stand outside his role and display it, as if it were a separate object, not treating it as an emotional bath for him or for you. What he wants is your observation and reaction. "So that's how Puerto Ricans really felt when the U.S. took over their country."

One scenic arrangement of steps and doors, set in the center, is cleverly designed to serve a lot of purposes, and almost all the company play several parts apiece. The time is 1898-99, and the story ambles after a black man who gets in trouble in South Carolina by trying to vote, flees to Colorado where there is tension between Mexican and American copper miners, joins the army in Teddy Roosevelt's "splendid little war," then returns to Colorado where a strike is going on. It's a tour, more than a play—of issues of the time considered to be antecedent of present ones—and part of its intent is to crack marmoreal schoolbook history.

But, by their own definitions, that's not where judgment of the Troupe can end. They think of themselves as a radicalizing instrument, they speak in their money-appeals of "revolutionary fervor," and I don't know what their revolution is. They are against oppression, exploitation, racism, which is about as radical as Calvin Coolidge's report of the minister's sermon on sin: "He was against it." Radicalism, if it's more than rhetoric, is political; and politics, if it's more than rhetoric, is programmatic. What is the Troupe's politics? The (mostly young) audience thought it knew: at least they cheered all the catch-phrases. But I don't know. In the 1960s and up to the death of Mao, I would have assumed that the radicalism of such a group was anti-Soviet and pro-Mao: and Maoism was a clearly articulated program that revised social organization and, heeding the Soviet failure, tried to revise values. But our newspapers are now full of Mao's failure in this second regard. It's probably only a matter of time until he is reviled as viciously as is his widow in the new China of Pan Am hotels and McDonald's fast food. Could the Troupe specify its radical model? Albania? Cambodia? Something that the members have devised on their own? What is their theater work moving *toward*? Something more than anti-flagwaving that is as facile as flagwaving?

I came to this performance just after finishing some work on *Danton's Death* with a group of student actors who agreed that the current stories from China make a perfect epilogue to the play. One of the themes in Büchner's disquieting masterwork is that, under political fervor however sincere, is, in some measure, politics as egocentric fantasy. This is not negativism: truth cannot be negative. I couldn't help wondering what Büchner would think of the Troupe.

The Elephant Man

(February 17, 1979)

The Elephant Man is the best new play by an American that I've seen or read since Sam Shepard's *The Tooth of Crime* (1972). This opinion needs qualification: and the qualification is the base of the comment that follows. The author, Bernard Pomerance, is an American living in London. Shepard, in fact, was living in London when he wrote *The Tooth of Crime* and it had its premiere there, but that was mere coincidence; Shepard's play is American in every molecule. Pomerance's play is not, and not just because of its subject.

The subject is factual. A young man named John Merrick lived in the London Hospital from 1886 to his death in 1890. He was grossly deformed from birth. His face was distorted hideously, his right arm was a long lump (though his left arm was perfect), great blobs of spongy brown flesh hung from his skull and torso, and he gave off—before hospital care—a stench. A surgeon named Frederick Treves discovered him in a carnival where he was being exhibited as The Elephant Man. Eventually, Treves took him into his hospital, the London, and a fund was raised to tend Merrick for life, which was short. During that life, Treves discovered that Merrick was exceptionally intelligent and imaginative. Because Treves was known, his ward became known. In time, many of the famous and high-born, the celebrated actress Madge Kendal and the Princess Alexandra among them, visited Merrick and became friendly with him.

Pomerance read about Merrick in Treves's memoirs and in *The Elephant Man* by Ashley Montagu. Presumably, four aspects of the story drew Pomerance to write a play about it: the isolation by deformity; the contrast between the outer and the inner man; the fact that so many distinguished people enjoyed his company; and the fact that, during his years in the hospital, Merrick worked on a model of a nearby church, St. Phillip's, which he finished just before he died. (The model and Merrick's bones are still at the London Hospital.)

Now the reason why this American author's residence in London is not a coincidence, is absolutely central, is that he has written an English play. *The Elephant Man* has a superficial resemblance to Brecht: each of the twenty-one brief scenes has a title, in the program anyway, taken from the text of each scene, and the audience is sometimes directly addressed. These incidentals, plus the fact that Pomerance did a version of *A Man's a Man* produced in London two years ago, have brought this play the label "Brechtian" in some comment. Not remotely true, for at least two reasons: his aims have nothing to do with "presentation" or *Verfremdung*. Pomerance is writing in one line of the post-Angry English playwrights (there are other lines), a group that includes such people as Charles Wood, David Hare, Ann Jellicoe and Alan Bennett. Unique though each is, they share some qualities; and the head of their line, I would hazard, is the early John Arden—and *his* antecedent, as I think he once owned, was John Masefield, the Masefield of *Pompey the Great* and *The Tragedy of Nan.* Those in this "school," differing widely in subjects, share a style of poetic pin-point understatement, poetry through understatement. The diction is spare, tart, nuggety. The dialogue is engraved with tense rhythms and small flowers of lyricism. The dialectic—the tension—comes from flash-and-silence in the language itself, as well as from the drama of the action. These writers combine burnished English phraseology with the English stiff upper lip. The fire, which is there, generally seems to filter through reticence.

The fundamental strength and the oddity of this new play are that the American Pomerance has written it—well—in this quintessentially English style. In the last scene, the head of the hospital, Gomm, reads Treves a long let-ter that he is sending to *The Times*, explaining what he will do with the residue of the fund for the deceased Merrick. Gomm asks Treves whether he wants to add anything to the letter. Treves declines and leaves. Gomm reads the rest of the letter aloud. Treves returns.

Treves: I did think of one small thing.
Gomm: It's too late, I'm afraid. It is done.

End of the play.

This spareness, which governs the structure as well as the writing, very pleasurably embraces leaps of time and place, collapses complex action to clear strophes, condenses development of relations. So it's no irrelevant nationalist interest which makes me underscore that Pomerance has written in an English manner. Obviously, because his subject was nineteenth-century England, he had at least to attempt some period flavor. But beyond that, he chose an English dramaturgic style, which, in diction and structure, carries a vision of what one wants a play and the theater itself to be. That style is the play's under-pinning, even when other matters falter.

Pomerance was not rooting out the pathetic in Merrick's story, though his play has pathos: he wanted to use Merrick as a metaphor. Immediately, one thinks of another relatively recent play about a physical anomaly, Peter Handke's *Kaspar*, in which there is no pathos whatsoever but which transforms the story of Kaspar Hauser, the teenage boy who grew up without any knowledge of speech, into a superlative dramatic poem about language as liberator, certifier, doom. Pomerance was after the thematic significances in the Merrick story, but the results in metaphor—and this is the play's thinness—tend to be patent or a bit strained. At any rate, they don't enlarge us, as *Kaspar* does. Pomerance explores the beauty in this appallingly ugly man; Merrick's visible loneliness among people whose loneliness is less visible but there; his visible deformation within a society whose deformations are less visible; and the fact that each of his visitors finds in Merrick what he or she needs to find. (Treves says to a bishop: "He makes all of us think he is deeply like ourselves. And yet we're not like each other. I conclude that we have polished him like a mirror, and shout hallelujah when he reflects us to the inch.") These insights, as used, are not much more than serviceable. The most suggestive of the lot is the one that is touched most lightly. At one point, the actress Mrs. Kendal, speaking of women's good looks, says: "It is a rather arbitrary gift." Near the end, an orderly, bringing Merrick his lunch, talks about a young woman's sudden death. He says: "It's all so—what's that word? Forgot it. It means chance-y." He leaves. Then Merrick, who (as the doctors know) is dying, dies. The orderly returns and, before he notices that Merrick is dead, says: "I remember it, Mr. Merrick. The word is arbitrary."

That is the granite of the play. Clearly, it's not only death that is arbitrary. Life, as Merrick's extreme case shows, is much more cruelly so. For those of us who can't quite believe that Merrick's affliction was somehow an element in a Grand Design, the hard job is to find a pattern of sorts for one's self amidst the arbitrariness. Man's great blessing/curse, the gift of logic, keeps ramming into the "chance-y" illogic of existence. That, for me, is the great theme at which the play only glances. (There's irony, too. Merrick's chief labor is a model of a place consecrated to the idea of a Divine Mind, and the model itself is a triumph of *his* power to design.)

But in terms of its theater rather than its themes—and *The Elephant Man* is proof that a play can be seen that way—it lives on the stage with a wiry, quick intelligence, with a quick and lasting grip. The scenes move well, join and grow like crystals. There's a necessary and good basic theatrical device. Pomerance, for several reasons, didn't want to load the actor who plays Merrick with horror-film make-up that would make Quasimodo look like Puck, so the actor simply contorts his speech and body and is first seen, clad only in breech-clout, while Treves addresses the audience pointing at slides of the actual Elephant Man. Thus we know what Merrick is supposed to look like and we see how people react to him, but the actor is able to perform and we are able to watch.

What we watch is the growth of models and the (implicative) poignancy and futility of that growth: not just the model of the church, but the models of behavior and thought, which Merrick takes mainly from Treves, and the model of the lost paradise through Merrick's relation with Mrs. Kendal. (In an inevitable scene, she shows him her body, because he has never seen a woman and because she knows he is dying.) There is a wry dream episode—Treves's dream in which he and Merrick exchange places—that gives us the chance to see Merrick as normal and that underscores the arbitrary fate that kept him from it. With its English astringency of diction and structure, the play itself is an *enclosing* model.

The production understands the play excellently. Two quick reservations about the direction by Jack Hofsiss. I disliked the solo cello music used throughout, especially the appearance of the cellist himself on stage at the beginning of Act Two. And the symbolic handling of the church model once or twice becomes blatant. Otherwise I can only congratulate Pomerance on finding a director who understands the mode and delicacy of his play so well, who concentrates on refinement of the acting rather than a self-serving "concept." I saw Hofsiss's work once before—Thomas Babe's *Rebel Women*—but that play was so cumbersome that it handcuffed him. Here he makes the most, legitimately, out of a really responsive script.

Kevin Conway, the Treves, is fine and once again surprising. After some blustering, easily effective parts, Conway moved well ahead with his George in *Of Mice and Men*. Then he did some more blustering in two films, *F.I.S.T.* and *Paradise Alley*. Now he is acting again, moving forward again. That he comes up with a credible toff's accent is not nothing, but more important, he gives us a quiet, vulnerable, humane man unlike any role I've seen him in, and solid.

Philip Anglim, the Merrick, creates, without any attempt at heart-tug, the prisonhouse of flesh and its prisoner. Carole Shelley, an English actress who has been here since 1964, has been notable before mostly as a merchant of birdy brightness. As Mrs. Kendal, with the help of Hofsiss, she is lovely with nuance and feeling. Richard Clarke, as Gomm, has the right tired stiffness. I. M. Hobson, who looks something like a gentile Zero Mostel, is much more than a spherical actor living by his width. In three roles—carnival man, bishop, hospital orderly—Hobson's unctuous slyness or benignity or efficiency helps to furnish the scene.

(May 12, 1979)

The Elephant Man by Bernard Pomerance, which I reviewed Off-Broadway, has been moved to a Broadway theater, and the transplant is working. David Jenkins's set, a bit enlarged, now gives the director Jack Hofsiss a chance to get more fluency out of the movements around the edges, to give these peripheral actions a feeling of respite and preparation that helps the texture. (I still don't like seeing the cellist—the source of the play's incidental music—sitting at the side. Why must we always be aware of how careful he is not to move during action in the center? Why does he have to be visible?) Beverly Emmons's lighting is better articulated here. Almost all the actors are the same as before, and all are just as good as before except that Carole Shelley as the actress now spins out her pauses to the last split second that they will bear. Only one of the two pinhead girls now appears to the dying Merrick (the Elephant Man), which is a loss, but the very last spotlighting of the church model is out, which is a gain.

A second viewing makes the play at least as enticing as before, a good work with great ambition. Its assets now seem stronger: the large theme of the arbitrariness of existence, posed against a hunger for design—in everyone but especially in Merrick. The weaknesses are now a bit clearer too: the occasional soft patches in the lean, evocative dialogue; the patness of such moments as the doctor's entrance just when the actress bares her bosom for Merrick; the fact that the play's metaphors don't sufficiently deepen.

This last defect—the major one—arises because Pomerance hasn't fixed the center of the play. It begins as the drama of Treves, the doctor who finds Merrick; then most of the action focuses on Merrick; and only near the end, by means of a lengthy scene between Treves and the bishop, does Pomerance try to move the focus back to the doctor. It's a good scene, but it can't quite do that job. This split is what makes the second act waver a bit and what keeps the metaphors visible, rather than ingested. Admittedly, it's difficult to keep Treves at the center because Merrick is more theatrical. To cite a lofty analogy, it's the problem that Melville faced in *Billy Budd*, in which Vere is the protagonist but Billy takes the stage. The slight muzziness of that wonderful work comes from the attraction of the experience (Billy) over the experiencer (Vere). The greater muzziness of this lesser work comes from the same trouble.

But, having seen seven more candidates since February, I can still maintain that this is the best new American play since 1972, the year of Sam Shepard's *Tooth of Crime*.

Sweeney Todd

(March 24, 1979)

Sweeney Todd is a monument of misproportion—in a wide cultural sense and in the instance. First, the instance.

The production of this musical is large—an immense setting, a complex score—and it's all invested in a puny nineteenth-century melodrama, tricked out by modern hands. The process was standard in opera at one time. Who would want to see the play on which *Il Trovatore* is based? But Verdi kept the tone of his adaptation so consistent, took the human elements in the piece so seriously, and supplied music so invigorating of the feeble original, that he created a new, immediate work. In *Sweeney Todd* the feeble original has been patronized, inflated, and badgered: and nothing in the music completes the sketchy drama.

In 1847 William Dibdin Pitt made a melodrama called *Sweeney Todd, the Demon Barber of Fleet Street* out of a popular novel by Thomas Preskett Prest. The play was a hit, and in the nineteenth century, a hit meant revival in many theaters over many decades. Lately it was re-adapted in London by Christopher Bond, and from the new version Hugh Wheeler drew the book of this musical. Stephen Sondheim wrote the music and lyrics, and Harold Prince directed. (Note: it's only the usual figure of speech to say that Sondheim wrote the music. What he wrote was the piano score, which was orchestrated by Jonathan Tunick. If an artist does the cartoon for a mural that is then finished by others, do we give the first man credit for the whole work?)

Why was this old play chosen? The question ought to be superfluous, and isn't. For grim social comment? This is boldly promised at the start, but the promise is quickly fiddled. For Grand Guignol thrills? Everything scary is so telegraphed and the throat-cuttings (many of them) so much like an abattoir instead of sheer madness, that bored disgust arises, not horror. For macabre humor? Only the attempts at it are macabre.

The real reason, I suppose, is that Sondheim and Prince thought they would be adventurous again. Adventure to them means shopping: for what's "in" outside the mainstream. (*Company, Follies,* and *Pacific Overtures* are past examples.) Sondheim and Prince run a kind of Bloomingdale's of musical theater, bringing the chic to the center. Here, apparently, their gelded daring took the form of an urge to create a new *Threepenny Opera*, sort of. To do this job, they—helped by Wheeler—chose a trumpery piece of early Victorian claptrap presumably because it's from the same period as the Brecht-Weill work and because its hero is a poor man mishandled by the powerful. What Sondheim-Prince overlooked was that Brecht-Weill transposed an eighteenth-century work to the nineteenth century in order to bite the twentieth century. But all Sondheim-Prince want to do is to please the twentieth century, while they earn credit-by-association.

They reach hard for that association. The set they commissioned echoes Douglas W. Schmidt's set for the Richard Foreman production of *Threepenny Opera* at the Beaumont in 1976. Schmidt put his show in a great empty warehouse, with a beam stretching across it that could be lowered and with iron wheels up high to pull back a traversing curtain. Eugene Lee's set for *Sweeney Todd* is an empty ironworks with *two* beams high across the stage that roll back and forth on iron wheels, sometimes lowering a catwalk.

After a sanctimonious prelude on an organ in the auditorium, which is never again touched, the show begins with a grim audience-confronting chorus, much like that in Foreman's production and with a comparable opening number: instead of the ballad of Mack the Knife, the ballad of Sweeney Todd.

Up through a trap—a valid Victorian entrance—comes Sweeney, and we are promised a single-minded tale of revenge. He's a barber who was transported to Australia fifteen years earlier so that the judge who sentenced him could have Sweeney's wife. She then reportedly killed herself, and Sweeney's daughter, now grown, is the lecherous judge's ward. The Demon Barber sets up shop again, hoping to get the judge as customer. Meanwhile he practices on others, especially those who threaten his plan, cutting their throats as he shaves them, then tipping his chair so that the corpses slide down a chute. How it all ends doesn't matter. En route to the end, however, the corpses land in the establishment downstairs of Mrs. Lovett, a vendor of meat pies, who chops them to practical use.

I gather from theater histories that Mrs. Lovett was originally Sweeney's equal in grimness. Here she has been converted into a goofily comic character for Angela Lansbury. The role is thin. Lansbury has to blink and twist her mouth and cock her head—in short, to mug like mad—in order to give it presence. She also has some comic patter songs, but as usual with Sondheim's patter lyrics, they read better than they speak. Lansbury is not always comprehensible even though she is miked and articulates athletically.

Sweeney is played by Len Cariou who, for me, is Mr. Understudy. Whenever I see him, I feel that the actor who usually plays the part is indisposed. He works hard, sings forcefully, and ends up dull. I've been watching him since the Guthrie in Minneapolis in 1966 and have yet to see anything but plenty of good intentions with little grace or command.

Wheeler's tale of revenge, blazoned as another *Count of Monte Cristo*, wobbles badly as he tries to woo us. He padded or sidetracked his book to keep it going for two and a half hours and to rouge it with charm. There are subplots about an Irishman pretending to be an Italian barber, a youth involved with Mrs. Lovett, a romance between Sweeney's daughter and a Jolly Jack Tar. These plots all would have been weak at best, and here they're at worst. All these secondary roles are wretchedly acted and sung.

Some of Prince's staging is moderately graphic, but he simply can't resist living beyond his directorial means. Once again—it's the third time this month that I've seen it—desultory action leaks on to the stage before the actual start, while the house lights are still up. (Of course there's no front curtain: do you think Prince is square, for heaven's sake?) Once again supers lounge around the fringes of the stage during the show, watching the action in the center. This décor of actors has become a meaningless commonplace since, at the latest, Peter Brook's *A Midsummer Night's Dream* nine years ago.

Inevitably, of course, a musical rests on its music. Shows with good scores have got by with books and casts not much better than these. Sondheim is simply defective in invention. He can supply the necessary changes for numbers like the opening chorus or the patter songs, which are really only matters of mild rhythmic acuteness, music which need not be—and isn't—memorable in itself. But when melody is absolutely required, as in the love songs, Sondheim just spins series of notes, which could just as easily be other notes. He has studied Weill for pungency, for spicy irregularities of stanza, but in Weill those things enliven his melodic gift. And that's where Sondheim limps. In the past he has sometimes found one tune for a show—like "Send in the Clowns" for *A Little Night Music*. Here there is none, only failed Weill and failed operetta.

Franne Lee's costumes rightly work for sharpness of line and detail rather than range of color. Ken Billington's lighting is poor: it doesn't do much to mold forms or evoke atmosphere and sometimes just doesn't give enough light.

But the most monumental misproportion in the whole affair is the size of the Broadway maw—which is what the vast size of the Uris stage suggests—chewing away at true ideas and genuine art, chomping them down to salable bite-size. Once again the upper and lower dentures, clacking away, are named Sondheim and Prince.

Zoot Suit

(April 21, 1979)

"Will Broadway produce a Chicano version of *Hello, Dolly* now that it has produced a Black one?" So asked Luis Valdez, head of the radical Teatro Campesino, in 1970. In 1979 *Zoot Suit* by Luis Valdez arrives on Broadway via the Mark Taper Forum in Los Angeles. It's not exactly *Hello, Dolly*, still, it's Broadway's bet that there are bucks in Chicanos.

Valdez founded El Teatro Campesino in 1965 as a result of his work with the San Francisco Mime Troupe. I never saw the Teatro's work but read much about its passionate involvement with Chicano problems in California. Reportedly Valdez tired of taking Chicano problems to Chicanos, when the trouble lay with Anglos, so he accepted a commission to write and direct *Zoot Suit* for the Mark Taper. It was a success there, and the Shuberts have brought it east.

The fact that *Zoot Suit* turns out to be a mess does not entail the classic sell-out of a radical under the gold of show biz. I don't believe, on the evidence, that Valdez did much selling out; but also, on the evidence, I don't see that, in terms of talent, he had much to sell. His play is loosely based on the Sleepy Lagoon murder in 1942 in Los Angeles, which resulted in race riots. As a piece of writing, it's ludicrous. It's filled with Good People and Bad People; the former are Chicanos and the latter are Anglos, and the worst thing the Good People ever do is sometimes lose their temper because they have pride. The writing is honest, but in the hands of such incompetence it turns out phony—verbal posturings and inflations that couldn't be worse if Valdez's intentions were sheer hack. The construction is like a string of little fat sausages: a conflict swells, is settled and diminishes: then a new, virtually unconnected conflict swells, is settled and diminishes, and so on.

The disgusting aspect of the script is that it portrays every Chicano male in the cast, without exception, as a *macho* imbecile. Obviously even *macho* imbeciles ought to be free of police harassment and economic oppression, but it would have been encouraging to see one male who showed that there was hope for more in Chicanos than swagger, sexual strut, and a belief in women as appurtenances. The male dream climaxes when, toward the end, the hero is forced to choose between two girls who adore him equally.

Valdez doesn't dramatize the root cause: the zoot suit and the *machismo* are consolation and defiance within a ghetto precisely because the ghetto exists. There is a prototypical Chicano who acts as a chorus, a companion for the hero, and an arbiter of the play's action (played with slinky, arched-back sententiousness by Edward James Olmos—a one-note performance that has been sillily overpraised). But this character doesn't illuminate, he is merely the projection of the posturing ideals of the adolescents around him.

As for the production, its worst element is the choreography by Patricia Birch that Valdez encouraged or permitted. With lindy-hop and jitterbug, Birch makes sure that we see enough of girls' bottoms so that we don't get too depressed by social woes. But some of Valdez's staging is vivid. It reminded me occasionally of the Federal Theater's Living Newspaper productions in the 1930s, which means that it has a faint, faint flavor of Piscator's political theater in the Berlin of the 1920s. For instance, Valdez makes some attempt to use the material of the story as décor. When we enter, we see a wide, shallow flight of glitzy steps, over which hangs a huge blow-up of a front page of a Los Angeles newspaper in 1942. The play begins with a huge knife slitting the page vertically, then the choric Chicano steps through. And, throughout the play, tightly packed bales of newspapers serve as seats, desks, judge's bench. That's a bright Piscatorial idea—introducing a prejudiced press as furniture—brighter than anything in the writing. And from time to time Valdez gets some good dramatic sculpture out of groupings on those steps. (There's not a stick of formal scenery.)

The response to this show in Los Angeles was strong. In New York the Hispanic population is much more Puerto Rican than Chicano, and the Winter Garden is a big musical-comedy barn. (The Mark Taper is much more intimate, seats 742, and has a thrust stage.) Both factors pose questions for this show, although on the night I was there, small pockets of "ethnics" scattered in the conventional Broadway audience cheered individual speeches and gasped when a son raised his fist to his father.

But Valdez has said he wants primarily to bring Chicanos to non-Chicanos. Possibly he will succeed. An odd coincidence is that a new film has just arrived that deals with present-day Chicanos in East Los Angeles. *Boulevard Nights*, written by Desmond Nakano, is essentially just another street-gang flick, but it has some similarity in story to *Zoot Suit*—a strong older brother and a weak younger one. What's more, on a utilitarian level, in terms of bringing Chicano problems to people who were unaware of them, *Boulevard Nights* is going to have greater effect than *Zoot Suit*, even in New York where Valdez's gussied-up play is running—at a $22.50 top.

Taken in Marriage

(April 21, 1979)

Meryl Streep, now attracting international praise in *The Deer Hunter*, is playing in *Taken in Marriage* Off-Broadway, extending her range and confirming her brilliance. Here she is a much-married upper-class New Englander, airy and disconsolate, risible and depressed, who with sarcasm and aggressive-defensive laughter, is making her blithely unhappy way through a disordered life. The difference from the supermarket checkout girl in *The Deer Hunter* is not only in detail but in coalescence of detail. Like a good novelist, Streep observes and stores the life around her, selects from her treasury for the work in hand, and then fuses the detail inward and downward to keep it from being a mere construct. This much is true for any competent actor. Streep goes further. Everything—the cigarette fondling, the commenting gesture, the smiling insult—seems inevitable for the character yet also is recognizably Streep. This dual quality, contradictory-complementary—authentic characterization plus authentic individuality—marks the talent that stands out among talents.

Robert Allan Ackerman's direction is as busy as Karen Schulz's setting. Nancy Marchand and Elizabeth Wilson do unsurprisingly well as Streep's mother and aunt.

Thomas Babe, who wrote the piece, is one more of the quarter-baked writers whose activity is taken as proof of our theater's liveliness. Last year it was the fevered and footling symbolism of *A Prayer for My Daughter*. Here it's a sort of realistic chamber-piece, a small group brought together for a purpose and compacted into revelation. Once again Babe got an idea, then failed to write a play.

A prospective bride (Kathleen Quinlan), her older sister, her mother and aunt come to a New England church basement to rehearse the wedding. Before the men arrive, Things Develop. The men never arrive—on stage, anyway—and nothing really develops. Babe puts in a catalyst character—the stunningly original concept of a Southern show-biz quasi-floosie whom I hadn't seen on stage or screen for at least four days—but she just helps to bring out some information. Babe confuses this with development and drama. He thinks that, if he reveals that the bride's sister has been sleeping with the prospective groom and that the maiden aunt is a lesbian, he has written a play. In any genuine sense his play has no action whatsoever and articulates not a wisp of theme. And since most of the information is either revealed or guessable by the end of the first act, the second of the two acts is a long portentous wait for someth : ng that never happens and whose omission we care about less and less.

Whose Life Is It Anyway?

(May 12, 1979)

Whose Life Is It Anyway? began as a TV play and it still is one, although it's been on several stages and is now on Broadway. Since I'm using the term as a value judgment, I'll try to make clear what it means to me. First, I'm referring to plays written for TV, not adaptations; second, I'm discussing TV plays at their best, which usually means British scripts. (Below the top level, they're not worth derogation.) A TV play lights on an easily definable subject—a concrete issue like drugs or euthanasia, or a social-personal problem like corroding values or the vitality of love—examines the subject with some fairness and frankness, and is expressed in dialogue of some sting and tartness. The point of the script is its subject, not the drama arising and taking over from the subject, which is true of good "non-TV" plays. Sooner rather than later, we become aware in the TV play of neatness: the strictures of time on TV press toward arrangement—not happy endings necessarily but a sense that the real reason for starting the thing was to finish it in sixty or ninety minutes. This subtle oppression by time-form underscores the esthetic fact that the script is demonstration, no matter how effective, rather than drama. Turgenev said that he had long wanted to write a novel on the Young Generation and that it was crystallized for him by "the striking personality of a young provincial doctor." It was then that he began *Fathers and Sons.* This is not the customary sequence for TV writing.

Yes, Aristotle said that character is subsidiary to action, but he was speaking in an age when virtually all the plots (of serious plays) were known in advance and authors varied only in their treatment of them. Yes, there are plays/series on TV that are exceptions to the description above. The British series *The Glittering Prizes* by Frederic Raphael struck me as such an exception: its shortcomings were those of the author, not of the process. But the TV play as described is so common as to provide a useful critical term. Brian Clark's *Whose Life Is It Anyway?* is a TV play: a humane inquiry into the right of a hopelessly disabled, hospitalized person to end his life. The key word is person. Color it Fred or Harry or, as Clark does, Ken.

Ken was in a car accident and his spine was snapped; he will never again move his arms and legs. Clark dresses him in characteristics. Ken is Scottish, which gives him a wry accent; young, which gives his future a long perspective; witty and sexy and bright, which gives his condition some snobbish garlands of sentiment. (Snobbish because it appeals to bonds of superiority between him and us. Clark would not risk his case with a stolid Ken, less bright than ourselves, although the paralysis would be no whit less grim.) Gary Jay

Williams, reviewing the Washington production of this play some months ago (*Theater*, Spring 1979), noted that Clark has made Ken a sculptor so that the idea of immobility-as-end hovers aptly over the play and that, equally aptly, Ken has driven away his fiancée before the curtain rises and has already had his last visit from his parents. Thus he has been stripped of emotional attachments.

All these factors do not create a man, they construct a polemic instance. Clark never convinces us that he is interested in Ken: his interest is in the theme. He certifies this by rigging a supporting cast of puppets: the sympathetic woman doctor, the blinkered-by-duty medical chief, the draconian head nurse, the shy new nurse, with whom—surprise!—an orderly flirts. Clark is serious, writes reasonably supple dialogue, and has a smidgen of wit. What he doesn't show as yet is an ability to make his play grow out of his people, to imply that, like Pirandello's Six Characters, these *people* have absolutely demanded a theater in which to present themselves.

Tom Conti, who was in *The Glittering Prizes*, plays Ken—with his head alone, of course. His performance is good but, for a competent actor, easy. It's the sort of part that, as they say in the theater, an actor would pay to play: it's "in" before it begins. Jean Marsh, inflated to theater stardom by TV success (*Upstairs, Downstairs*), is the doctor and doesn't act, she dispenses English toffee. Philip Bosco, the medical chief, is a good actor fallen upward, into the higher registers of his voice. He was up there last year in *Saint Joan*, and he hasn't come down yet. Does he think this gives him "modernity"—to contrast with all the classical roles we've seen him in? The director, Michael Lindsay-Hogg, shows a grip here equivalent to what he showed in the film *Nasty Habits*; movement, rhythm, interplay are all orchestrated nicely. Alan Tagg, whose rightly precise set for *Hedda Gabler* I saw at the Royal Court in London in 1972, does the rightly quasi-abstract setting here. It combines the rectangular reality of hospital rooms and—by using a few panels of ceiling lights instead of an actual ceiling—a suggestion of the immensity that the protagonist is facing.

Dispatches

(May 12, 1979)

To some degree I've admired everything Elizabeth Swados has done, from her music for Andrei Serban's *Trilogy* to her recent children's musical, *The Incredible Feeling Show*. I'm sad to report that this "rock-war musical," based on Michael Herr's book, is bad. It doesn't pass the fundamental test that Herr's book passes easily. Herr—anyway, one feels this—waited ten years or so before he published his book about the Vietnam War so that he could test every line, bite every phrase, to make sure that it was not counterfeit or trite, to make sure that he was adding to our knowledge and imagination of the war, to avoid any suspicion in himself of exploitation. None of this applies to Swados's musical.

Apparently she was hugely moved by Herr's book, and she kept her rendering simple: little dramatization, just various members of the cast of eleven performing numbers while a seven-piece band sits on a ledge above them and the lights change. But her settings of various passages of Herr's prose, done in her regular range of pop styles, contribute nothing. (Worse, if it weren't for the electric sign above the stage that flashes some of the words, we wouldn't even understand some of the over-miked songs.) Good songs, as hard and fresh in their own way as Herr's prose, might possibly have added something to the book. But these songs seem merely to be riding on the book. There was no point in this show unless it could *add*. As is, it risks the charge of exploitation.

Swados remains the most adventurous artist in our musical theater. On to her next.

Postscript. Speaking of Swados: I've just seen again—for the eighth time—the La Mama Theater production of *Fragments of a Trilogy*, directed by Serban with music by Swados.(*Medea* has been restored.) I'd like to see these magnificent versions of three Greek plays every year, because of such actors as Priscilla Smith, Joanna Peled and William Duff-Griffin, because of Serban's imaginative vault and, certainly not least, the thrilling music. But *Trilogy* has been revived only because the La Mama company has been invited to Jerusalem to perform it. It may never be revived again. What a cultural disgrace it is, in our humdrum theater, that means are not available to keep this company together permanently, working under Serban, with Swados, to move further among the mountain ranges of drama.

Talley's Folly

(June 9, 1979)

This is another piece of Lanford Wilson's front-porch knitting about the South Central states, full of the click-clack of theatrical needles that obviously brings joy to critical hearts nostalgic for old fashions. The play is a two character hokum-jokum—a self-styled "waltz"—which, as we're told in advance, runs ninety-four minutes and ends happily. The way in which the man of the pair addresses the audience at the beginning and end; the ungainliness and self-doubt of the woman; the loneliness of two wounded people; the seedy elegance of the setting; the inclusion of inserted jokes—these are all Tennessee Williams derivatives. The difference from the best Williams is that no authentic mood or character is ever generated, just a series of facsimiles that lead to revelations whose only point is to justify the series of facsimiles that led to these revelations whose only point etc. . . .

This protracted dialogue between a St. Louis Jewish accountant and an Ozark hospital aide, set during World War Two, ultimately uncovers two secrets: an experience of hers has left her sterile; he (not credible in this buffoon) is the child of tragically harassed European Jews and doesn't want children. This, after ninety-four mechanical minutes, brings them together.

Judd Hirsch is deft enough in what is really a vaudeville turn, not a role. Trish Hawkins is less appealing as—the name exemplifies Wilson's wit—Sally Talley. Their performances, like the glibly summoned nostalgia, the distant band music, the southern summer evenings, are just further deployments of familiar theatrical devices.

Yet the huzzahs range across the (alleged) spectrum of critics. And intelligent "civilians"—people not specifically engaged in the theater—go to *Talley's Folly*, and other plays that could be cited, then leave with their heads shaking: in wonderment at the praise and in despair about going back to the theater.

All New, All American

(July 7 & 14, 1979)

James McLure's two one-act plays are about the effects of the Vietnam War on its veterans. *Pvt. Wars*, played first though billed second, is set in a veterans hospital and has three characters, all inmates: Gately, a southerner with mechanical aptitude, Natwick, a well-bred Long Islander, and Silvio, a breezy "operator." The play moves in a series of short, astringent scenes, and through this oblique process, it reveals the differing wounds of these three men. Gately *must* keep on repairing a damaged radio even after the man he's doing it for has died—the work is his being; Natwick is still fearfully oppressed by his mother; Silvio must continue to dominate as king *macho* even though his genitals were blown off in combat. All three inmates say often that they could get out any time they like, which is literally true but psychologically unlikely.

The strength of the script is in its method. By sliding past the pathos, the play touches it. A frontal attack might well have missed or, worse, might have emphasized that the play is nothing *but* an appeal for pathos. The method shows McLure's awareness of the danger, his insistence on the importance of this pathos if it can be reached without theatrical corn that would falsify it. The three actors, Gregory Grove (Gately), Clifford Fetters (Natwick) and Tony Campisi (Silvio), play in a way that suggests the tart tonality of modern understated fiction. An actress who was my companion said that she thought the director, Stuart White, had worked by suggesting images to his cast—animals hiding, for instance. I agree.

White directed the première of the second play, *Lone Star*, at Actors Theater of Louisville, where both plays were first done, but here *Lone Star* is directed by Garland Wright who has fashioned exceptional "visual" productions at the Lion Theater such as *K* and *Music Hall Sidelights*. Here Wright shows a different and almost equally strong aspect of his talent. *Lone Star*, also with a cast of three men, is Texas-realist, set in the yard behind a bar in a small town, with old car-seats as benches and a décor of old license plates. (The scenery is by John Arnone who did the delicate work for Wright's other productions.) The title operates in several ways besides the nickname of the state: the name of a beer that is swilled a lot, the sighting of the first star that is wished on, and sometimes the emphasis is on the adjective.

McLure's script is written in beer-proletarian-rural, menace-and-solitude poetics, somewhat in the vein of Sam Shepard or, latterly, William Hauptman. Powers Boothe, a tall and trenchant actor, is Roy, who drinks and hells around today pretty much as he did before he went to Vietnam, but this life used to be enough and now it isn't: everything seems different. Leo Burmester is Ray, his beefy, adoring, dumb, younger brother, and Clifford Fetters of the first play does a sort of Jimmy Carter imitation as Cletis, a newly married nit. As the play moves on, Cletis confesses to Ray that, earlier this night, he has taken Roy's beloved car without permission and has smashed it. That car is the dearest thing in Roy's life after his wife, Elizabeth. Cletis asks Ray to tell Roy about the wreck and take the blame. When the brothers are alone, Ray tells Roy that, while the latter was in Vietnam, he and Elizabeth slept together, more than once. Fury bursts forth—but within the bonds of brotherly affection; and by the time Ray gives Roy the news about the car, the fury is even less. Ray has told the truth, strategically.

Wright's direction gently and firmly polishes the theme under the action: ideas of value. In these two men, brotherly love is more that marital betrayal, but the news of that betrayal takes the sting out of the destruction of a tribal symbol, the car: and all these matters are blanketed by the general lingering numbness of Vietnam. The play is something like a field-trip in anthro-pology—with an echo of *Tobacco Road*—but it's cogent, authentic, well worked-out.

It's not James McLure's fault that his two plays have been snowed with the Confederate-currency inflation of our theater criticism. In spite of the blown praise, his double bill has some modest rewards and is worth seeing.

Michael Weller, on the other hand, is himself inflationary. His new play *Loose Ends*, which is also a post-Vietnam number, is an improvement over his hippie-licking *Moonchildren*, but that's not to say much. The inflation begins in the very first of the eight scenes. Two young Americans, Paul and Susan, are lying on a beach in Bali where they have just met, in 1970, and presumably made love. She is floating around the world with a girl friend; he is on his way back from two Peace Corps years in a remote country. The opening account of his experiences there is couched so squarely in platitudinous bitterness (a tale that ends predictably with his getting drunk to forget) that for a time we hope that the clichés are the character's, not the author's. This hope vanishes when Susan's girl friend bursts in followed by a Balinese with a fish, and we get a

local-color "cameo-bit" which is completely unrelated to the play and is a battered cliché about American-abroadism.

The succeeding seven scenes take us through the 1970s and through the
Susan-Paul story, and each scene executes more or less the same pattern: an initial positing of a situation that seems ticked off from the author's checklist of
current problems, the burrowing into the trouble for a while in language that
struggles toward but never quite reaches incisiveness, and the lapse into one or
another theatrically worn poignancy to conclude matters. The characters are
also off a checklist: the hearty bearded friend who is full of health and hump-
ing; his woman who bears three of his children liberatedly, confiding—like the
girl in Osborne's *Inadmissible Evidence*—how much she loves sex; Paul's sleek
salesman brother who is enjoying his selling out; the gay interior decorator
whose "cameo-bit" seems a belated counterpoise to the earlier Balinese fisher-
man.

Chiefly, the scenes seem patterned and the "bits" seem tailored because the
whole play is a duty tour of Contemporary Life by an author who has absolutely not one iota of his own vision on the subject. In the second half of his play,
desperate to keep his drama dramatic, Weller hauls in the issue of children:
Paul wants them, Susan doesn't. (For those who think that this is a "today"
issue, related to women's rights: this was the plot nub of *Bulls, Bears and Asses* in
1932.) The couple, now married, split because Susan has had an abortion
which Paul finds out about only afterward. The breakup scene on a rooftop is a
paragon of dramaturgic clumsiness (besides being incredible in Susan's
character); and anyway the issue is revealed as a sham in the last scene. A year
after their divorce Paul and Susan meet and have a sex reunion in a country
house (an echo of the end of Bergman's *Scenes from a Marriage*), and we learn
that Paul is now living with another woman; but there is no mention of his
hunger to have children, no word that a wee one is on the way.

Roxanne Hart, the Susan, is fairly pleasant, but she has a voice that tends to
dullness in its middle range, and in general she has to work too hard to keep
our interest to be genuinely interesting. So, also, Kevin Kline, the Paul, who is
not an actor of much depth and who often makes choices in his performance
that seem remembered from performances he has seen, rather than observed
freshly and distilled. In their faintly tired strophes, the actors are abetted by
Alan Schneider the director, who did the first production at the Arena in
Washington and whose deployment of stage conventions—the textbook turn
or cross or pause—is familiar. The total is a long evening that, in every way,
does nothing but remind us of what we have already thought or felt.

Getting Out by Marsha Norman, like McLure's double bill, originated at Actors Theater of Louisville, then proceeded via the Phoenix in New York (where
I saw it last year) to its present home (where I saw it again). A southern
prostitute-drug addict is released from prison and is determined to straighten

herself out. It's misleading to say that Joan Crawford, alive and starring today, would want to film it; it's truer to say that this script, with its language scrubbed, could have been done—figuratively *was* done—in the 1930s.

The lack of anything more than naturalistic varnish on one more Girls in the Big House story is purportedly disguised by a stale theatrical device. There's a multiple set—several settings in one—and there are interwoven scenes of the protagonist at two ages, as an adolescent and as she is today, played by two people. The youngster is a hellion, absolutely unvaried from beginning to end; the older woman is trying to resist temptations to slip back into an easier life than the dishwashing that lies ahead of her. Apparently, no one—from the author to the raving critics—has noted that there is no connection between the two people. How and why did Unregenerate Number One become Regenerate Number Two? So long as there's plenty of (alleged) nitty-gritty—from the kid's heavily prophetic story of the killing of some pet frogs to the howlingly trite scenes with the ex-pimp who wants his non-job back—that question isn't asked. It's squelched by the old naturalistic tinware dragged out and rattled again, with facile squirming and kicking and easily induced hysterics.

Jon Jory, who directed all three productions of this play, has been praised for his work presumably because the light cues are snappy in various parts of the stage, cell-doors bang and doors slam on cue, and all climaxes are built patently and paused after pregnantly. (I can't remember a play with a multiple set whose direction wasn't praised.) But the moments that call for some subtle vitalization of stage space, like those between the woman and a new woman friend, are simply left untended. Jory shows himself more of a stage-manager of technical effects than a director with a knowledge of acting or character texture or true stage motion.

Evita

(Saturday Review, November 11, 1979)

The program of Evita identifies the lyricist and the composer but no author of the book. This is puzzling before the show but not after it begins, because the narrative of this musical is carried entirely in the score by Tim Rice and Andrew Lloyd Webber. Ths show tells its story through one relatively formal song after another, sometimes connected by isolated stanzas or versified passages set to music. Evita is thus in a new form which, like many new forms, is a refurbished old one: the secular oratorio.

But far from that term's suggestion of stiff choristers and statuesque soloists, Evita is steeped in theatricality. Writing about the 1968 production of Hair, Gerald Bordman says in American Musical Theater, "Staging was coming to outclass even librettos as the mainstay of the modern musical," and the Evita people almost seem to have taken Bordman as their text. The settings by

Timothy O'Brien and Tazeena Firth materialize and disappear with suggestive fluency; the lighting by David Hersey, which is the most dramatic element in the show, uses even a semicircle of lights sunk in the floor to help mold the playing spaces graphically; and the entire action is placed against film projections that reinforce the story with newsreel shots of the (real-life) principals, atmospheric shots of places, oceanic shots of crowds. Harold Prince staged the piece, much more flexibly and incisively than he staged *Sweeney Todd*. If it's sometimes hard to see where Prince's direction leaves off and Larry Fuller's choreography begins, that's surely part of the production's method. Yet after virtually everything that sheer stagecraft can do has been summoned up to galvanize *Evita*, it runs into a stone wall. It remains narrative, not dramatic; and the authors never make clear why they chose the subject in the first place.

Possibly there is a benighted yak-driver somewhere in Mongolia who doesn't know what that subject is. For that yak-driver: Evita is Eva Peron, wife of Juan Peron and co-dictator of Argentina with him, who died in 1952 at thrity-three and whose short life-span is disproportionate to her effect as politician and personality. We've all known for a long time that histrionics is essential to dictatorship: Eva Peron was the only dictator—or co-dictator—who had been a professional actor.* We've also known that part of the effect of Hitler and Mussolini was their sexual attraction for millions of women; Eva Peron was the first woman in a position to exercise comparable sexual-political power over millions of men. Her story, tyrannies and all, is fascinating, but more fascinating to read than to see in *Evita*.

Rice and Webber shortchange her. They reduce her to a cunning small-town singer who slithers her way to Buenos Aires, sleeps her way into radio acting, then sleeps her way up the power scale. Whatever her sexual tacking and luffing may have been, boudoir navigation was far from the whole story. She had been a labor organizer, had helped to form the national union of radio employees, had led mass demonstrations: she did considerably more for her future husband than (as she does in the show) advise him to wait for the opportune moment. (And he himself had done more than is shown: he had already headed a secret military group that had overthrown a previous government.)

No one expects a musical to be a political handbook, particularly about a country so remote—tragically remote, I would say—from our close concerns. But when Rice and Webber chose this subject, they assumed some obligation to make the Perons' rise to power credible in the theater, rather than relying on the extrinsic fact that they *did* rise to power, just as they had some obligation to shape the materials into a cumulative and discerning drama rather than relying on the fact that the actual lives were dramatic. (It's a pitfall that traps many biographical playwrights.) Rice and Webber simply stitch together a line of

---

*Possible exception: Jiang Qing, Chairman Mao's third wife and his widow, who had been a film actress.

events, leaning on the lurid ones, then end with Eva's early death from cancer, which is treated more or less as if it were her biggest mistake. (They begin with the death, too: the story is told in flashback.)

Beneath the dramatic feebleness, and causing it, is the sorry truth that Rice and Webber have nothing to "say" about Evita. They provide no insight into her extraordinary combination of beautiful actress's flash, vindictive ego, and real concern for working people; they don't even fashion a cautionary tale like Brecht's *The Resistible Rise of Arturo Ui*. They just pick up a glittering figure from the shelf of history, twirl her a while, then put her back.

They must have had a sense of the show's flatness because, trying to give it some tension and bite, the authors put in a commentator whom they call Che. We're obviously meant to infer that this is Che Guevara, who was a revolutionary in his native Argentina before he went to Cuba, but this Che is not a character, he's a utility infielder. Sometimes he's bitter about the Perons and gets slugged by their police; sometimes he helps out in the stage-management when the scene needs it; sometimes he's a mere chorus. Instead of deepening the texture he adds to the show's spurious gravity.

Still, despite all the above, the show might have been gripping if the score were good. One of the great myths of the opera and musical-theater worlds is that bad libretti can drive good scores off the stage. I'm not arguing for bad books—even subsumed books, as in *Evita*—but the music is finally what keeps a musical piece alive, or doesn't. (Look at the problematic books of *La Bohème* and *Show Boat*.) The score of *Evita* is banality trying to make a virtue of itself, trying to pass as anticonventional. Like the previous Rice-Webber show, *Jesus Christ Superstar*, this score has just one striking phrase, not even one complete striking song—"Don't Cry for Me, Argentina." The rest is only a series of appropriately wrought stopgaps.

The casting of Evita has the same stopgap quality. Patti LuPone was one of the few bright spots in John Houseman's dreary Acting Company, with a nice nubile vivacity, but here she just can't fill the bill. She sings and acts competently, but it's a bit like the young Debbie Reynolds playing a dazzling cobrasaint. Bob Gunton resembles Peron and sings well enough, but he too leaves the charisma question dangling. As the ubiquitous Che, Mandy Patinkin tries to make bricks without straw, but anyway one can't throw bricks at straw figures.

What Rice and Webber have shown in their two big shows so far is a talent for titles and subjects. I remember the sting of excitement when I first read the title *Jesus Christ Superstar*, the expectations of a new Vulgate, a show that would possibly both use and transcend pop forms. What we got, however, was a *religioso* bath for adolescents. Undashed, I felt the same sting when I read the title *Evita*. But it too is just a fumbled utilization of a rich subject, with (allowing for the switch to Latin rhythms) the same kind of rhetorical score. The mysteries of political power, of political personality are named but not even slightly explored; yet Rice and Webber have arranged things so that the audience can go home, as it did after *Superstar*, feeling good that it has been at more than a mere musical.

Ladyhouse Blues

(Saturday Review, January 5, 1980)

Are American playwrights awake? It's a fair question to ask many of them—and I mean many of the most serious. They seem not to know of a fundamental change in all the arts during the last few decades. A lot of playwrights in other countries are aware of this shift, but not a lot of ours.

The change is in the artist's relation to truth. For about 150 years, until the middle of this century, the basic drive of art was to be more and more truthful. From romanticism to surrealism, progressive artists saw themselves as breakers of shackles and bringers of light. Not today. Few progressive artists now think of themselves in anything like those terms. Truth, at least in the aspects that inspired realists and naturalists and the others, comes to us now through the social sciences and the informational barrage of the media. In the pop phrase, the artist can't keep up with the headlines. So he has turned, very fruitfully in numerous instances, to other powers in art: to explorations of consciousness, to validations of reality, to rummaging in the mysteries of the artistic process itself. To put it too simply, Brecht is followed by Beckett.

But this change, which has nothing to do with vogue or novelty, has not yet registered notably with American playwrights, even the ones who might be expected to be most responsive, the ones not focused on Broadway. Numbers of these last still have their minds fixed back several decades, still rush in breathlessly to Tell All. Last season Off-Broadway, Marsha Norman's *Getting Out* told us about a woman ex-convict at the depth of a 1930s Warner Bros. weepie; Michael Weller's *Loose Ends*, about young people in the 1970s, had all the penetration of a TV special.

The line stretches on. Prominent in the new Off-Broadway season is *Ladyhouse Blues*, by Kevin O'Morrison, a play that has been cosseted by grants, conference workshops, and previous productions, including an earlier one Off-Broadway. And what has all this huffery and puffery brought us? One more kitchen-sink opus. If it had been written in 1919, the year in which it is set, it might now be revived as a modestly rewarding example of early American naturalism. Today it's dramatically, socially, psychologically comatose.

Worse, it's still one more remembering of Mama. Just after World War I, a countrywoman is living in a St. Louis apartment surrounded by four daughters—three resident, one visiting. The title refers to the postman's name for buildings from which all the men have gone off to war. No drama is made out of this fact, but then no drama is really made of anything. It's all just a recital of "realities."

Each character symbolizes a social fact, with an invisible sign around her neck. One daughter has been married to a German, one is going to marry a Greek, so we know that the attack on ethnic prejudice has begun. One daughter is socially mobile upward, one is in the labor movement. And the mother is the nineteenth-century figure against whom they are all measured. In her stubborn, brave way she is supposed to exemplify old virtues; but she comes out short-sighted, selfish. (Her son dies in the navy and, out of pride, she refuses the insurance, though she badly needs it.)

Absolutely nothing is intended in this play except to show us what these people were; and that simply is not enough. In style even more than in subject, this is very old ground to trudge over again. The acting and direction match the play, jigsawing along close to the profile of prosaic representation. The mother, Jo Henderson, is predictable. It's one of those programmed parts—suffering, staunch, humorous—in which the performer merely has to do nothing egregiously wrong in order to wow the imperceptive.

Still, the acting is better than the writing. O'Morrison wants to tell the truth, but he is so inept that it comes out false. As happens so often with such writers, his sincerity is corrupted by bad dramaturgy. The long opening expository scene, in which two of the daughters mostly tell each other things they already know so that we can learn them, reeks of the typewriter. Time after time, a character bursts in with news, then—in stale imitation of the Nurse in *Romeo and Juliet*—delays reporting it to build suspense. Devices like these mar the play's tiny ambition to be veristic.

Despite the critical heralding and hailing, any importance of *Ladyhouse Blues* is not in the play itself but in the fact that it is a clear instance of the disconnection between our playwrights and contemporary esthetic sensibility. Of course this isn't true of every American playwright: Sam Shepard, still our preeminent talent, is one who has shown, with differing success, from *La Turista* to *Buried Child*, the reach of transformative imagination. And, of course, not every playwright who moves past realism is successful: I can't find much of interest in the mellifluous meanderings of John Guare (*Landscape of the Body, Bosoms and Neglect*) or the pretentious trickery of Arthur Kopit (*Wings*). And, most certainly, none of this is to decree that there can never be another good realistic play, one that says something enlightening *about* its facts. But the majority of serious new American plays strive only for honesty, and are trapped in it.

That's a dangerous phrase, perhaps, but it's an apt one for our culture, which still envisions the artist's life as centrally a battle between principle and commercialism. The prime, often exclusive way that a good writer is identified in America is by his refusal to sell out: honesty is not the best but the sole policy. Other virtues are nice but sort of secondary. And the way that the artist proves his honesty—by contrast with Broadway and Hollywood writers—is by not tampering with facts. So what we get, in great measure, are fact-fastened, Rip van Winkle plays, instead of imaginative plays that make demands on us.

Sugar Babies

(Saturday Review, January 5, 1980)

Sugar Babies is spurious nostalgia. Does anyone really miss burlesque? A few of the stripteasers were exciting, a few of the comics were wonderful, but it's hard to generate a genuine pang about it all. In these permissive days, all that one can feel about burlesque is lost innocence, and innocence is exactly what it wasn't aiming at. However, there is now a steady market for nostalgia, true or forced, and this show is a plastic-wrapped package of it.

It isn't really a revival, it's a sporadically amusing requiem. The show has no strippers (a tacit admission that burlesque is out-of-date), just fan and belly dancers. Most of the gags hang in limbo between wit and history, neither fresh nor old enough to be endearing—not even "*Meet* me 'round the *cor*-ner *in* a *half* an *hour*," with a bump and drumbeat on each accent.

Besides, there never was an Ann Miller in burlesque. Her dance numbers, impressive only because she is of a certain age, are out of orthodox musical comedy. And Mickey Rooney, though he knows the mechanics and is very smooth, has dead eyes. He's a skilled technician without a dram of warmth.

Standards apply in burlesque, just as elsewhere. When I see a Hamlet, I can't help measuring it against Gielgud's. When I see the old courtroom sketch—the lubricious judge and the luscious witness—I measure it against Bobby Clark and Gypsy Rose Lee. Even the unlucky ones who never saw *Star and Garter* (1942) may feel that Rooney and Miller are more fabricative than funny.

Bent

(Saturday Review, February 2, 1980)

Imagine an inmate of a Nazi concentration camp protecting himself by pretending to be Jewish. That could have been true, says Martin Sherman, if the man had been a homosexual, because homosexuals were rated lower than Jews. Sherman's play *Bent* memorializes the German queers—I'll use his pungent term—whose persecution and murder have generally been ignored. His aim to award a first place in suffering (which is historically debatable) is less engrossing than the suffering itself; and it's less pertinent than the play's implicit point: society keeps on making homosexuals suffer grossly.

Sherman is American, but his play was originally done at the Royal Court Theatre in London, where I also saw it. The protagonist—played here by Richard Gere, the star of such films as *Days of Heaven* and *Yanks*—is a Berlin queer who lives with a male nightclub dancer. After the June 1934 purge of Ernst Röhm and associates, after the homosexual hunt is heated up by the new government, Gere and the dancer live on the run. Captured at last, they are slung onto a train bound for Dachau. The officers torture the dancer, and Gere, under duress, proves that he hates queers by helping to beat his friend to death. Then, offstage, he further proves that he is not queer, is really the thoroughly heterosexual Jew he claims to be, by copulating with a dead little girl. Thus he earns (!) the yellow Star of David and avoids the pink triangle of the queer.

On the train Gere meets a labeled queer, arrested for political offense. This man quickly discerns Gere's sexual nature. In Dachau the two are assigned the senseless job of continuously moving the same pile of rocks from one side of a yard to the other. This monotonous rock-lugging is the chief physical action of the second half of the play, the ostinato under the dialogue of the two men, which is carried out in sidelong snatches under the guards' eyes while working or while standing at attention during the three-minute rest periods. Sometimes during the rest periods, the two men manage to have sexual "intercourse" through verbal stimulation.

When the friend sickens, Gere pretends to the captain that he himself needs medicine, since a Jew stands a better chance of getting it than a queer. To get it, Gere performs a sex act for the captain, apparently tolerable in a Jew but not a queer. After the deception about the sickness has been discovered—and punished—Gere is so deeply stirred that he moves to a self-sacrificial act of loyalty.

The power of the subject sustains the first half of the play. When I worked on farms as a boy and learned how to split wood, I was told to let the fall of the axe do most of the job. In effect that's what happens in Act One: the sheer impact of the situation stuns us despite the two-dimensional writing. Also Act One has some vivid secondary characters. The dancer, played by David Marshall Grant, who recently made his film debut in French Postcards, is a silly little poodle of a fellow, immediately endearing. The transvestite star of the nightclub where the dancer works is engraved à la George Grosz by Michael Gross. Gere's uncle, a fastidious rich old queer, is neatly managed by George Hall.

But by Act Two the subject is familiar, and there are no vignettes. It's in Act Two that Sherman has, so to speak, to write his play, has to justify the progress of Act One. And he wobbles. After the rising action of Act One, we get only a plateau decorated with a macabre vaudeville. Only near the very end does Sherman return to drama.

Both the filler-material and the return, however, are destructive. I daresay that, in Dachau and the other camps, there were moments of comic irritation, possibly of boredom, but the banter between Gere and his friend—tolerably acted by David Dukes—is not ironic, it's footling. ("I'm going cra-a-azy," intones Gere comically as he carries rocks.) And the finish is even phonier.

The falseness comes from the mixture of two plays. Sherman wrote one play about homosexual persecution and another about moral regeneration. The protagonist begins as a dedicated sensualist, partying around Berlin. Except for one flicker of honor in Act One, he shows nothing but self-concern. At the end he suddenly changes; and he decides to die to consecrate the change. I don't contend that the hero had to be a homosexual Albert Schweitzer, but, first, the choice of this character strengthens the popular fallacy that being a homosexual means living a degenerate life and, second, the change turns Dachau into a moral gymnasium. Concentration camps perhaps ennobled some of their victims—anything can happen among millions—but it's sentimental to see uplift as the inevitable result of suffering. And to use the transformation in this structurally unprepared manner smacks more of Technicolor than growth. Worse, Gere's final action is basically patronizing, as if to prove that "even" homosexuals can show nobility. Paradoxically, the terrible truth of the persecution ultimately wilts under the trumped-up heroics that Sherman uses to convey it.

As far as I can remember, Robert Allan Ackerman's staging resembles the overall design of Robert Chetwyn's staging in London. The all-white lighting by Arden Fingerhut tends to wash out faces. This is unlucky for Gere, whose features, like his acting, are rubbery.

Night and Day

(Saturday Review, February 2, 1980)

Maggie Smith has apparently stopped acting and gone into business, but at least it's a well-run business. The woman who once played Hedda Gabler in Ingmar Bergman's London production, whom I saw as Desdemona to Olivier's Othello and as Masha in The Three Sisters, now concentrates on marketing one commodity: her own brand of lazy-incisive high comedy. She did it in Private Lives and in the film California Suite, she's doing it again in Tom Stoppard's play Night and Day, but she does it enjoyably.

The play itself, garrulous yet thin, is said to signal a new Stoppard. The new one is actually old-fashioned. The earlier Stoppard was shallow but glittery and adventurous. Now he lumps through a relatively conventional play that he tries to brighten with some grabs at his first fine, careless, rhetorical rapture. Stuck in a stock play, his allegedly diamond dialogue now looks the rhinestone it really always was.

The scene is a turbulent African nation, the ostensible theme is the worth of journalism. Members of the press sift through the home of an English mine manager and his wife (Smith), providing occasions for discussion of the theme. But the real center—affectively, anyway—is Smith, her love life and interior dilemmas. (Most of the latter are couched in cinematically lighted asides.)

I saw this play earlier, in London, and both times it was pointed up nicely by the same director, Peter Wood. But the American supporting cast, except for the president of the African country, is very much better than the English cast, particularly Paul Hecht and Peter Evans as reporters. They seem to have helped Smith: she's better here, too—all vocal slink and razor-keen inflection, precisely interwoven with delicate facial play. The latter-day comic merchandise of Maggie Smith Inc. may perhaps pall in time, but that certainly hasn't happened yet.

Betrayal

(Saturday Review, March 1, 1980)

The hero of Harold Pinter's new play is Peter Hall, the director. Hall, head of the National Theater in London, has directed the premières of all of Pinter's plays since *The Homecoming* (1965). Twice, with that play and *No Man's Land*, most of the original cast was brought over for the production here. Twice, with *Old Times* and this new play, Hall redirected in New York with different actors. In the past, Hall developed out of each Pinter script a polyphonic performance that enriched the work; he found the life of the play, which, with Pinter, means the mystery that gives the play its life, and he exalted that mystery without trying to "explain" it. But in this new work, *Betrayal*, Hall had to do more: he had to supply the mystery. To read an earier Pinter play is to see how delicately Hall responded to it. To read *Betrayal* (published by Grove Press) is to see how well Hall buttressed it.

The play centers on three Londoners: Jerry, a literary agent, Robert, his best friend and a publisher, and Emma, Robert's wife, who eventually opens an art gallery. "Eventually" is an imprecise word because the play proceeds in reverse chronological order. (Three of the nine scenes occur *after* the scenes that precede them, but the overall movement is reverse.) It opens with a 1977 meeting between Jerry and Emma. They haven't seen each other for two years but were lovers for seven years before that, had even rented a flat for their afternoon meetings—Jerry is married, too. The last scene is a party in 1968; Jerry, who had been best man at the Robert-Emma wedding, declares his love for her. In a long moment of quiet, during which she considers the affair we know has happened, the play ends/begins.

Betrayal can breathe in the theater only in the rarefied air of high comedy. The play needs a very English kind of acting, built on social (not theatrical) pose and vocal arch. Without polish, which includes the polished pause, this script would wilt into a lot of "What?" dialogue. ("It's Torcello tomorrow, isn't it?" "What?" "We're going to Torcello tomorrow, aren't we?") On paper such passages—they're plentiful—lie limp, unlike most Pinter dialogue. Under Hall's hand, the actors endow these passages with tease, duelling wit, calculation, and even inviting ambiguity.

The three principals are fine. That's Hall's central triumph: to have brought three American actors, not native to this social-theatrical style, into control of it. Blythe Danner's success as Emma is no surprise; from Viola in *Twelfth Night* to the heroine of Langdon Mitchell's *The New York Idea*, she has sparkled and delighted. But of Raul Julia (Jerry), so clumsy in *The Threepenny Opera*, and Roy Scheider (Robert), so pallid in numerous films, I expected little, and was happily stunned. All three had help with their English accents from Timothy Monich, the unsung aide on foreign accents for several New York productions. But it was Hall who put his cast at ease in a society of egotism-as-ethics even between lovers, a world-as-my-drawing-room society. And it's this sense of milieu, beyond the actors' grip on their characters, that gives the trio their impeccable timing.

The performances are matched by John Bury's sets, costumes, and lighting. I can't remember the last time I saw a production designed entirely by one person. It's a blessing here. Bury, who has often worked with Pinter and Hall, has provided sets in sharply compressed perspective, like shadow-box picture frames. (The year of each scene is flashed on the ceiling of the set before it begins.) In Bury's generally remorseless lighting, the sets give us the feeling of *tableaux* very *vivants*, pieces of a puzzle being fitted together. This feeling is heightened by the Hall-Bury device of starting each scene with the actors motionless in dim silhouette (city sounds in the background) and having them move as the lights blaze up. More, this device suggests that fragments of the past are being brought to life again.

But Pinter's play itself disappoints. First, the writing. Pinter couldn't write a careless line, but care is only one ambition. Much of the dialogue in *Betrayal* is at the boulevard level of Simon Gray's *Butley* and *Otherwise Engaged*, both of which Pinter has directed. Only twice does *Betrayal* burst into the full sardonic music of the best Pinter—in two speeches of Robert's, one about Venetians (when he and Emma are in Venice) and one about modern prose. I don't argue that Pinter's style must not change; I was among those who praised the new, lively lyricism of his two one-act plays *Landscape* and *Silence*. But the dialogue of *Betrayal* is the least implicative of any Pinter that I know.

The quality of the writing leads to—in a good dramatist it is inseparable from—the question of the play's theme. The title sounds promising, but the promise isn't kept. Who is betrayed? In even the most conventional triangle-play manner? Robert knew of his wife's affair, we learn, but he did nothing about it; he was in fact having affairs of his own. Jerry and Emma were faithful (or is it "faithful"?) to each other during their affair. Does the title mean betrayal of the idea of marriage, of honor, of self? Pinter never even hints. Not one of the three people is shown to have been directly affected by the affair. (Robert and Emma break up in 1977, but not because of Jerry.)

It's possible that, consciously or not, *Betrayal* is a spin-off from some lines in *No Man's Land*. At one point Hirst tells Spooner that, years before, he seduced

Spooner's wife: "Proposed that she betray you. Admitted you were a fine chap, but pointed out that I would be taking nothing that belonged to you, simply that portion of herself that all women keep in reserve, for a rainy day." The word "betray" sounds oddly rigid in contrast with the casual comment that follows. The title *Betrayal* has the same relation to the entire play that follows it, a play in which extramarital affairs are practically de rigueur for everyone. The backward journey shows us little more than that the desire which started an affair was bound to fade in time.

Time. That is the play's one true Pinteresque resonance. In his previous two plays, time is esthetically and thematically of the essence. *Old Times*, which I think will prove a lasting contribution to dramatic literature, blends present and past into a third time-state. *No Man's Land* is dramaturgic cubism, different views seen simultaneously. Then Pinter wrote his wonderful *Proust Screenplay* (published but not filmed), an adaptation of the world's greatest work on the dominion of time, *A la recherche du temps perdu*. It seems to follow that, drawn for his own reasons to the slight, familiar, linear story of *Betrayal*, Pinter colored it with that instrumentality of time which had become important to him, by reversing the chronicle.

This reversed structure is not a new procedure. (The most familiar American antecedent is *Merrily We Roll Along*, by George S. Kaufman and Moss Hart.) And that reversal doesn't in itself much magnify what is only an adroit little comedy. But it does permit a good production to enlist the poignancy of passing time that underlies every human action. Peter Hall has made the most of his chances. Under the lapidary shine of the comedy, he has recurrently touched the greatest of mysteries, the humorous-melancholy immanence of mortality. This time it's the director, with the designer's important aid, who has given a Pinter play its quintessential Pinter being.

The Lady from Dubuque

(Saturday Review, March 15, 1980)

Fate has not been kind to Edward Albee. I don't mean only the bitterness of early success and subsequent decline, though that's hard enough. Worse: he was born into a culture that—so he seems to think—will not let him change professions, that insists on his continuing to write plays long after he has dried up.

It's a notable fact (I've noted it previously myself) that some of the glowing names in the history of English drama wrote imperishable plays when they were young and then went on into other lives. Congreve, Wycherly, Vanbrugh, Sheridan, Barker, all spent most of their later years in other occupations. Apparently each of them felt he had written all he could or wanted to in play form, and changed. But today, pinned to public account by the intensities of hype, the dramatist evidently feels that to change professions, even if he might be good at another job, would be to admit defeat. Though exhausted —like Albee and Miller and Williams—he trudges on, to our embarrassment, if not to his.

Look at Albee's career since its peak, which I take to be *Who's Afraid of Virginia Woolf?* produced eighteen years ago. Three adaptations, *The Ballad of the Sad Cafe, Malcolm,* and *Everything in the Garden,* all deplorable. (The very fact that he began making adaptations right after the success of *Virginia Woolf* was a sign of nerve tremor.) Then *Tiny Alice, A Delicate Balance, All Over,* and *Seascape,* a long torpid decline interrupted only briefly by a pair of short, passable attempts at the Absurd, *Box* and *Quotations From Chairman Mao Tse-Tung.* What marked the full-length plays, right after the realism of *Virginia Woolf,* was Albee's use of mysticism and death. I mean use, utilization, not inquiry or dramatization. The big words and ideas became weapons to club us into awe of the works' profundity, a conclusion that was inescapable because the works themselves were so tenuous, even silly. Allegory (*All Over*) and symbolism (*Seascape*) were also called into service creakingly. Overall, Albee seemed compelled to write plays just to prove that he is still a playwright, and he grabbed at sonorous subjects and august methods to cloak his insufficiencies.

The bottom, so far, is reached in his latest play, *The Lady from Dubuque.* There *is* a lady from Dubuque in it, or she says she is, only so that the title could refer to Harold Ross's remark that the *New Yorker* wasn't edited for the little old lady from Dubuque. Which has nothing to do with the play. Which, in pertinency, lines up the new title with *Virginia Woolf.* Even more strained is Albee's attempt once again to place himself at the center of mysteries, though again he ends up in the center of gas.

Lady begins realistically with party games (once again!) in a living room, with Albee's latter-day salty language that offends because it's so self-consciously salted on. The realism is mechanically lightened with an ancient dramaturgic device: the actors know they are in play, and they address the audience from time to time. Since no reason, narrative or textural, is ever adduced for the device, we soon realize that it's Albee who is addressing us, not the actors, assuring us that he is a clever-deep master of the stage.

The scene is the metropolitan home of a young couple, and we quickly learn that the wife is dying, presumably of cancer. She feels licensed to be candidly harsh about her friends, so we get disclosures of rivalries and dislikes under the initial chumminess. None of it is enlightening or amusing or moving because the patterns of discovery are trite and the characters are stock—those that are well-enough developed to be stock. As the tired first act is obviously coming to a close, it dawns on us that we haven't yet seen Irene Worth, the star. The guests leave, the hosts go upstairs, and Worth enters through the front door, accompanied by a suave black man. She puts a finger to her lips to enjoin the audience to be quiet about her presence. Then she speaks a portentously veiled line or two, and the curtain falls.

Our hopes for the second of the two acts are, therefore, low. They rapidly sink further. After the relative realism of the first act, the play suddenly goes symbolic. Worth and her black friend turn out to be Mysterious Beings. We never learn much more about him than his first name and the fact that he has a black belt in karate. Worth says that she's the young wife's mother, but her "son-in-law" doesn't recognize her when he comes downstairs the next morning, and the playwright keeps the "daughter" so agonized that when she joins them she never even really looks at Worth, who embraces her. Much superiority is given to Worth and her friend (they constantly exchange knowing looks and chuckles at the puzzlement of the others) and much hollow gnomic dialogue. Someone says to Worth: "Who are you—really?" She replies: "Who are *you—really?*"

All through the second act, reminders of the numinous guardians in Eliot's *Cocktail Party*, and of Hellman's *Toys in the Attic*, in which Worth played a character with a black lover, are mixed with windy wisdom. "The thing we must do about loss is hold on to the object we're losing." Patently, we're meant to think of divine messengers, but there's no intrinsic reason why we should. The suffering wife is comforted by the two visitors but in no way that others could not have done. She dies, and they go.

And we're left with the conviction that still another Albee play was written chiefly because Albee felt he had to demonstrate that he's still a playwright, that again he chose immense subjects as armor to cover his dramatic skinniness. Inarguably death is haunting Albee's mind. One way or another, death has figured in all his long plays since *Virginia Woolf*—but to no artistic end. It may be critically overwhelming but it's thematically apt to raise the name of this age's prime dramatist of mortality, Samuel Beckett. Unlike Beckett, Albee can't face death without a lot of spiritualist's hokum, let alone add to our apprehension—any kind of apprehension—of the idea.

The cast and director, Alan Schneider, can scarcely be criticized because they virtually had to fabricate everything. They had neither whole characters to deal with nor tenable symbols nor real currents of dramatic motion. This is most painful with Irene Worth, an actress I call great with whatever truth is left in that worn adjective. To see her try to give weight to this trumpery role is rather like what it would be to hear Dietrich Fischer-Dieskau sing "White Christmas." For Worth's entrance and exit Pauline Trigère, who gets large billing, designed a tailored scarlet coat, a long black stole, and a wide black hat. That costume provides the only drama of the evening.

Albee is now fifty-two. What will become of this intelligent, valuable man? He has a third of his life left—more than that, I hope—plenty of time for another career if misconstrued pride doesn't deter him. I've long thought that he would make a first-class dramaturg—not "resident dramatist" as he's supposed to be for the reorganized Vivian Beaumont Theater in New York but dramaturg in the European tradition that is beginning to prosper at American institutional theaters—an in-house critic (Albee's writing and interviews show sharp critical acumen about everyone but himself), a literary manager and production adviser, and occasionally a director (he directed his own *Seascape* and has done more directing since then). Some of Albee's recent comments show a movement toward dramaturgy. I hope it grows.

It's not a matter of renunciation. Why should he flatly renounce playwriting? But the evidence of the last eighteen years doesn't justify Albee's investment of all his remaining life in his own plays. What a courageous act it would be for him to opt for dramaturgy. How helpful to a theater, to other writers he can advise, to the changing of a cultural pressure that is wasteful, to the fullest use of his own gifts. Will he insist instead on serving out the term to which, presumably, he has let our culture sentence him?

The Haggadah

(Saturday Review, May 1980)

"Why is this night different from all other nights?" It's the first question asked by the youngest son at the seder table in the home of a Jewish family on the first night of Passover. He reads it from a service called the Haggadah. And why is *The Haggadah* different from all other musical shows? Except those by Elizabeth Swados? Because, like most of her shows—*Nightclub Cantata*, *The Incredible Feeling Show*, and more—it's a work of irresistible imagination, theatrical nativity, warm feeling, and true originality. The flight of her inspiration, never higher than it was in her collaboration with Andrei Serban on *The Trojan Women*, soars beautifully this time.

Swados calls this piece "A Passover Cantata." The word haggadah comes from the Hebrew *higgidh*, "to tell," and here she retells the story of the liberation from Egypt. ("This night" is "different" to celebrate anew that liberation.) The bondage, the plagues, the crossing of the Red Sea, the wandering in the wilderness, the arrival in the Promised Land—all these Swados, who also directed, has dramatized with ethnically mixed singing actors, with dance, mime, narration, and puppets, all accompanied, all exalted, by her music.

She hasn't stuck closely to the text of the Haggadah: she interweaves bits of the Old Testament, bits of Elie Wiesel and others. This is part of a threefold process. She started with the original; she let her response to it jet-propel her into cognate materials; and she assembled it all in honor of the original. The result is a rich fantasia on one of the world's great exemplary stories, untainted by too-perfect sufferers, ending in the proclamation of a key codex of our ethos, the Ten Commandments.

The wonderful masks and puppetry are by a magician named Julie Taymor, who also designed the scenic pieces, wooden and sculptural, at both ends of the hall in which the show is performed. (The one sag in the piece, a gathering of old Jews around a table in eastern Europe, is redeemed because all the old men are Taymor puppets.) Swados insists in the program that her cast of nineteen, her musicians, and others, contributed conceptually to the event. Why shouldn't we believe her? Still it's noteworthy that her collaborators contribute well when they work with Swados.

She uses some traditional Jewish music and some that sounds like it, but the score is built on jazz and rock. This is her honesty. Verdi didn't try to go ecclesiastical when he wrote his Requiem; it sounds much of the time like great opera. Swados, who deserves this gigantic comparison at least in method, doesn't desert the contemporary idioms she loves just because she's deeply serious. For the rest of my life, when I read the lines "By the waters of Babylon, there I sat down and wept," I'll hear a rock beat behind them with strong accents on "sat" and "wept."

The central figure is the boy Moses. He moves through the whole piece right to the Promised Land—played by a winning nine-year-old named Craig Chang, who seems fluent in Hebrew. (A lot of Hebrew in the text and some Yiddish, sufficiently translated.) The musicians are led by the keyboard artist Judith Fleisher, a fixture of Swados shows.

By the time this appears, *The Haggadah* will probably have finished its run in LuEsther Hall at the Public Theater, but work of this quality can't be ignored. Anyway that was only its first run, I hope. Besides the fact that it ought to be recorded, it ought to be revived every spring.* It does more, unpretentiously, for Passover that Gian Carlo Menotti's *Amahl and the Night Visitors* does for Christmas.

BAM Begins

(Saturday Review, June 1980)

Any review of a new repertory production ought to be an interim report. In a true rep company, a new production ought to be seen only as the first performance in a series that recurs and ripens through more than a single season and as only one example of a permanent ensemble's varied work. In neither way does it resemble the usual go-for-broke, one-shot production that makes it or not, first crack out of the box.

This report is doubly interim, then, because of the above and because in this case the company itself is new. The BAM Theater Company—its name acronymically derived from its home, the Brooklyn Academy of Music—has taken a deep breath and dug in for the long haul, against the odds for rep suc-

---

*It has since been revived in several springs. Avoid, however, the "live" TV version, which barbarizes it.

cess in the metropolitan area. Clearly its aim is to be what is possible only to repertory: a "living museum," fixed yet progressive, of plays worthy of remembrance. The artistic chief is David Jones, an associate director of the Royal Shakespeare Company in England, whom I've admired since his RSC production of Gorky's *Enemies* in 1971. At BAM Jones means to work with a stable group of actors, directors, designers, and others. His first season will include five productions, and two are now in repertory.

BAM opened with Shakespeare's *The Winter's Tale*, directed by Jones. Some first bite. This late play is so steeped in artifices of romance that it calls for an audience almost as skilled in its conventions as the audience for Kabuki theater in Japan. The story can live only by mile-high suspensions of disbelief. Leontes, king of Sicilia, apparently happily married to Hermione, becomes murderously jealous of her amiability to their guest, Polixenes, king of Bohemia —so much so that Leontes puts his pregnant wife in prison and tries to have Polixenes killed. In prison Hermione gives birth to a daughter, and Leontes, suspecting the child's paternity, orders her abandoned to the elements. Hermione is reported dead. The daughter is secretly brought up in Bohemia as a shepherd's child, meets and loves Polixenes's son, is returned to her father. Her mother, who has really been hidden, is "restored" to life, and Leontes recovers reason and love.

With a considerable stretch, the symmetries and coincidences of the plot, like the notorious bear that kills off an old courtier conveniently, might be taken as part of the pastoral atmosphere, the way that comparable matters are accepted—even treasured—in the much superior *As You Like It*. But Leontes's ragings in the first two acts are so real and vile that they prepare *against* the light, fanciful matters that follow. Coleridge, contrasting Leontes with Othello, spoke of the Moor's "solemn agony" but of Leontes's "wretched fishing jealousies." Those jealousies are so fishy that they would be a shaky start for a tragedy, which indeed is what Victor Hugo called the play, shakier still for a romance.

What this comes down to in actual theater practice—never mind the literary value of Shakespeare's verse for the moment—is that, within a very few minutes, Leontes has to become scorchingly jealous without one wisp of convincing evidence, has to do it credibly if the play is not to collapse, yet has to stay within the bounds of our sympathy so that, when he recovers at the end, we can accept him back.

This opening comes off splendidly under Jones's hand. I should say, his ear. He is one of the rare Shakespeare directors today who believe that the theatrical life of the play lies in plumbing its language, not in imposing directorial concepts to make up for Shakespeare's deficiencies or to keep him up-to-date. That belief faces a particularly hard test in *The Winter's Tale*, and on that score Jones comes off well. In the ridiculously short time he has had to blend an ensemble as such, he has worked to center his company on principles of language-as-theater, and none has responded better than Brian Murray, the Leontes.

I can't say that Murray's performance makes the evening: the show falters when it gets to Bohemia because of some weak actors and because of some of William's least funny writing for clowns. But before Bohemia, Murray, principally, makes the evening possible. He carves stature out of the air with voice and presence. A veteran of the RSC, Murray has been acting (and directing) in New York for several years, sometimes well and sometimes pallidly. Touched by Jones, he is a new, big actor, who gives us a lot to hope for.

Marti Maraden has lovely dignity as the wronged Hermione, and Sheila Allen (Mrs. Jones), as the queen's loyal friend, puts fine force into that loyalty. David Gropman's raked stage, on which Jones moves his actors with sharp economy, is pleasantly simple in Sicilia, but an abstract awning from a SoHo gallery somehow slips into Bohemia. Bruce Coughlin's music misses at the moment when Hermione's "statue" comes to life—a few feeble guitar plinks where some woodwind chords would have made wonder.

With the second play, John Lee Beatty's setting, visible at once because there is no curtain, announces a change of acting styles as well as place. It's a huge, wood-paneled anteroom of a Southern governor's office, with three sets of doors and an elevator. Whenever you see plentiful doors, especially swinging doors, prepare for bustle.

Johnny on a Spot is a farce by Charles MacArthur, co-author of *The Front Page* and *Twentieth Century*. It was first done on Broadway in 1942, but not for long—four performances. I didn't know the play, but I was glad when I heard that Jones had chosen it, glad that he showed a healthy appetite for vulgarity, a recognition that some of Broadway's chromium-plated slam-bangers are among the best plays that America has produced (like it or not), and a refusal to take past failure as a final judgment.

In proof MacArthur's play is torpid. It has a good farce idea: a governor, who is running for the Senate and is a shoo-in, dies on election eve; his body is hidden for twenty-four hours so that he can seem to have died of joy at the election results and the new governor can appoint a successor. But ideas are not plays. The structure of *Johnny* uses an OK formula, but the dialogue badly needs the florid, snarling humor of MacArthur's former collaborator, Ben Hecht. The basic dramaturgic principle here is money; the play reflects an era when actors came cheap. If your script sagged, you threw in more subplots with more actors, even cameo bits. You didn't strengthen the essence, you swelled the cast. This worked for George S. Kaufman more than once, but it doesn't help here. It just makes for more limp dialogue lying there, waiting for a joke man to come in and jazz it up.

The size of the cast makes revivals of this genre nearly impossible for any but a large resident company like BAM. Roxanne Hart and Gary Bayer, who have bits in the Shakespeare play, play the leads here, the governor's aides, and they jog in and out a lot, trying to pump energy into the show. Hart in fact is more vocally vital than she was in the recent *Loose Ends*. (Incidentally, Bayer's role was done thirty-eight years ago by Keenan Wynn.) Most of the others, except Jerome Dempsey as a likable old fuddler, do what actors do in plays with hordes of reporters and pols. Edward Cornell, an American, directed, and when MacArthur lets him, which is to say after the sluggish first act, Cornell gets the right surreal mania boiling on the stage.

So, interim report. Two differently dubious first choices, one of which will surely improve in performance, with the other presumably being phased out. Generally firm, stylistically apt directions for each. A company that has some promises of excellence, much promise of competence, and a few hopeless cases. With a little purging and strengthening and, above all, with time in Jones's care, a possible *company*. Thus some reason to hope that the city which is the cultural center of the Western world may at last be getting a repertory theater of substance.

BAM's next plays: Gorky's *Barbarians* and Rachel Crothers's *He and She*. More later.

BAM Continues

(Saturday Review, July 1980)

BAM, the repertory theater at the Brooklyn Academy of Music, has now finished its first season with Gorky's *Barbarians*, Rachel Crothers's *He and She*, and *The Marriage Dance*, two one-act farces by Brecht (right, Brecht) and Feydeau. The state and fate of BAM are nationally significant as an index of the chances for repertory in the United States today. The first season just about manages to provide us with some reason for hope.

Barbarians is lesser Gorky, and he's not a major dramatist to begin with—grave and humane but with little of the power to evoke the invisible from the visible that lay to the hand of his revered Chekhov. *Barbarians* tries to epitomize Russian change around 1900 through the arrival of a railroad in a sleepy town, but it proceeds by thickness, a clutter of characters, rather than by depth or vision. It was directed by David Jones, the head of BAM, whose previous Gorky productions with the Royal Shakespeare Company I've admired. Here Jones seemed hobbled by the caterpillar script and by the quixotic idea of egalitarian repertory casting, spreading the big parts around. The important role of a lady-killing railway engineer was played by Jon Polito, who was inadequate, while Brian Murray, who would have been right for it, etched a small role well.

Rachel Crothers, whose plays about women populated Broadway from 1906 to 1937, is one of those once-celebrated dramatists who, on reexamination, deserve their present oblivion. *He and She* (1911) is about a married couple, sculptors who compete for a big commission. She wins. She then has to try to find a way to save her unsteady marriage. Crothers finds it *for* her, mechanically.

He and She may have seemed daring in 1911, though it's hard to see why. It was thirty-two years after *A Doll's House* showed a woman refusing suffocation through wifedom, and twenty-one years after James A. Herne's *Margaret Fleming* did a much inferior job to Ibsen but a much better job than Crothers on the same theme. Today *He and She* is a period piece with a little perfume and a lot of poppycock. Emily Mann directed with enthusiasm, so much of it that she allowed Laurie Kennedy, the wife, some incredibly girlish outbursts. And did Kennedy, as an elegant Edwardian, have to say "beeyoodiful" for "beautiful"? Again the leading male role was miscast: Gerry Bamman is a minor chromatic comedian, not a central actor. But Jerome Dempsey, who was so dopily pleasant in *Johnny on a Spot*, was crustily pleasant as Kennedy's conservative father.

The two farces were performed upstairs in the large Lepercq Space, with two sets of audience bleachers facing a platform stage between them. Andre Ernotte, a Belgian, directed both and succeeded once. The Brecht piece, a youthful one called *The Wedding (Die Kleinbürgerhochzeit)*, is about a marriage feast whose pretenses of amiabilty collapse along with the homemade furniture. It's more satire than farce, it's predictable early, and drags late. The dumpy, laborious tone of the production was exemplified by Christine Estabrook as the bride.

Georges Feydeau's *The Purging (On purge bébé)* is a farce masterpiece and is BAM's best-realized production of the year. Ernotte rose with the lift of this piece and was helped by two fine performances. Brian Murray, whom I'd never seen in farce, was insanely, hilariously intense as the chamber-pot manufacturer frantic for an army contract, and Roxanne Hart, who showed comic mettle in *Johnny on a Spot*, came on marvelously frowsy and blowsy as his fierce wife.

Their performances are clues to the best hopes for BAM. Murray, an established actor, got chances to range, in Shakespeare and Feydeau, that he might not have had otherwise. Hart, a young actress, showed territories in herself that might otherwise have lain undiscovered. David Jones might take these achievements—in *acting*—as his guide and goal. His company needs rigorous weeding, some strengthening, less worry about developing "stars," and more concentration on sheer quality of acting as its chief reason for existence.

Manifesto, esthetic or otherwise, won't help. Work on the pinnacle of the first half of *The Winter's Tale* (the Sicilia section) and *The Purging* will make BAM an artistic necessity instead of the semicharity case it is at the end of its first season.

Not even charity can excuse Jones's choice of plays so far. Only the Feydeau—I don't except *The Winter's Tale*—fully justified itself. More (differingly) satisfying plays are needed, but that's a need relatively easy to answer. What's harder, and absolutely essential, is a more trim company working more consistently at the pitch of the two high points noted, a company whose justification—it would eliminate the need for justification—is concerted excellence. A big order, but Jones, out of the RSC, must have known that when he started. All of us who care about the survival of the repertory idea will hope for him.

BAM Concludes

(Saturday Review, November 1981)

Time to drop the other shoe. Some readers may recall that, in June and July 1980, I commented at length on the first season of the BAM Theater Company, a repertory group sponsored by the Brooklyn Academy of Music, and I expressed some qualified hope. I saw all five classic revivals of the second BAM season and need to finish the discussion. Criticism of those five revivals is now superfluous—the company has disappeared, with not even a whimper, let alone a bang—but something must be said about the whole venture, in itself and as an instance.

Recently the Academy announced its plans for the 1981-82 season and, on the second page of the press release, said that the BAM Theater would suspend production "due to the lack of sufficient funds." Nonsense. I don't doubt that money was tight, but if the Reagan arts cuts had been increases, the BAM Theater would still have closed. It was dreadful. The one attribute that would have kept the company going—despite funding problems, despite its slightly but not impossibly inconvenient location in Brooklyn—was indispensability. I've rarely seen five productions I could more easily have done without than those of the second BAM season.

My intent is not to beat a horse that was embarrassingly moribund before it got around to falling. An important cultural issue is involved. As soon as the BAM demise was announced, out came the predictable bitter protests from the high-minded apostles of repertory. New York/America demands instant success, they told us yet again; the public and the critics want hits, want stars, want glitz, want smart new scripts, won't judge an allegedly growing ensemble by standards different from those used on Broadway. All the usual moans were moaned again about American philistinism in the face of an attempt to build a repertory theater.

To those high-minded people, it is apparently irrelevant that the plays of the second season, like most in the first season, were intolerably performed. The apostles presumably feel—and the theater is the only art where such a feeling exists—that we ought to go regularly to a company's bad productions just to keep the company alive, so that they can grow to give good performances for the next generation or perhaps the one after.

Paradoxically, some of these apostles seem not even to know what the term "repertory" means. They think that it means putting that word in the name of a stock company; then—particularly if you alternate performances within a week or a month—you've got a repertory theater. One essential of the form as it applies to dance was well stated by Anna Kisselgoff, of the *New York Times* on September 6, 1981:

> Dance being a repertory art, it is in the nature of the beast—of the form—to build up a body of works that is repeated from season to season. Continuity is the byword.

That is not the contemporary nature of the theater beast. (Occasional revivals are a quite different matter.) The BAM Theater had already shown that it was not going to be a true repertory, but that fact doesn't deter those who moan its loss.

Do I buckle too easily under modern social pressures? Am I unaware of what repertory can do for an actor's development? Well, I was myself a member of a true repertory company for ten years before World War II and perhaps have an inkling, but I still think that society ultimately makes its theater, not vice versa, and that the theater doesn't exist primarily for actors' development. And I certainly don't think that, in order to combat disliked social pressures and to help actors grow, repertory ought to be judged less stringently than straight-run shows. Quite the reverse.

I was excited by the start of the BAM Theater Company because it would be wonderful for the American theater, in spirit and as a model, if the U.S. theater capital had a good repertory group presenting the best of old and new plays; and because the man chosen to lead BAM, the gifted English director, David Jones, seemed aware of his short- and long-range responsibilities. (His own opening production of *The Winter's Tale* was the BAM high point.) But in every aspect except design and lighting, Jones made bad decisions, one after another, and I think it more healthful to state that opinion than to wail once again about American philistinism.

Among the best theater experiences of my life, most have come from repertory companies: the Old Vic of 1946, Grotowski's Polish Laboratory Theater, Andrei Serban's Greek productions with the La Mama Rep. I have my debts, therefore; and therefore I also have my hopes. But I see no sense in rushing to the defense of every company, mediocre or worse, that uses the term "repertory." We have been drugging ourselves on that term for decades in this century, often without even genuinely understanding it, even more often with a quasi-mystic belief in it as cure for all the theater's ills.

I'd like to see a performance by a good or visibly promising repertory company every week, particularly of something from the world's treasury of great drama; but I can live without more bad performances of fine plays produced just because a company's organizational heart is in the right place, or somewhere in that vicinity. Serious theater people, including serious critics, ought to re-read Ibsen on the dangers of sentimental idealism and the austere but wholesome blessings of reality.

Home

(Saturday Review, July 1980)

New York has at least 75 institutional theaters—permanent establishments that plan seasons of plays year after year, rather than *ad hoc* producers who put on shows when they find scripts. Of those theaters, the one that I go to with the highest anticipation is the Negro Ensemble Company. Whatever the quality of the particular play, which is usually a première, I know that the acting is going to be good. I've had my doubts about many of the scripts, but I've never been disappointed in the company. And amid all the hunger these days for the ensemble concept, few have noted that the NEC's actors have come as close to it as any company around. Their range is somewhat limited, but they work like people who know and grow together.

Last winter I went to their Off-Broadway base to see *Home*, written by one of their actors, Samm-Art Williams (who isn't in it) and directed by Douglas Turner Ward, co-founder and artistic director of the NEC. Now *Home* has moved to Broadway, with the same cast of three, the same direction and setting. I've seen it again, and again it's impressive in two ways: as a winning, simple, little theater poem and as a work built on the strengths of the NEC by someone who knows the company. The weaknesses of *Home*—its patches of facile rhetoric, its overly neat structure—are surmounted, even vitalized, by the performers. It's *their* piece, made for them, and they fulfill it.

Home isn't a conventional play. It's an unbroken narrative, running from the late 1950s to the present, about a young black North Carolina farmer. He comes to manhood loving the land, goes to prison because he refuses to be drafted, then drifts to the city, is whirled in its whirl, and finally makes his way back to the farm which is his again in a romantic finish that comes out of a romance begun earlier. The story is in the pastoral tradition about the virtues of nature, a young man who strays from them, returns, and finds clarity. What's important, beyond the lovely production, is the strength of the protagonist's feeling for the land, a theme that has been present in black American writing since Jean Toomer's novel *Cane* (1923) but that has been obscured by latter-day dramas of urban agony.

Charles Brown, the farmer, has warmth and strength and wit and more than enough stage presence to validate the evening. All the other characters are women, a lot of them, and they're all sketched vividly by two actresses, L. Scott Caldwell and Michele Shay. Under Ward's loving hand, *Home* has the effect of a homespun ballad.

In its thirteen-year existence the NEC and Ward have come in for a considerable barrage from radical groups, blacks and others, because their work generally centers on the life of black people rather than the changing of that life. I'm glad that there are other black groups concerned with such change; I wish they all had the talent of the NEC.

The Pirates of Penzance

(Saturday Review, October 1980)

"Sweet," said William S., "are the uses of adversity." Even when the adversity strikes William S. This summer Joseph Papp didn't schedule his usual free Shakespeare in Central Park because New York City's budget was too tight to help subsidize it. A special grant was arranged, but Papp declined it because he wanted official budget recognition or nothing. However, he was willing to accept another grant, from a different source, for an outdoor production of *The Pirates of Penzance* in the park.

Hence the sweetness of this adversity. I've seen very many of Papp's Shakespeare productions, before Central Park, also in and out of the park. A few were interesting, some had good individual performances. But, with the exception of A. J. Antoon's *Much Ado About Nothing* (1972), none showed the control or gave the sustained pleasure of this production of Gilbert and Sullivan's *The Pirates*.

Wilford Leach, the director, and William Elliott, the musical director, were the twin kingpins of the enterprise. They set the overall tone with generally intelligent and charming choices. Patently they didn't want either to imitate or to buck the Gilbert and Sullivan tradition of the D'Oyly Carte Company, the keepers of the G&S flame. Imitation, however good, is always quasi-apologetic; and to buck tradition arbitrarily would have been, as in loonier Shakespeare "concepts," to be different for the sake of difference. Leach and Elliott have produced *The Pirates* like contemporary Americans who love and respect this great Victorian work but who will not try to mimic Victorian Englishmen or their descendants.

Leach does just a bit of kidding. Sometimes, like the very opening, it's amusing—a view of a tiny cut-out ship on a cut-out ocean, followed by the ship-in-large coming around the edge of the stage carrying in the pirates for their first chorus. Sometimes it's a touch strained—the pirates' antics on a runway that circles the pit band in front of the stage itself. But most of his direction shows affectionate understanding, affectionate invention. Only the slapstick of the chorus of policemen, choreographed by Graciela Daniele, begs continually for laughs, without much luck.

Elliott, who has done scores for previous Papp productions and the vocal arrangements for *Ain't Misbehavin'*, had to face the facts of outdoor performance and the small band (eleven) allowed by the budget. (As I recall, the D'Oyly Carte people, using Sullivan's orchestrations, had an orchestra of around twenty-five.) Some of Elliott's devices bump the ear: not, for instance, the synthesizer as such but the use of it to make "wah-wah's" during the "Most Ingenious Paradox" trio. By and large he deploys his small group well, the flute and rolled cymbal especially; and he conducts with fun and fire. And in "Hail, Poetry!," a wonderfully incongruous chorus, he evokes an equally incongruous, meaty Carnegie Hall sound.

Two numbers have been inserted in the show, from *H.M.S. Pinafore* and *Ruddigore*. I object, less out of purism than economics: they aren't needed.

If the program said the performer of the heroine, Mabel, was Mary Jones, you might think her a pretty and sweet soprano, quite capable of handling Sullivan's limited coloratura requirements but quite incapable of acting. Her name, however, is Linda Ronstadt. Frederic, her lover, is played by another big pop singer, Rex Smith, and he, much more than Ronstadt, sometimes phrases his music in pop style out of Sullivan's rhythms (notably in "Oh, Is There Not One Maiden Breast"). But his voice is light and easy, and personally he's very appealing. If only he and some others in the cast—Tony Azito, especially, the police sergeant—could understand why classical singers study diction.

That brings us to the production's own "ingenious paradox." George Rose, as Major-General Stanley, and Patricia Routledge, as Ruth, the "piratical maid-of-all-work," are clear as tinkling crystals with their British English and are flawless in their native musical-show tradition. But just because of those things, they are out of key with the others. The ideal combination here is in sparkling Kevin Kline, the Pirate King, who has all the fluency and clarity and comedy one could want and who belongs in this production. Rose and Routledge stick out—not like sore thumbs but like guest stars. (Nationalism is not the point in this instance; production unity is.)

But there's a bigger paradox. The true new stars of the occasion are the world-famous authors, making—in a way—their debut. It's been quite a while since the last full professional Gilbert and Sullivan production in New York. Some in the bowled-over audience had apparently never seen such a production. Well, if it was a shock to them to discover how excellent W. S. Gilbert and Arthur Sullivan are, it was a shock to me to realize how long this audience has been deprived. Years before I saw the D'Oyly Carte troupe, I was feasting on the annual G&S repertory of the domestic Aborn Opera Company, some members of which have never been surpassed. And in 1960 I saw Tyrone Guthrie's production of *H.M.S. Pinafore*, done with freshness and delight. No more protracted waits for G&S, please.

The joy of Gilbert and Sullivan is in the "and." Together, they make one splendid genius. Apart, Gilbert was probably the better of the two; his comedy *Engaged* is a neglected gem, and there is no finer comic verse in English than the *Bab Ballads*. What work of Sullivan's survives other than his Gilbert collaborations? (Oh, all right . . . "Onward, Christian Soldiers" and "The Lost Chord.") But collaborating, though their personal relations were troubled, they blended and bloomed. It wasn't so much that each grew through collaboration as that each became half of a miraculously larger being. Yes, Gilbert's social satire is more nudging than trenchant; yes, Sullivan's thematic developments and orchestration are sometimes commonplace. In union, there was transmutation. When the two combine—Gilbert's pearly patter and lyric love verses, Sullivan's exquisite Donizetti parody that frequently goes past parody to excel its model—the whole releases energy that sweeps us toward an idea of perfection. What more can art do?

This tale of a youth accidentally indentured as a baby to pirates; a youth who leaves the pirate band when he's twenty-one and, minutes later, falls in love with a general's daughter; a youth who is about to lead the police against his former mates when the Pirate King proves that the youth is still indentured because the deed runs to his twenty-first birthday, not his twenty-first year, and as the youth was born on a February 29th, he has a lot more birthdays to go—my sentence is almost as serpentine as the recitative in which the Pirate King explains the paradox—this tale is a mockery of all subjects save one. The plot mocks plots, logical cause and effect, evasion and self-esteem; the music flies with it and through it. But neither music nor words mock love. As in much nineteenth-century opera, no matter how ridiculously one arrives at a love scene, it is always taken to heart. Readily risking mawkishness, *The Pirates*, like other G&S works, says that everything human beings do is a trifle silly, except love. Just as the collaboration of the two men raised their individual talents to a third plane, so their joint genius distills both vanity and romance to a poetic quintessence.

At the end of this production the whole cast, principals and choruses, waltzed with one another. I wanted to waltz with them. Which leads to a last paradox. Joseph Papp's Shakespeare has frequently had a taint of culture-for-the-masses, more populist than good. This *Pirates* is populist *and* good. New York's budget crisis, in this case, turned out to be a proverbial ill wind: it blew away, for a season at least, some shaky Shakespeare and gave us a lesser masterwork, better done.

42nd Street

(Saturday Review, December 1980)

"Hear the beat / Of dancing feet," says the title song in *42nd Street*, and never did a lyric fix a show's essence more neatly. What it's about is tap dancing, dozens of feet in unison, choreographed by the late Gower Champion on 1930s models. How rare a sound in these post Agnes De Mille days, how reassuring. For a couple of hours that brisk tapping protects us from the uncertainties of today. (It didn't do much for the people actually in the 1930s, but nostalgia is a drug, not history.)

The songs, too, by Harry Warren and Al Dubin—mostly taken, like the story, from the 1933 Warner Bros. musical—feel snug and comfy: that title number, "We're in the Money," "Shuffle Off to Buffalo," and my favorite, "You're Getting to Be a Habit With Me." Phillip J. Lang has orchestrated them refreshingly, with some woodwinds rarely heard in a Broadway pit.

And that's about it. But since that's the bulk of the show, that's enough. The book, which is the grandma of all backstage musicals, never makes up its mind whether it's straight or parody. The physical production, as is the general Broadway case these days, looks cheap, although I'm sure it cost a modest mint. The musical numbers are all built alike: solo start, dancers and singers joining for seeming conclusion, pull-back and new start, then wham finish with arms high above heads. If they did the second act first or shuffled numbers within acts, it wouldn't greatly matter. The show is just chunks of agreeable stuff that makes us feel things were better back then if only because we were younger or unborn.

The leading performers are, again as usual in musicals these days, a bit below what's needed because there isn't a populous commercial theater to provide talent. Tammy Grimes is passable, though far from overwhelming, as a big musical star. Jerry Orbach, who plays the director, is like the second-best actor in your local theater group. And the night I saw 42nd Street there was an added plot twist. The show is all about an unknown who goes on in the leading role in an emergency and becomes a star. When I saw it, an unknown, Karen Prunczik, went on for Wanda Richert, the now well-known who usually plays the unknown. Near the finale Orbach says to her: "You're going out there a youngster and you're coming back a star." Prunczik went out there a youngster and came back a youngster, but she was pleasant all the way.

The nostalgia market is apparently insatiable. At the moment Broadway has Ain't Misbehavin', Brigadoon, A Day in Hollywood/A Night in the Ukraine, Morning's at Seven, Sugar Babies, and Tintypes, all of them dealing one way or another with that market. Few of them connect more directly than those dozens of tappers in 42nd Street. During one number I found myself reaching in my pocket to make sure I had a nickel for the subway ride home. Pavlov, thou shouldst be living at this hour.

The Suicide

(Saturday Review, December 1980)

In the last few years we've seen the arrival of some directors from Eastern Europe: Liviu Ciulei, Andrei Belgrader, and now Jonas Jurašas. Each of these men is obviously cultivated, experienced, theatrically energetic. Each of their productions that I've seen—a total of six—was disastrous.

No one production of the six can exemplify all, but The Suicide, directed by Jurašas, comes close. Before the lights go up (no front curtain) we see that the scene design flows out into the auditorium along the walls. In fact these extensions are little used later; principally their purpose is to tell us beforehand that this director is no proscenium-bound hack. When the play begins, another play also begins at once: a counterpoint of action, devised by the director, that embroiders the action of the text.

The Suicide is a comedy about Senya, a simple and sore-beset Soviet citizen in the early 1920s, and the first thing we see is Senya in bed with his wife, uneasy while she sleeps. Immediately numerous arms appear behind the bed, announcing the arrival of a commenting chorus invented by Jurašas that will appear and disappear throughout. This is only one thread in his embroidery, but it's enough to manifest his rousing vote of no-confidence in his script. Evidently he feels he has to explicate, moment by moment, scene by scene: more accurately, he *wants* to feel he must do it, because it gives him so many chances for self-display.

What we get thenceforth, as in Ciulei's production of The Inspector General, is, for the most part, a series of derivations from the work of Vsevolod Meyerhold, the giant of the Soviet theater. Descriptions and photographs of Meyerhold productions tell of the same use of many doors, of sharply different levels, of acrobatics (Jurašas uses a fireman's pole), of a long banquet table stretched across the front of the stage, of sculptured masses of people, and more. Derivation in itself doesn't much matter: Andrei Serban, the best of the current East Europeans, has been charged with it. A big difference with Serban is that, for his Greek productions, he spent several years molding an ensemble, thus following the Meyerhold spirit as well as the letter. For The Suicide, a jobbed-in bunch of actors, mediocre and worse, with different styles and with no style, have been signed up and thrown into imitative poses.

In the theaters of the Soviet Union where Jurašas made his reputation, where possibly he had real ensembles to work with, where certainly he was more subtle in the language, his work may have been whole and enriching. Here, in The Suicide, where those things are not true, his direction seems muscularly intrusive, extrinsic, impasted on the play in self-promotion. What's worse, it's so singularly unoriginal that Jurašas doesn't even create a good substitute play, as some "conceptual" directors have done with their impositions on texts. All he does is make us hungry for clarity, for the *play*.

I've left the play itself until last because, in a sense, that's what Jurašas does. And that brings me to another discomfort. The work of Eastern European writers is often overpraised because, often, their moral and physical courage is beyond praise. (Jurašas too has had troubles in the Soviet Union.) Nikolai Erdman, the author of The Suicide, died in 1970 at the age of sixty-eight but because of this play, written in the late 1920s, he was effectively throttled as a writer for most of his life. How enjoyably bitter it would be now to talk about the belated birth of a satirical masterpiece. But The Suicide is like much of the work that comes from the East: with a veracity that is, in its own right, heroic, it shows us a grave subject: but as art it isn't nearly up to that subject.

Senya is harassed by the circumstances of Soviet life into announcing his forthcoming suicide. His family can't dissuade him, and various persons come forward, not to stop him but to ask him to "dedicate" his suicide to their interests: the intelligentsia, the romantics, and others. In the end, as we foresee (it *is* a comedy), he doesn't kill himself, though he's nearly buried when dead drunk. In this version, the play ends with him back in his bed with his wife. The whole play has, apparently, been a dream.

It's a pattern, not a play: a cautionary tale with puppet characters. Once the premise is given, we just wait—through a lot of set-piece scenes—for the end. Not once are we engaged, either in pathos or doubt or insight, though there's an occasional funny line. We just endure the tracing of the obvious design, while Jurašas engorges every possible point with his nonvirtuosic display of nonvirtuosic actors.

One exception—the star, Derek Jacobi, the English actor best-known here as the emperor Claudius in the PBS series, whom I've seen play Shakespeare robustly in Britain. Jacobi has some breadth of style and a good voice, though it tends to what the English call "plummy": it's rather counsciously inflected and enjoyed. In the role of this nobody, he is sorely miscast; he has to work hard to be affectingly ordinary. The worst of his performance is that we can see him strive against the miscasting; the best is that the very qualities that make him wrong for the part give his long second-act monologue the warmest life of the evening.

The American Clock

(Saturday Review, January 1981)

Like every child of the Depression, Arthur Miller can't forget it, but all he has done in his new play is remember it. *The American Clock* ("inspired by Studs Terkel's *Hard Times*") is not much more than a superficial ramble through the lives of a New York Jewish family in the Twenties and Thirties. Presumably it's somewhat autobiographical, with a narrator-reminiscer who makes us think of Miller himself. This narrator, called Lee, very soon pulls up his trousers to look like knickers and takes us back to his adolescence and flush times, with Mom and Dad in evening clothes worshipping the stock market; and after this depressingly platitudinous start, the play never improves.

The family's plight when the market collapses, the move to cheaper Brooklyn, the adjustments to grim changes, the strategies for survival, Lee's gropings toward jobs and education—these parade past in shallow, unexplored scenes. The only consistent effect is the instant pathos that attaches to memory, especially when the rememberer is standing before us, stepping into and out of the past. The play is performed before what looks like a satellite weather map of the U.S., with furniture and lighting changes for the many scenes, and Vivian Matalon has staged it with complete adherence to the sentimentalities of its stock splitting of time-planes. Any stock form can of course be used well—Miller used split time-planes well in *Death of a Salesman*;

but here he merely leans on the form slothfully, meandering through material that must by now be substantively familiar even to those who didn't live through that era.

Occasionally there's a sharp line. ("Any girl with an apartment of her own was beautiful.") Mostly it's the easy heart-tug of this easy form, sometimes varied with equally easy hindsight irony. ("This Hitler can't last six months.") After a ramble down Memory Lane that could have been either shorter or longer because it has no intrinsic shape, the play ends with Lee talking to us about his mother, who is seated upstage at her piano, telling us that she is just like this country: full of contradictory views on a number of subjects. But this would have been just as true of her in Scene One. Why did we need to travel the length of the play to reach that end? And what did the Depression have to do with it? It would have been just as true if Wall Street had never crashed.

As the mother, Joan Copeland (Miller's sister) has a role carefully carpentered with wry wisdom and infallibility, full of charm and poignancies at the piano. No competent actor could muff the part, and Copeland is competent. John Randolph, the father, blusters along with his usual sincere face-making, and William Atherton as Lee is gulpingly passable, but why, for this youth, did they choose an archetypal WASP? The most imaginative, incisive acting of the evening is done by Edward Seamon in three small roles: a smart speakeasy owner, an irritating welfare applicant, a down-and-out farmer from Iowa.

In much of Miller's past work, one could at least discern what he was reaching for and fumbling. Here he seems only to be exploiting his position as a "great" playwright and the fact that he lived through the Depression. It's sad, especially because of the press campaign before this première to present him as a master maligned by critics, a master who would be vindicated by this new work. Despite the campaign and despite the popularity of Miller all over the world (which is also true of some American playwrights who are even worse), *The American Clock* leaves Miller essentially where he was—a "great" American playwright whose work is mostly mediocre.

A Lesson from Aloes

(Saturday Review, January 1981)

Athol Fugard, a white South African, has written many plays about black-and-white South Africa, preeminently *Boesman and Lena*, which is not only his best work so far but which after ten years' acquaintance, seems to me an addition to the world treasury of drama. His new play, *A Lesson from Aloes*, is on the same general subject—South African race tensions and their consequences—but, though it's no less genuine a work, it's feeble.

Boesman and Lena has three characters, a "colored" man and wife and a black man, and deals with them specifically but so powerfully it grows to include the lives and secrets of everyone in the audience. *Aloes* also has three characters, a white man and wife and a black man, but it not only doesn't transcend its specifics—something that one cannot demand of a play, even a good one—it doesn't deal adequately with them.

The aloe is a spiny-leaved flowering plant indigenous to southern Africa, and Piet Bezuidenhout, an Afrikaner, collects the many species. He lives with his English wife, Gladys, outside Port Elizabeth, and from the beginning it's clear—stagily clear, alas—that something is wrong with her and between them. The entire first half of the play, moving between the backyard and the bedroom of their house, details matters of the past, data and events already known to husband and wife. Yet they keep telling each other these things so that we can learn them, and they do it in that flakily disguised way which shows that the author is embarrassedly trying to pass off this exposition as emotional and character development. At the end of the act, we know that Piet has somehow been involved in political activity, that the police raided their home and confiscated Gladys's diaries, that the shock of this raid and later interrogation unbalanced her, that she has spent some time in a mental hospital, and that Piet's considerateness is almost getting on her nerves. One other fact: Steve, a black friend, is coming to supper with his family this night to say goodbye. Steve and his family are emigrating to England. He has just served a prison term for breaking a banning order—a limitation on his movements because of his politics—and he wants to live free of harassment.

After a first act that does nothing but tell us what has already happened, we look forward to some present action. It arrives, belated and insufficient. Steve comes alone (we learn later that his child is not sick, as he had said; his wife just didn't want to come), and after some laborious reunion stuff between him and Piet—the past revisited again—the play slogs down to an accusation that it was Piet who informed the police about Steve's breach of the banning order. Piet is willing to let Steve believe it in order to "help" his friend to emigrate, but the charge evaporates. This is the sole moment of present-tense drama. Steve goes, and the white pair resume their suspended-animation marriage—until Gladys returns to the mental hospital.

Patently, Fugard wanted to create a private agony that symbolized a nation's agony, but the grinding mechanics, the saturation in neurosis, and the relatively petty climax after the long preparation defeat him. If small-scale symbolism doesn't generate implication, it grows even smaller. The elaborate politesse of British-style marital discourse, Gladys's flitterings about her new diary (which turns out to be portentously blank), the chat about supper and aloes and good times gone, all these sink the play under their light weight. The authenticity of Fugard, a man valiant and scarred in his struggles within his country, is beyond question, but this play is misconceived and unfulfilled. We see a side effect of a national tragedy, rather than an epitome of it.

Maria Tucci makes Gladys's neurosis credible but, because of the writing, the more credible it is, the more remote and clinical. Harris Yulin, as Piet, doesn't seem much like a bus driver only recently awakened politically, but his quietness holds the stage until James Earl Jones enters in Act Two and takes possession. Jones, who was the first American Boesman, gives a performance full of colors and meanings insinuated almost physically, conveying his difference from his friends both in inflection and movement. By his physical being and behavior, he emphasizes the gap that even affection cannot quite close. Fugard himself directed and only underscores the play's flaws and didacticism, down to the very last moment when Yulin, left alone, sits on a bench and touches an aloe—from which he and we are supposed to have learned "a lesson." (Hardiness to survive and thus ultimately to flower, I guess.) That last moment closes the heavy circle that begins with the unfortunate title.

Amadeus

(Saturday Review, February 1981)

Here is Lionel Trilling on Rameau's nephew in the Diderot novel of that name: "His command of the musical repertory is prodigious. . . . But despite his native abilities and the cruel self-discipline to which he has subjected himself, he must endure the peculiar bitterness of modern man, the knowledge that he is not a genius." That passage could be the epigraph for Peter Shaffer's *Amadeus*. It crystallizes the theme, and it fits the play's historical moment, the era when modern self-consciousness began to form. Diderot wrote in 1762; most of *Amadeus* takes place later in that century.

Shaffer is dealing with the "peculiar bitterness" in Antonio Salieri, the once-famous Italian-born Viennese composer—specifically, with Salieri's jealousy of the genius in Wolfgang Amadeus Mozart. That jealousy is commemorated in the myth that Salieri poisoned Mozart, which , paradoxically, almost no one believed except Salieri himself when he grew old and dotty; apparently it was his psyche's guilty revenge for his jealousy, the guilt abetted by Mozart's early death at thirty-five. The play investigates the theme of justice, whether it exists and can be hoped for, not in law but in the possession of artistic gifts, in the tensions between talent and genius.

This is a potentially fertile idea, but good ideas don't necesarily result in good plays—especially, as *Equus* showed, in Shaffer's hands. Once again Shaffer has had the acumen to discern a large-scale possibility, and once again he has reduced it with gimmicks. *Amadeus* begins in 1823 with the aged Salieri believing the murder-myth of thirty-two years before. All Vienna is now whispering about it, he thinks, and so do a couple of gossip-gathering aides whom he employs. They are given a lot of brisk, short dialogue at the beginning, to convey information to us, which they do, and to create a *School for*

Scandal glitter, which they don't. Then Salieri steps forward to address us, not in the torment we might have expected from the "overture" but rather wryly, à la Tom Stoppard. He wants us, the future, to be his "confessors." He invokes us to appear—the house lights come on for a moment after he summons us with music—so that, on what he says is the last night of his life, he can tell us his story.

The evening is about ten minutes along by now, and our hope for a serious play—drama or comedy—is already waning. The tricky devices, the preening witticisms, the uncertainty of tone suggest that after Shaffer got his good idea, he was frightened, and began to grasp at ways to reduce it so it might be manageable in his hands

Of course we soon flash back, to 1781 when Mozart arrives at the court of Emperor Joseph II and unwittingly threatens Salieri, the court composer, simply by being a genius while Salieri is not. Intrinsically there is only one dramatic action now: Salieri's blockage of Mozart's advancement, which he contrives even though Constanze, Mozart's wife, consents to sleep with him for his help. But we all know that Mozart did not advance, and Shaffer knows we know it, so he had to develop other elements. He chose two, one factual and one imagined.

The first is the "revelation" of Mozart's true character, and it's of limited use. Any reader of a Mozart biography knows that this miraculous genius had a tough time getting commissions while lesser men prospered, and must have concluded that he was difficult. Emily Anderson's edition of Mozart's letters (1938) shows that he wasn't merely difficult, he was bumptious and foul-mouthed; other sources reveal that he didn't confine those qualities to his letters. The real Mozart, contrasted with the schoolbook figurine, can't shock anyone with some knowledge of the man, and it can't long shock others.

Still, the theatrical problem is that the scabrous Mozart, like Iago against Othello, is more attractive than Salieri; yet the play is supposed to be about the better-behaved man. Whenever Mozart leaves the stage and Salieri, who is on throughout, steps forward, we think: "Oh, yes. Nice old humdrum him." It's even worse than that because Salieri is a moral accountant: he seems to think that enough brownie points for good behavior ought to earn a man genius. When the harsh facts dawn on him—rather late in life—he assails the supposed fount of justice, God. (Mozart's middle name, the play's title, means "God-lover," possibly "beloved of God.") This is Shaffer's second dramatic element, meant to strengthen Salieri vis-à-vis the fascinating Mozart, and in itself it's an ancient major theme, the calling of divinity to account. But it crumples Shaffer. At the end of the play's first half, Salieri has a long speech berating God, which ends: "To my last breath I shall *block* you on earth, as far as I am able." If the rhetoric is empty, at least it booms; but then Salieri addresses *us* dryly: "What use, after all, is Man, if not to teach God his lessons?" The facile Stoppard-type crack blows away whatever weight Shaffer has managed to scrape up. Once again the bantam author is giggling around his Promethean subject.

The second half of the play is even weaker than the first. There's no mileage left in the shock of Mozart's character as such, and Salieri's struggle with God is flimsy, fabricated, facetious. It all just winds on and down through Mozart's death and Salieri's survival for a couple of years after he cuts his throat at dawn following his "last night" with us.

But there are some rewards. When Shaffer isn't sweating to be cool, he can write a good line. Salieri remembers the God in his small-town church to whom he promised fealty as a youth: "an old candle-smoked God in a mulberry robe, staring at the world with dealer's eyes."

And the production sparkles. John Bury designed it, which means, as with Pinter's *Betrayal*, that he did everything—scenery, costumes, lighting. He distills the rococo for us with an ingeniously flexible setting and gorgeous *usable* costumes, and his lighting runs a helpful counterpoint throughout. Again as with *Betrayal*, Peter Hall directed, much as in the London production, which I saw: dexterously, rhythmically, with a discreet sense of character. (In one way it's too much like London. Why does Hall insist that Salieri be sitting on stage while the audience files in? At the Olivier, which has no proscenium, this was necessary. At the Broadhurst, it's just a pointless gag, tired too. The show would be better off if it began with the rise of the curtain.)

Ian McKellen, Salieri in New York, is a rising British classical actor, which is easy to understand. He has depth and strength. Oddly, he has more gnarled strength as the young Salieri than as the old one, who is too much like a pantomime gaffer. McKellen mispronounces Italian, although he's playing an Italian-born man, and he overuses that too-precise enunciation that sometimes passes for comic acting with the English; but he has almost enough command and presence to compensate for Mozart's greater attraction.

Tim Curry, best-known here for *The Rocky Horror Picture Show*, is Mozart and is fine. His abrasive aspects are parts of a man, not tags appended to him, a man impatient with the short-comings of the people around him and with the world's inability to give him everything he wants right away. (The spoiled child prodigy, seen later.) Curry is especially moving as the sick and dying Mozart; he gives us the poignant fright of punctured arrogance. As his wife, Jane Seymour has the loveliness to fill out a two-dimensional role.

I kept thinking of the London production for two connected reasons. One, the play here has been considerably cut and altered—streamlined. For instance, Salieri's valet, Greybig, a considerable part in London played by a prominent actor of the National Theater, is reduced here to a mute without a name. Two, in London, *Amadeus* was one item in the National's repertory, with no crisis air about it. In New York, as a solo million-dollar production, it seems to strain to be this year's one serious Broadway hit.

Probably it succeeds. But it carries a (hidden?) sting in its limp tail. At the very end the ancient Salieri totters forward to address us: "Mediocrities everywhere—now and to come—I absolve you all! Amen!" Sounds grand, until one thinks about it. What power of absolution does he have, and what is he absolving them of? His legacy of jealousy, of a sense of God's injustice? Of a wish to be more than they are? The best guess may be that, at the last, Salieri is addressing his author.

Piaf

(Saturday Review, April 1981)

One of the great romances in Western history is the theater's love affair with itself. Since Aristophanes, the theater has been addicted to plays about how important, wonderful, and glamorous it is; and as the centuries have twirled along to our day, that reflexive love has embraced entertainers as well as actors. The latest "affair" is *Piaf*, a play by Pam Gems about the French singer who was in fact a genius of pop. *Piaf* is also one more of another curious breed, the show that asks a performer to perform like a famous star: Bessie Smith, Fats Waller, and the Marx Brothers are others who have lately had their impersonators on Broadway.

Pam Gems is English and has had one previous play produced here, Off-Broadway at the Manhattan Theater Club, *Dusa, Fish, Stas, and Vi*, which I thought fairly static. It meant to show the struggle for liberation of four young London women today, and three of them stayed the same throughout. *Piaf* is certainly not static; and show-biz adulation though it is, it too seems designed to show a woman's struggles in a world dominated by men. Its first trouble is that, as an example of a woman's struggle against male domination, Edith Piaf is a poor choice. She had gifts that would have made her outstanding in an Amazon society, and she was so active sexually that it's hard to think of her as being exploited sexually by males. True, early in life she was reputed to be a prostitute, a male-oriented trade, but there's no indication that she was much less promiscuous when she wasn't for hire.

The play's muzziness continues. *Piaf* was first done in London—by now almost a routine comment for serious plays on Broadway—the star is English, and the dialogue, which is gamy, is in Cockney to suggest the street argot of Paris. At first this seems even more apt for America because it makes the play sound foreign at the same time that it's comprehensible; but then Piaf sings most of her many songs in French, which leaves us with madly mixed conventions.

The script itself is a surfboard ride over a complex life: from the streets of a working-class quarter to cafés, then stardom and adulation and international tours and international friends, through husbands (several) and lovers (who's counting?), to a finish in drugs and disease at the age of forty-eight in 1963. (I read her biography some years ago and was especially struck by the fact that, even toward the end, racked and maimed, she drew young men both in sex and devotion.) Gems's play skims the story so synoptically that all the characters other than Piaf—and one lifelong pal, a woman who whored with her—are like props for the star. The play runs over two hours, but it has the texture of a skit.

Now even this effect, like the use of Cockney, might have turned out well: a play with the shape and speed of a cabaret skit about the life of a cabaret performer. This reinforcement of content by form seems intentional: the stage holds a large raked platform; behind it sit the three musicians who accompany and set moods; bits of furniture are placed and removed, with most of the "scene design" done by lighting; around the platform sit the actors who, other than Piaf and pal, all play many parts. Further to the cabaret mode, the director Howard Davies has paced the piece with egregious pizzazz and often has the actors play front. I don't merely mean they face front: they "take" front—they show their reactions, like vaudevillians, to an audience they know is watching. And the life-as-show feeling is heightened by the free-form neon light over the playing area that changes from red to blue at peak moments.

But this idea—mimesis of the story by the form of the play—is done so breathlessly fast that it never breathes: it's a whiz-past of mannequins. And two other troubles weaken it further. First, that star-imitation syndrome. Jane Lapotaire, the English actress who did the part in London and does it again here, knows that she's no Piaf and has said so, but disclaimers are no help. The play is built around a lot of Piaf's performing, and that performing has to be what everyone on stage says it is or the whole thing's down the drain. If Lapotaire were anything like as good a singer as Piaf, she wouldn't be playing Piaf, she would be Lapotaire. It's not a criticism of Lapotaire to say that she's not Piaf: but it was a mistake to center so much of the show on her singing. As for her acting, that made me a bit uneasy, too. Lapotaire, a scrawny little woman physically right for Piaf, commits herself to the role in a way that suggests immersion rather than acting, more an induced self-deception than imaginative recreation. It's the way Will Geer used to do Robert Frost or the way Liza Minnelli keeps trying to do her mother. There is no edge, no view of the part, which good actors give us at their most convincing. It's almost like watching a nut case instead of an actor. If Lapotaire had been playing a fictitious or nonfamous performer, there might have been more acting and less intoxication.

And then there's that theater self-love. A lot of the play, as it goes on, is about going on: how much every performance takes out of a real performer, how little the audience knows or cares. Why the hell should we care? It's a bit like the president of the United States complaining about the burdens of office after he has fought to get in. But in a quite different way, the audience does care. The Star's Ordeal, in itself sentimental self-aggrandizement, has become the great fake agon of our time, a way for the viewer to go through catharsis on the cheap, without any real self-roiling, with plentiful caressing of frustrations.

(For two hours, you too, John or Mary Bloggs, can know what it feels like to be a star.)

But there's something deeper, more important, in *Piaf* that holds an audience. I'm not predicting its success, though it was one in London, only commenting on what I saw and felt when I was there. To explain, I go back a step.

Despite the Broadway box-office boom, there's much talk these days about the end of the theater, not the usual facile gloom (of which the theater has always been secretly proud because the gloom was always proved false), but the esthetic finish lying ahead of it because of technology. A talented actor told me lately of advice from one of the most active theater figures in New York: get prominent as fast as you can because in ten years it will all be cable television and they'll want names. One of our few intelligent theater critics, Gordon Rogoff, has commented comparably on the theater's future after seeing preparations for a TV-tape of an opera—preparations far beyond any theater's means.

Saturnine though I am, I doubt the completeness of these predictions, and the *Piaf* production is one reason why. Its audience was getting something it liked and can't get elsewhere. I don't mean live actors: I've doubted the indispe ibility of "liveness" ever since I began to understand a bit about film. I mean intrinsic and inseparable theatrical form.

If you go to see *Lunch Hour*, the Jean Kerr bore now on Broadway, you sit in front of something—an awkwardly designed Long Island beach house with script and performance to match—that you'll be able to see again in a few years at your local movie house and a few years after that on your TV screen at home. The other media will require only a little adaptation, nothing fundamental: *Lunch Hour*, more or less as it is, can be done on stage or screen or TV. Not *Piaf*. It could exist only in a theater: with its bare platform, its continually flexed and unrealistic lighting, its actors waiting in view, changing clothes for different characters in view, its musicians waiting and playing in view. Now any experienced playgoer will recognize that all of this is highly unoriginal but will also see that it couldn't happen anywhere but in a theater. (The few exceptions—some of Fellini's films, for instance—*are* exceptions.)

The audience at *Piaf* likes the show's reliance on its imaginative collaboration. The challenges to imagination here are hardly deep or new: they are aimed at the center of a soft viewer's soft daring. But they couldn't be issued anywhere but in a theater; and they give the audience, unconsciously, some feeling of stretch, of adventure, of accomplishment. *Piaf* itself is only a failed tease of a play about a bawdy humane genius, but at least the production does move toward one aspect of the theater's uniqueness, the selfhood—under the smarmy self-love—that is possibly the theater's best life insurance.

Lolita

(Saturday Review, May 1981)

When Donald Sutherland strode on stage as Humbert Humbert in Lolita, he radiated at once the odd combination of modesty and assurance, ease and skill, charm and reticence that has made his screen presence a pleasure. We felt immediately that this man was completely in command and meant to do all he could not to flaunt it. As he addressed us—and about fifty percent of his role was direct address to us—he implied a promise that he would make this eccentric story absorbing, would tickle its devilish comedy, and would also touch its lyric stature—in short, that Vladimir Nabokov's masterly novel would be honored.

That opening moment—say ten seconds—was the high point of the evening. The warm surge of those ten seconds still lives in my memory: the rest is drowned by Edward Albee's deplorable dramatization, which itself is now deservedly sunk. But since it was written by another of America's spurious "great" dramatists—how rich we are in them—a bit of post mortem is in order. Especially since Albee this time mixed debacle with desecration.

He began by confessing failure. The backdrop and wings of William Ritman's setting, within which various scenic pieces moved clumsily during the evening, were covered with graffiti—fragments of Nabokov's language. That décor seemed Albee's admission that Nabokov's genius is in his prose, that the prose is in the novel as such, and that the play would have to be lesser. It was, inevitably, shorter than the book; it was also so much shallower that it became a different, corrupted work. A complex, gorgeously orchestrated black comedy, a poem of an obsession faced poetically, a slyly dramatized clash of the defects in European and American moralities, became a drooling account of a clinical perversion and its mucky end.

The film of Lolita (1962), directed by Stanley Kubrick from a screenplay attributed to Nabokov—who subsequently published the screenplay precisely as he had written it—had severe faults but some merits, too. Nabokov himself called the film "first-rate" while stipulating that Kubrick's view of the novel was not his own. Kubrick was at least able to transmute into cinema language some of the neon-lighted fabric of America, some of the dizzying prism of characters, some of the ludicrous agonies of the motel odyssey that enwrap this love story of a thirty-eight-year-old foreigner and his twelve-year-old "nymphet" stepdaughter. Transmutations like Kubrick's are impossible in the theater. Then what was Albee left with, if he could not do with Nabokov's prose at least something of what the film could do? He could extract the sex stuff. He could make the script an act of daring, giving the cast things to say and do that would have been absolutely taboo twenty years ago. Albee's Lolita was nothing more than another exploitaton of the sexual license that he and some coeval playwrights apparently wish they could have had when they started.

Albee not only stripped, he added. In the published screenplay, Nabokov used the fictitious editor-psychiatrist of the foreword as narrator. Albee used the author himself, coyly dubbed A Certain Gentleman, used him throughout as companion to Humbert Humbert, though visible and audible to no one else; and Albee gave this Gentleman dialogue of excruciatingly banal pseudo elegance. In this role Ian Richardson, heroically managing to stay awake, uttered such witticisms as "No doubt" and "I daresay" in a sophomoric caricature of suavity.

Shirley Stoler played Lolita's mother whom Humbert marries en route to the daughter. Stoler is so gross that Humbert's marital duties, demanded constantly by her, boggled more than the imagination. Blanche Baker had the snap role of Lolita: any young actress who could look the part could do it. Clive Revill, a failed protean actor, continued to fail in the senselessly curtailed character of Clare Quilty, the hunter and hunted of Humbert. Frank Dunlop's direction acutely hit every chance for vulgarity-posing-as-wit.

Nabokov said he published his screenplay as a "vivacious variant" of his novel. Albee's dramatization was a vitiated variant. But I'm grateful for those ten Sutherland seconds.

Rockaby

(Saturday Review, June 1981)

The most recent play by the world's greatest living dramatist runs fifteen minutes. Samuel Beckett wrote Rockaby in response to a request from Dan Labeille who teaches theater, film, and TV at Cayuga County Community College of the State University of New York. In the fall of 1979 Labeille wrote to Beckett, announcing that SUNY was planning a celebration of the Nobel laureate's seventy-fifth birthday in 1981, and he invited Beckett to contribute. In June 1980 Labeille received the manuscript of Rockaby. A pretty good morning's mail, one might say.

Funding was found both for a professional production and a TV-taping of the production. The play is for only one performer, a woman, and the English actress Billie Whitelaw was engaged. Whitelaw had done the London première of Beckett's Not I, and he had written Footfalls for her. The American Alan Schneider, a Beckett familiar, directed the world première of Rockaby at SUNY in Buffalo in April 1981, where it was taped. The production was then given three performances at La Mama in Manhattan and was taken to Paris. (Because of the brevity of Rockaby, Whitelaw preceded each performance with a reading of Beckett's odd love story, "Enough.")

Rockaby is one more of Beckett's border crossings. Conceive of the crossing from life to death as a border between countries: conceive, too, that it is possible to see across before going, to float above the border a bit, and to itemize one's final hope and hopelessness, memories and bitterness and joy and relief, as if in a customs declaration done in the form of a laconic poem. Under this conception would come such recent short Beckett plays as *That Time, Footfalls, Not I* (one woman speaker), *A Piece of Monologue* (one man), and *Rockaby* (one woman). Further, as has been his concern since *Krapp's Last Tape*, Beckett is trying to "disembody" the voice, to make the voice a self that can speak to the self that contains it, the self that has been perhaps repressing it. In *Krapp's Last Tape* an old man listens to recordings of himself when young. But in *Not I* the Mouth, which is presumably part of the Auditor, seems to have attained independence *at that moment* from the Auditor, a hooded figure of "undeterminable" sex: one of Mouth's few pauses in the play comes as Mouth "recovers from vehement refusal to relinquish third person." This idea of "disembodiment" recurs in *Rockaby*.

The play opens as all of Beckett's plays open—with an arresting theatrical image. Alone in a circle of light, seated in a rocker with her feet on a footrest, is a "prematurely old" woman with "unkempt grey hair" and "huge eyes in white expressionless face." Her costume: "Black lacy high-necked evening gown. Long sleeves. Jet sequins to glitter when rocking." After a long pause, she speaks the single word "More." Her chair rocks, and her recorded voice is heard. After a few minutes, the words and the rocking stop. Again after a long pause, she speaks the word "More"; more recorded words and rocking for a few minutes. There are four such sections in all, each begun by her speaking the same word and followed by recorded monologue, each a bit longer than the previous section. At the end, her voice and the lights fade, as the rocking stops.

Each of the four recorded sections begins with the words "till in the end" or "so in the end"; each is in the third person; each is in short lines as of verse; each contains the ambiguous phrase "time she stopped." The three later sections contain much of what was in the first section, adding or altering, so that the effect is incremental.

The first section tells us that at the "close of a long day" she was looking

high and low
for another
another creature like herself. . . .
another living soul
one other living soul

The search continues through the other sections (says the voice, as the silent old woman rocks in what we learn is her mother's chair and dress), but she is at last at her window

facing other windows
other only windows

In the closing section she goes "down the steep stair" and discovers that she

was her own other
own other living soul

She is done with rocking, says her voice now, as the rocking slows. Having realized her complete solitude, her solitary completeness, that she is "her own other," she says

> fuck life
> stop her eyes
> rock her off
> rock her off

And the play ends.

Its delicate cumulative quality, its oboe-like winding toward the revelation of absolute loneliness, the shock of the consequent obscene renunciation of existence, the end of rocking felt as the end of her pulse—all these I discerned from the printed page. (*Rockaby and Other Short Pieces*, published by Grove Press.) None of these subtle beauties is achieved or even outlined in the performance directed by Schneider. Whitelaw's recorded voice just chants, not always intelligibly, with no inflection of growth or resolution, no clarity of design. It's all blind Beckett worship, not acute Beckett performance. Schneider has had long experience with Beckett, but experience is not equivalent to sensibility. I wish that a better performance—perhaps with Whitelaw under a better director—had been taped. *Rockaby* does not open new reaches in Beckett, but it's a valuable bead for his unique rosary of lasting last rites.

The Little Foxes

(Saturday Review, July 1981)

"I'm so excited I can hardly stand it," said the woman behind me. The lights had dimmed, the curtain was about to rise on *The Little Foxes* with Elizabeth Taylor. I liked the woman's remark, her excitement—which the audience shared—at the start of a play. That sense of trembly anticipation is rare in our theater these days, and even if it has to come from glamour, well, glamour is an ancient and venerable factor in the theater, not automatically to be despised.

And with her first appearance, with her appearances throughout, Taylor fulfills the glamour expectation. Her face is lovely, she's well wigged and costumed, and though her bosom is now more of an international phenomenon than a personal attribute, she conveys it and the rest of herself around the stage with some poise, some good use of her stardom.

But the glamour is not enough. Taylor's first performance on the stage seems to have been judged by the fact that it's her first performance on the stage. By that gentle criterion, she does some things passably. She moves with an attempt at line. She knows how to listen fairly well. Although her hands look surprisingly large, she uses them with some deftness and restraint. But an actor's sustaining of a long scene needs more than our wonder that a film star, used to short takes, is actually playing a long scene. To use a camera term, Taylor seems repeatedly to go in and out of focus during scenes. Worse, in the climaxes, her force comes from her throat, not her spirit; the result is only noise. A Martian, ignorant of Taylor's film past, seeing her for the first time here, might wonder how an actress of her age could have developed so little technique and could have become a star with so little ability to take command.

Lillian Hellman's play, first done in 1939, is about a wealthy Southern fin-de-siècle family who want to be wealthier—the Hubbards, consisting of Regina Hubbard Giddens, her brothers Ben and Oscar, Oscar's son Leo. Differing from them are Regina's husband Horace, their daughter Alexandra, Oscar's wife, Birdie. All the latter are Good; all the Hubbards are Bad, rapacious, not linked by their greed but scheming against one another because of it. A few commentators have wondered why Taylor chose Regina for her theater debut, a role without a romantic or appealing touch, a woman made of aggressions, sometimes gloved, sometimes naked. They forget that several of Taylor's most effective film roles—like those in *Suddenly Last Summer, Reflections in a Golden Eye, Who's Afraid of Virginia Woolf?*—depended on her (and her director's) ability to work up a clawing hysteria. Taylor's career has relied less on audience seduction than any other film-star beauty I can think of. (Bette Davis was never a beauty of that rank.) The contrast between Taylor's violet-eyed softness and those rages brought her considerable success; now she has merely chosen a stage role that carries the contrast further.

By luck or design, the actors around Taylor have been chosen so as not to show her up. The one competent performance is by Novella Nelson as the maid, Addie. Regina's bullied aristocratic sister-in-law, Birdie, is played by Maureen Stapleton, who suggests a risen kitchen maid more than a fallen blueblood. Stapleton has long ceased trying to act; she has become a beggar for pathos, like a dog sitting up and begging for biscuits, and she does it with increasing clumsiness. Anthony Zerbe as Ben, Joe Ponazecki as Oscar, Dennis Christopher as Leo are all slovenly and inadequate; and they suggest a decline in American acting. If you think the word "decline" is just the maundering of an old playgoer, see the 1941 film of *The Little Foxes* in which those three roles are played by Charles Dingle, Carl Benton Reid, and Dan Duryea, and Birdie is played by Patricia Collinge, all of whom were in the original Broadway production. The invalid Horace in this revival is Tom Aldredge. As is often the case, Aldredge's acting is so thin as to be nearly invisible: I'm never quite sure whether he's on stage or off. Alexandra is done by Ann Talman, a colorless young woman who, says the program, is a student of Austin Pendleton, the director.

Talman and Christopher are the second and third Pendleton students to make their debuts in a Pendleton production this season. (The first was Patricia Cray Lloyd who was equally unimpressive in *John Gabriel Borkman* at Circle in the Square.) The idea of Pendleton as acting teacher—I've seen a lot of his acting as well as his directing—is depressing, and his direction of *The Little Foxes* does little to reassure. His work here apparently consisted of giving Taylor some confidence, devising stagy patterns of stage movement for the whole cast, and interrupting those movements with stilted groupings as for old-time photos. The overall impression of his method is of actors obeying orders to move and occasionally obeying orders to stop, to have their pictures taken.

If Pendleton's ineptness needed confirmation, it comes with the final curtain. Regina has connived at her invalid husband's death, has bested her brothers in business skullduggery, is well on her way to riches and power. She starts upstairs to her bedroom, then says (quite incredibly, by the way) to her daughter: "Would you—would you like to sleep in my room tonight?" The daughter replies, "Are you afraid, Mama?" The stage directions say:

> Regina does not answer, but moves slowly out of sight. Addie *then* comes to Alexandra, squeezes her arm with affection and pride, *then* starts for the other lamp, as the curtain falls. [Italics added.]

Pendleton makes Addie move *before* Regina is out of sight: thus he obscures the sting of the daughter's line in Regina, and he muddies Taylor's star exit up the stairs.

Hellman—regardless of the fact that Regina's last-second qualm is unbelievable—has enough stage wile to have ordered it otherwise, just as she was wily enough to construct a pathos number for Birdie in Act Three that virtually flashes its own "Applause" sign at her exit. But the play as a whole is monochromatic. Once its premise is set, it's just financial ploy and counterploy among the Hubbards and against Horace. Fundamentally, nothing grows or changes; it's just a continual barrage of tricks on more or less the same plane until it's over. And even then it's over only because the final curtain comes down: Ben has suspicions about Horace's death, which means that, if the curtain were to rise again, the play might still be going on. (Seven years later Hellman wrote a three-act prologue, *Another Part of the Forest*, which showed that, in effect, *The Little Foxes* had been going on twenty years before its first curtain rose.)

Because of the two-dimensional characters and the assorted contrivances, the drama never really entails more than the snarlings of a dog fight. But Hellman wants her play to have resonance, so she pastes on her own aggrandizements. Says Ben, in his last scene:

> There are hundreds of Hubbards sitting in rooms like this throughout the country. All their names aren't Hubbard, but they are all Hubbards and they will own this country some day.

And just before the end, the seventeen-year-old Alexandra tells her mother that she'll be fighting her uncle "as hard as he'll be fighting . . . someplace where people don't just stand around and watch." Don't queston where the girl got that impulse or what the line means; just observe Hellman's considerateness. She includes with her play hints for college-senior essays on its themes.

These final fake pronouncements don't deepen the gimcrack play, don't make it any more than reverse sentimentality, a bath in theatrical vice instead of theatrical virtue. Not long ago a revival of Hellman's *Watch on the Rhine* revealed it—still more clearly—as a tawdry insult, through melodrama, to its theme of anti-fascism. *The Little Foxes*, though less clankily constructed, is equally superficial in the treatment of its theme, American materialism throttling the American dream. The quotation marks plead to be printed in acid when one refers to these plays as native "classics."

Cloud Nine

(Saturday Review, August 1981)

Cloud Nine is the first play by the English writer Caryl Churchill to be produced in the U.S., and flawed though it is, it adds to our understanding of why some current British playwrights, a lot of them under forty-five, are among the most important in the world today. Their importance is not just for their work but for the confidence they restore in the act and art of playwriting, a confidence that not many American playwrights inspire.

Anger has prevailed in most good British playwriting since the phrase Angry Young Man was launched in 1956, but these latter-day writers are not knotted up in bilious personal frustrations, like John Osborne; they wrestle with the largest possible questions of society and politics and spirit. Very often these radical probings of subject matter are expressed in radically untraditional dramatic structure. Churchill's play is a strong example.

Cloud Nine is in two acts, widely separated in time and place. Act One, set in an unspecified African colony in 1880, deals with the British colonials: Daddy, who is the governor, Mummy, their nine-year-old son Edward, their two-year-old daughter Vicky, Mummy's mother, their nanny, their loyal black servant, and two other English people, a lone explorer and an attractive widow neighbor. The first act is Somerset Maugham savaged three ways. First, conventional pukka Victorian attitudes are stretched to ludicrous extremes. In the opening, which is written in rhyme, Daddy says: "I am a father to the natives here / And father to my family so dear." Mummy says: "I am a man's creation as you see / And what men want is what I want to be." The servant adds: "What white men want is what I want to be."

These domestic-political attitudes are laid out in a kind of music-hall presentation, with some music. Then—the second attack—these attitudes are stripped to the truths under them in a style that's like a series of skits. We see that:

Daddy is bedding the widow; Mummy is chasing the loner, the loner has already had little Edward who loved it and wants more, but meanwhile the loner is meeting the black servant in the barn; the nanny lusts for Mummy but is forced by Daddy into marriage with the loner in order to coat two problems with respectability. Meanwhile, a native uprising is squashed bloodily offstage, and the act ends with the servant raising a gun to shoot Daddy in the back. Little Edward, who loathes Daddy, sees the gun raised and says nothing; he merely covers his ears with his hands.

The third attack is in the casting. Mummy is played by a man, the black servant by a white man blacked up, the boy by a young woman, the little girl by a dummy, the nanny and the widow by one woman. This technique, reminiscent of Jean Genet, further barbecues the platitudes and fakeries by blatantly impersonating the characters rather than acting them seriously.

A bit of condensation would have helped Act One; we fairly soon get the idea that petticoats are being overflounced so that the satire will be sharper when they are flipped up. But Act One is retrospectively reinforced by Act Two, set in London 1980. A number of places are called for in the published script; Lawrence Miller's unit setting—a few rows of park benches on a raked stage—encompasses them all imaginatively and makes a good seedy contrast to the vaudeville-drop feeling of Act One. Though Act Two is a century later, Churchill says that "for the characters it is only twenty-five years later." This device allows the calendar to jump ahead drastically while allowing characters *and* actors to connect with the past. For instance, Jeffrey Jones, who has been airily funny as Daddy in Act One urging his young Edward to be manly, now plays a thirty-four-year-old Edward who is gay. Veronica Castang, one of the most satisfyingly versatile actresses in our theater, who was Daddy's prim and frustrated mother-in-law, is now a young London lesbian divorcée.

Act Two begins with a monologue by another gay (played by Zeljko Ivanek, who was Mummy in Act One), in which he details a homosexual pickup and act in a train compartment during a six-minute trip. What's especially significant about the monologue is its tone, its assumption of our understanding, as if he were telling us about finishing the *Times* crossword in six minutes. This gay, like every other character in Act Two, is acted, not cartooned. Everything has moved closer to reality.

The story winds through sexual weavings and unweavings of some modern Londoners, including Edward, his sister, her husband, the gay man, the gay woman. One particularly poignant monologue comes from Edward's mother, an elderly widow called Betty (which was Mummy's name in Act One), telling us how lovely she finds solitary sex after a life of conjugal sexual numbness. One intrusive sequence brings in the ghost of the lesbian's brother, a British soldier just killed in Belfast, who tells us that what he chiefly misses is sex; his appearance seems engineered. And there a few revenant appearances by characters from Act One to do underscoring that is superfluous.

The two acts, each of which could almost stand alone, combine into a comedy-drama about the beginnings of escape from past cruelties into present quandaries. Men and women are at least attaining a sense of what liberation can be (says Churchill). Sexual freedoms grow, not only in practice but in acceptance; political oppressions have a harder time posing as unassailable truths. And all this change leaves Britain where? (Not just Britain, or the play would not bite us as it does.) Is this what all the struggle and upheaval have been about, just so that people can screw whom they like more freely? Is liberation nothing but an emptiness to be filled with uninhibited sexual activity?

Only in this society, Churchill hints in Act Two. What's needed is a new society in which freedom is not a vacuum to be filled with gonad satisfaction.

This political base links Churchill with her playwriting "group," who otherwise vary widely in temperament and art. Some of the outstanding names, few of them well-known in this country, are Howard Brenton, David Hare, Edward Bond, Barrie Keeffe, and Bill Morrison. (Pam Gems is also a "member" but in my view a lesser one on the basis of *Piaf* and an earlier play seen here.) Besides their true talents, they share anger. Auden wrote of Yeats: "Mad Ireland hurt you into poetry," then when on to say that Ireland hasn't changed because "poetry makes nothing happen." Mad Britain has hurt these writers into drama, which they hope *will* make things happen—they are all in some degree Marxist—but in any event they have all written some good plays. It's no more necessary to be Marxist to appreciate them than it is to be Catholic in order to value Bernanos and Mauriac. What is relevant is that these dramatists' rootedness in a culture, a culture that infuriates them, has moved them to levels of playwriting that almost no contemporary U.S. playwrights can approach. That's not an argument for Marxism; it's a truth about these particular talented Marxists.

In the current production at the Off-Broadway Theatre de Lys, American actors show again that they deserve better American playwrights. Especially notable besides Jones and Castang are Concetta Tomei as the boy Edward and the grown Edward's sister, and E. Katherine Kerr as the nanny and the saucy widow in Act One, the middle-aged widow in Act Two. They give us small-stroke acting built on deep feeling. The director, Tommy Tune, has a fitting name for a dancer and a director of musicals, which is how he started; we're just going to have to get used to it as the name of a dextrous and sensitive director of plays.

A Tale Told

(Saturday Review, September 1981)

If there were a Nobel Prize for Sincere Imitation, Lanford Wilson would be a leading contender in the drama department. It's impossible to doubt his sincerity; but not all of it seems to be his own.

Wilson became visible with a stream of short and long plays in the busy Off-Off-Broadway days of the Sixties. He ranged in style, with evident sincerity, from naturalism through poetic realism to abstraction. But none of his work made much mark until he began more patently to build on successful models, always sincerely. *The Hot l Baltimore* (1973), his first big success, was a smooth imitation of latter-day Tennessee Williams sleaze, complete with a young man passing through on a quest. After some unmemorable intervening work, Wilson then began a series of plays about a Missouri family named Talley; and all of the three written to date cling, with desperate sincerity, to apparent models.

Fifth of July, produced Off-Broadway in 1978 and re-produced on Broadway in 1980, climbed aboard the hip Chekhov bandwagon already carrying such young playwrights as Michael Weller (*Moonchildren*) and Robert Patrick (*Kennedy's Children*). To lean on Chekhov, according to these writers, you needed only to keep a substantial number of characters on stage at the same time, each following his or her own ego track, and out of it all would eventually come Loneliness. If, as Wilson did, you included in your cast a legless Vietnam veteran, his homosexual lover, a free-mouthed country singer and her cynical husband, who, along with others, are cooled-out survivors of the idealistic Sixties, if you put them all in the Talley house in Lebanon, Missouri (Wilson's hometown), and built much of the action around the singer's attempt to buy the old homestead for a recording studio—hear those axes from *The Cherry Orchard?*—you sliced right across the moral agony of 1977 America. Especially with that title. In fact, the first act took place on the evening of Independence Day.

All that, of course, was Wilson's hope. But the reliance on eccentric mélange rather than freshness and depth of perception, the greater reliance on superficial imitation of Chekhovian form, made *Fifth of July* a recipe being followed—with sincerity—rather than a drama being disclosed.

Talley's Folly (1979) was set in 1944, so Wilson chose a dramaturgic mode to fit *that* period—earlier Tennessee Williams, summer-and-smokey, tidied up with the single-stitch tailoring of a John Van Druten. It was a two-character play, two secretly wounded people, of course. Sally Talley, sterile because of an illness, and Matt Friedman, a European Jewish refugee now an accountant in St. Louis still suffering from anti-Semitism, meet in the Talley boathouse at night, meld, and decide to run off together, all in an explicitly predicted ninety-four minutes. The tonalities and pathos were as Williams-derived as the summer-evening dream effects, the distant band music, even the use of inserted jokes. Once again, more blatantly but no less sincerely, Wilson imitated. And not to miss out on his cute irony, Wilson set this play too on the evening of Independence Day.

With cuteness unflagging, the new Talley play, *A Tale Told*, is set on that very same July Fourth evening up at the Talley house. (Near the end Sally comes up from the boathouse to get her things and go off with Matt.) The year still being 1944, Wilson uses another contemporary dramaturgic model. This time it's Lillian-Hellmanized Ibsen.

Grandpa Talley is an ailing tyrant who still controls the family factory, now making wartime Army uniforms, though his middle-aged middling son is nominal manager. A soldier grandson is home on leave because grandpa is supposed to be dying. Another grandson is home uncorporeally; he has just been killed in combat, and his ghost wanders through in blue light. (This mars Wilson's Hellman imitation with a touch of David Rabe.) Among the several plot strands, the central one is the old tyrant's handling of the trouble caused by his son's impregnating a laundress eighteen years before. But the neatest stage trick in many a year comes when the dead soldier's mother gets the telegram announcing his death, and his ghost, standing behind her, catches her as she faints.

Again Wilson is sincere. Again his trouble is that he is following form: he doesn't really know any more about his characters than he tells us, he just puts them through their paces like an animal trainer with platforms, hoops, and cage. Each of the twelve in the cast is tagged early with virtues and defects and that's it, except for the untangling of some plotty plot lines. In Ibsen, what we learn early about his characters is where the play begins; in Wilson, as in some other Ibsen epigones like Hellman, that's substantively where the play ends. To put it another way, the play has no theme, just some action. Wilson has merely taken the extremely tired diluted-Ibsen ploy—revealing the frauds behind a mansion's respectable facade—and has run it through his typewriter yet again. Sincerely. A Tale Told could be called A Form Filled.

We're promised two more Talley plays. Why not twenty? Wilson needs only to choose a model that fits the period, then fill it from his ever-ready bowl of sincere dramatic dough as honestly as a baker fills a mold.

Marshall W. Mason, Wilson's usual director, had a special traffic problem here. Often a crisis occurs between a few characters, and the whole Talley family has to be hustled in to witness it, then hustled off when it's over. I thought of the way opera choruses scoot in and out at the Met. From most of his actors, Mason gets mediocre performances, adequate to their explicit roles. From the one fine actor, Fritz Weaver, Mason gets the worst Weaver performance I've seen—a basketful of leftover crusts from all the crusty family tyrants in stage history.

Misalliance

(Saturday Review, October 1981)

It's happened again. For the umpty-seventh time I've left a performance—really a three-hour brutalization—of a wonderful play by Bernard

Shaw hearing people mutter that it was "talky." In fact, the only reason that the audience was able to endure it at all was that Shaw's genius made itself at least partially felt even through the bungling. To cap the irony, that hardy genius then induced some critics to rave about the very performance that had inadvertently tried to strangle it.

Last season Stephen Porter directed *Major Barbara* at Circle-in-the-Square, and, though there was some hurtful miscasting, he had sufficient sympathy with that great comic-dramatic opera to perceive its designs. This season Porter has directed *Misalliance* at the Roundabout and has made the fundamental mistake of treating it as he did *Major Barbara*. In rough analogy, this is to direct *Twelfth Night* as if it were *Measure for Measure*. Shaw's Salvation Army play deals consistently and organically with several gigantic themes. Shaw's *Misalliance* is a very different glass of champagne. The themes in it are serious enough, heaven knows, but they are touched, passed, recovered—juggled, one may say, perhaps in mimesis of the practice of the acrobat-juggler who is pivotal in the play itself. The structure, far from the syncretic Handel-Molière majesty of *Major Barbara*, seems (repeat: seems) to follow the caprices of a bubbling imagination. Porter has utterly missed the difference. To him, Shaw is Shaw.

Written in 1909, *Misalliance* came four years after *Major Barbara* and one year after *Getting Married*, another full-length play designed to be played in one unbroken act. Shaw gave *Getting Married* the mockingly defiant subtitle "A Disquisitory Play," and *Misalliance*, with equivalent tease, he called "A Debate in One Sitting." I've never seen it done in one sitting—though, well-played, this would help it—and it's about as much a debate as *The Importance of Being Earnest*.

Like many of Shaw's plays, *Misalliance* begins innocently, as if it were a conventional theater piece—in this case, a weekend country-house comedy. Within two minutes we know otherwise. A young aristocrat named Bentley Summerhays, just arrived after a dull week in the city, feels like talking, wants to "argue about something intellectual" with his host's thirtyish son who is relaxing with a novel. The other man declines and tells Bentley that, if he wants to argue, he ought to go over to the Congregationalist minister, who likes it. Says Bentley: "You can't argue with a person when his livelihood depends on his not letting you convert him."

It all happens one Saturday afternoon in 1909 at the Surrey home of John Tarleton, the middle-aged, ebullient founder of Tarleton's Underwear. It starts as a comedy about family life—"comedy" implying for Shaw "surgery"—parent-and-child relations, marriage, the effect on them of changing ideas of class. The only specified misalliance is the engagement of Bentley to Hypatia Tarleton, rich but nevertheless a tradesman's daughter. Yet there are more misalliances than that, of several kinds. The form of the play—very subtly designed—is made to look like a series of coincidences which scoff at the ideas of arrangement, alliance *and* misalliance, that pervade the play.

Fairly early, Bentley happens to mention that he had a friend at Oxford named Joey Percival. Subsequently, Tarleton complains that Hypatia wants adventure to drop from the sky. In the middle of the play Joey Percival drops from the sky—he's an amateur flier, and his plane crashes into the Tarleton greenhouse—and in the course of the next hour, he takes Hypatia away from Bentley, to no one's surprise, least of all Bentley's, who is bright but spindly. Percival was carrying a passenger in his plane who in fact saved his life. That passenger, in breeches and helmet, turns out to be a beautiful woman—a Polish acrobat-juggler whose family creed for generations has been that every day you must risk your life at least once. And, before the play is over, Tarleton offers (unsuccessfully) to set up the Polish woman as his mistress; Bentley's father, Lord Summerhays, recalls having made advances to her in Vienna; and Tarleton's son proposes to her. (It's the last that enrages her.)

Now you have only to read these samples—out of a good many more similar incidents—to know that this is not the way things happen in life. It's not even the way things happen in farce, which, after an eccentric premise or two, proceeds with mathematical logic. *Misalliance* is *playing* with the serious, and the non-sense is not only amusing, it's all the more enchanting because every line spoken to advance the non-sense is expressed in language of sparkling sense.

A director who can't see the contrast between the extravagance of what is happening and the wisdom of what is said about it is stratospheres away from the play's style. That's Porter. But his work is worse than that: even as direction of "straight" comedy, it's clumsy from Moment One. At the start Tarleton's son is, says Shaw, "reclining, novel in hand, in a swinging chair. . . ." Porter has him sitting in an armless, straight-backed chair next to a table, just about the last position anyone would choose for relaxation. Why? Because Porter has to have him there for an (equally clumsy) encounter he's planning. This mechanical start is followed by more mechanics: People cross the stage just because Porter thinks a bit of movement will keep things bright, or they stand face to face for dialogue like Nelson Eddy and Jeanette Mac-Donald about to burst into song.

Philip Bosco, that valuable actor who was Undershaft in Porter's *Major Barbara*, plays Tarleton and has some flavor, though his Midlands accent comes and goes; but, as with Undershaft, he lacks the sheer powerful presence that is basic to the role. Patricia Elliott, whom I've often admired, makes the pride of the Polish acrobat false because it's all external, not generated from conviction. And her last great long speech, which should grow and grow, propelled by her fury at a marriage proposal that would move her from a life of valor to a life of knitting, is severely fractured by foolish little detours into irrelevant colors. The rest of the cast, especially Lord Summerhays, who is apparently played by an unemployed waiter, is inadequate, except for Jeanne Ruskin, the Hypatia. Despite her constricted voice, a better director could have elicited a good performance.

Yet Shaw, battered, condensed a bit, survives. The laser vision, the probing comedy, the twists that come from telling the truth instead of inventing twists, are indomitably there. And in *Misalliance*, as in a few of his other plays, there is an extra quality.

This play, like some of his one-act plays, like *Too True to Be Good* (1931), doesn't build on a traditional genre. *You Never Can Tell* (1896) and *Saint Joan* (1923) are superlative examples of high comedy and historical tragedy. *Misalliance* won't fit into such a category, but it does fit somewhere else. Even the few samples of the play given above will show that Shaw was both fathering and advancing the Theater of the Absurd.

Some have maintained, defensibly, that he was preceded by W. S. Gilbert, surely an Absurdist if the term means dramatic form that wryly reflects the difference between the range of mankind's vision and the limitations of mortality. But Shaw opened up much more and went much further. The critic R. J. Kaufmann (no relative—note spelling) wrote that Shaw "is godfather, if not actually finicky paterfamilias, to the Theater of the Absurd," that Shaw's "sense of art as medley, art as teetering on the edge of formal dissolution" is often like Ionesco and other Absurdists. I'd add that the reason Shaw is not often considered with the Absurdists is that he had other strings to his incredible bow, which is not true of them. He could write a *Mrs. Warren's Profession* or a *Pygmalion* when he needed to.

There's talk these days about a Shaw "revival," but the word is silly. He has never been away. (Been reading lately about children's rights? Look at the preface to *Misalliance*, in which he argued at length for children's rights in 1909.) It's a safe bet that, at any given moment of the day, every day of the year, a Shaw play is being performed somewhere on the face of the globe. The only other dramatist in the history of the world about whom the same bet could be made is Shakespeare. How can you "revive" a genius whose work (like Shakespeare's) even bad performances can't kill? The idea is small-a absurd.

Postscript. Subsequently I read Stanley Weintraub's essay "The Avant-Garde Shaw," first published in 1966, then included in his collection *The Unexpected Shaw* (Ungar, 1982), in which Weintraub advances and supports the argument for Shaw as forerunner of the Absurdists.

Nicholas Nickleby

(Saturday Review, December 1981)

Almost any comment about *Nicholas Nickleby* is true. This Royal Shakespeare Company production, eight and a half hours long, with forty-three actors playing 143 parts, is so multifarious that it embraces contradictions. The show has sags, yet length is of its essence; it sometimes follows

Dickens too faithfully, yet it sometimes distorts him; and so on. All these contradictory truths support a central truth: the production insistently *exists*. In some degree its contradictions are less artistic faults—with one howling exception, noted below—than the contradictions we would expect within any living organism.

What first struck this American viewer was that *Nicholas Nickleby* is a company effort by a subsidized theater. No U.S. producer could contemplate a show of this length, with thirteen musicians and hundreds of costumes, a show whose cast had done eight weeks of preparatory work before regular rehearsals began or a script was written, a show that requires physical renovation of a theater where it plays. (Two-tiered towers stand downstage right and left, connected by a runway around the front mezzanine.) The tickets are $100, but they would have had to be twice as much, I'd suppose, without the head start provided by subsidy. British taxpayers helped to make this show available to Americans.

Another fruit of subsidy is that this is a company work, done by actors who have been maintained as a group. The show was instigated by the directors, Trevor Nunn and John Caird, and the script was finalized by David Edgar, but the groundwork was done through improvisations and experiments by actors who had been working with one another for varying lengths of time. The spirit of ensemble is emphasized by the opening and closing of the two main sections; the entire company comes together on stage, as for a photograph. "This," they seem to say, "is *our* show."

In Dickens's novel, published in 1839, the hero and his sister, after their father's death, go from Devon to London with their mother to seek the help of their uncle, Ralph Nickleby. Uncle Ralph coldly finds hard jobs for the nineteen-year-old youth and his sister; and their pursuit of livelihood and happiness—thrust out of the shelter of a loving home into a brass-bound world—is the substance of a somewhat tacked-together plot. But in the RSC version, both the ensemble playing and some outstanding performances (another contradiction!) give the work considerable unity. Roger Rees is so fine as Nicholas that it's impossible to imagine the show without him. He is dark, lithe, sensitive—a perfect Dickens hero, innocent without being stupid, strong with a delicate strength. John Woodvine, as Ralph, is chilling granite, a man transmuted to rock by hard circumstance. Edward Petherbridge is his sodden clerk, Newman Noggs, a fallen gentleman and a walking social history, touched with charming rue. Bob Peck, who doubles as the hearty Yorkshire farmer John Browdie and the viciously insatiable Sir Mulberry Hawk, is magnificent in both. Most of the acting is at least good, occasionally sparkling. If I have reservations about Smike, the hero's pathetic friend, rescued by Nicholas from a wretched existence, it's not because of David Threlfall's acting but because the production drastically alters Smike from Dickens's skinny, lame boy into a complete grotesque. How could Vincent Crummles, the actor-manager who engages Nicholas for his troupe, possibly also have engaged this Smike?

Which brings me to the one dreadful blotch. After Nicholas and Smike have, in their adventures, met Crummles and been engaged by him, the Crummles company performs *Romeo and Juliet* with Nicholas as Romeo and Smike as the Apothecary. Dickens gives this performance one brief paragraph, saying only that both Nicholas and Smike were well received. The RSC inflates this paragraph into a very long, platitudinous mockery of a bad performance, with which they end Part One of their own show. No doubt the Crummles company would have been shoddy or worse, but we are not given a shoddy performance; we see an undergraduate parody of what ignorant amateurs imagine ham acting to be. Nicholas, with no experience whatsoever, could not possibly have been a good Romeo, but neither would he have behaved like a jackass, as this Romeo does.

I've never understood why actors like to ridicule blatantly the actors of the past instead of trying to understand a bygone style so that they can parody it intelligently. The RSC has committed this offense before, in their production of Boucicault's *London Assurance* (1974).

But overriding this facile vulgarity and some lesser flaws, the RSC tumbles a teeming Dickens world across the stage. More important, beneath the pleasures of the proceedings, a basic cultural link is completed. That link begins with the warm affinity between Dickens and the theater, which he loved, often refers to, sometimes employs (as he does with the Crummles troupe), and frequently uses for models of scene construction. And what was the theatrical genre that Dickens was particularly fond of? Melodrama, of course. We all know this; still, during this performance, I could hardly believe that the audience, on Broadway in 1981, was watching intently while, for example, a lecherous nobleman tried to seduce an honest working girl or an old crone cackled about secret documents. In a revival of any 1839 melodrama, such moments would now be something more than risible; here the audience, myself included, was held. Partly it was awe of the Dickens name, I guess, but awe alone couldn't have done it. Other factors helped—provided a context for those melodramatic moments.

First, the humor. We see the melodrama against the humor surrounding it, and we're persuaded that the man who saw life's ridiculousness so sharply can be trusted here. (Chesterton said that the serious thing in Dickens is his humor; such truth as there is in that comment helps us to accept the lurid passages.) Second, the details of dailyness, the family life, the doing of jobs in millinery shops and business offices, and more. (That's why length is essential to this show—we need the texture.) This dailyness is treated with such intimacy and conviction that it gives the melodramatic material a plentiful ballast of credibility.

Yet something crowns these elements, I believe. *All* of Dickens, the melodrama, the humor, the daily detail, even the narrative and descriptive passages—*all* are theater. Robert Garis illuminates this in his book, *The Dickens Theater*: "Dickens is a performing artist, displaying his verbal skills . . . in a theater created by the insistent and self-displaying rhetoric of his voice." The RSC seems to have recognized this truth—that, fundamentally, what they are performing is *Dickens*, not *Nicholas Nickleby*. They include, happily, more of the narration and description than is absolutely necessary, assigning parts of passages to actors stationed around the playing areas or, in a most memorable moment, having a large group speak in unison the wonderful description of London as Nicholas and Smike return to it.

So what we are seeing, esthetically, is the closing of a link. Dickens fed on popular theater, absorbed it into his very voice as well as into what that voice expressed; and now the RSC is bringing Dickens back to his source. This is hardly the first time that Dickens has been staged; *Nicholas Nickleby* itself was being performed in part while it was still being serialized, before its book publication. But the magnitude (in several senses) of this production, the intent to return to the theater a genius's transformation of the theater, combine to make this production a unique cultural act.

The production's final gesture—amidst the general happiness, Nicholas lifts another starving boy in his arms for the audience to see—attempts to conclude the whole event as a radicalizing social drama; but that gesture cannot prevail against what has been happening for eight and a half hours. The essence of melodrama is affirmation; no matter what troubles have been undergone, at the last, melodrama shows us justice being done. The greatness of Dickens is that he exalted the genre from popular escapism into a universally affecting myth, touching and ironic at one end of the intellectual spectrum, consoling at the other. It is the universality of this exalted melodrama that the RSC lavishes on us.

Mass Appeal

(Saturday Review, January 1982)

Mass Appeal by Bill C. Davis has only two characters, a veteran Roman Catholic priest and a young seminarian studying nearby. The priest is skillful and pastorally pragmatic, a man whose religious vocation has not kept him from developing charm as an aid to that vocation. The seminarian is consumingly devout but pastorally unpolished. The two roles have been cast with astonishing aptness. The priest is played by Milo O'Shea, a practiced charmer at his savory best. The seminarian is Michael O'Keefe, an appealing young man of fine feeling who is, artistically, a cub. O'Shea is a wise theater possum, canny in his native habitat; O'Keefe is emotionally genuine but has virtually no technique—I felt that someone had gone through his script and underlined the words for him to emphasize. Whatever control he can muster I think he owes to Geraldine Fitzgerald, the gifted actress who makes her directorial debut with this play. And I also think that she hadn't much more to do with O'Shea than to give him a bit of the rough side of her tongue when he caroled too freely.

The two-part set, reticently designed by David Gropman, contains the priest's office and the priest's pulpit. Davis's decison to use only two characters never makes his play thin or mechanical, though like many another playwright, he should light a dramaturgic candle at the shrine of Alexander Graham Bell. But Davis has wit, insight, and a turn for dramatic rhetoric; his comedy-drama is launched easily, sustained well, and is vividly, if incompletely, characterized. His play leaves us with a question about its author. He can write for actors, but can he write for himself? Which is to say, can he do more than construct a good show? Can he unflinchingly face the interesting issues that he raises?

Here he has taken a classic, still serviceable, dramatic situation. A comfily established mature professional—in this case a priest—is unsettled by the fervor of a beginner in his profession. The priest is both disturbed and touched by the youth. The older man tries to get the younger one to temper his fervor in his preaching debut so as not to attack the congregation's materialist vanity; he also tries to get the youth to temper the truth about his past to avoid expulsion from the seminary. On both counts the older man fails.

The second issue is the crucial one. Under questioning by the head of the seminary (whom we never see), the youth confesses that for three years before he entered the church, he tried to find love with women and with men; and he is expelled. He has no regrets about admitting the facts, but he wanted passionately to stay in the church. He tells the priest: "During those three years—whenever someone I loved, loved me, I did everything to keep it constant. . . . But to go through all that—to worry about who's got the upper hand—who's going to change first—it made the love worthless." Now that he has found the one constant love, free of maneuver, he must give it up because, in effect, he didn't find it first. The priest is so moved by the youth's expulsion that he preaches against it. He expects that his sermon will get him transferred to Iowa—apparently a synonym for Siberia—but there he will find street corners to preach on, as he did when he was a young deacon, which was the time when he felt closest to Christ.

But Davis doesn't fully confront the main questions that Mass Appeal presents. The priest tells us of his troubles with his parents and says: "By the time my father left and my mother died, I was so confused that I didn't want to be near man, woman, or piano leg. Celibacy came naturally to me." Naturally, perhaps, but when he first took over this church, he wanted so desperately to be loved by his parishioners that he broke out in a rash all over his body. And now we feel that part of his attracton to the seminarian is that the young man has known love, of differing kinds, that the older man has never experienced. I don't suggest that there ought to have been a homosexual relation between them; but this intelligent priest would have had some knowledge of this attraction, some curiosity, some sense of forbidden mysteries in the youth, possibly some fear of them. An immense and trembly psychological area is noted, then merely skirted.

Second, the ending. It's hemstiched. When the priest asks the youth what he'll do after expulsion, he simply says, "I'll be fine," then disappears. To what? He did a lot of social work when he was a prospective priest; will he be able to throw himself back into that work without the goal of priesthood? Is he going to have to fall back on physical love? Davis sayeth not.

Worse, he has tacked on an upbeat Broadway finish—the Iowa street-corner blather. The original ending, already published, is the priest's appeal for the youth from his pulpit, with no indication that he was really risking the loss of that pulpit. The priest had been genuinely moved by his experience with the youth, but not enough to change. The original ending was closer to reality. The new ending is closer to the box office.

Davis has shown that he can write plays; now let him write one. He has the charm of his priest. He needs the commitment of his seminarian.

Dreamgirls

(Saturday Review, February 1982)

Dreamgirls is not only a smash hit, it's a good show. Michael Bennett, who was responsible for *A Chorus Line*, has coaxed and imagined and hauled into being—with wonderful collaborators—a musical that occupies the stage for two and a half flowing hours. "Occupies" is a key word. The book, by Tom Eyen, about the trial and triumphs and let-downs of some black singers through the 1960s and into the 1970s, is a patchwork of spontaneity and afterthoughts. The score—lyrics by Eyen, music by Henry Krieger—is pleasant enough, in styles that don't offer endless chances for variety. But life—zingy real-fake stage life—leaps out on the stage from the first moment and never stops whirling. By the usual standards of book, memorable score, impact of theme—matters that *A Chorus Line* either handled well or victoriously ignored—*Dreamgirls* is problematic. But sheerly as a piece of theater practice, it breathes from start to finish.

The cast is almost all black. The show begins backstage at the Apollo in Harlem, early 1960s, when three girl singers arrive from Chicago to try out in an amateur contest. The verdict is rigged against them so that they will accept backup jobs for a male star. Love affairs with the star and the manager lace the story, though not very tightly. One of the three girls, the fat one, is bumped out of the group at the end of Act One; after some mechanical tribulations, she recovers and rejoins the group for the finale. A main trouble with the book is that, seemingly without being designed that way, the story has no center;

another is that the theme—with which presumably the whole project began—gets obscured in the Scotch-taped book. That theme is cultural integrity: a black entrepreneur tries to shift his singers from black rhythm-and-blues into what he thinks will be more widely accepted white popular modes. But this theme, though visible, is not the dynamics of the piece.

Three elements hold *Dreamgirls* together and move it forward. First is the fact that the music is almost continuous—very little of the show is spoken—and that a lot of Eyen's lyrics between the relatively formal songs are not in rhymed verse but in a lively cross of recitative and *Sprechgesang*—conversation rendered in ear-teasing song. Second is the fat girl, Jennifer Holliday, who belts into her songs like a fullback crossing for a touchdown. She combines sweetness, raucousness, and an engaging pleasure in her own power.

Third is the production, the work of Bennett; his co-choreographer, Michael Peters; the scenic designer, Robin Wagner; the costume designer, Theoni V. Aldredge; and the lighting designer, Tharon Musser. Wagner has provided structural—almost constructivist—settings. It's essentially a naked stage with four tall rectangular towers made of piping, each containing a "tree" of spotlights; and there are three battens—strips that hang from the flies—built much the same way. The towers move in and out and rotate when needed; the battens sometimes descend right to the floor and even carry people up with them. To these seven elements, mobile bearers of light, Wagner has added occasional steps and platforms, front drops like the fall of an old-fashioned beaded gown, and one solid back wall of dozens of soft blue lights. Absolutely integrated with the scenic pieces is Musser's lighting—most of her lights are *in* the scenic pieces, so scenery and lighting are twinned in a rare way. Together Wagner and Musser create an environment that combines backstage with the world seen from backstage, lushness spiced with spareness. (And, I could almost say, vice versa.) Aldredge's show-biz costumes are like tropical foliage gone artfully insane.

All this, underpinned by the consistently vital if undistinguished music, made me think, to my surprise, of Gordon Craig, the theater designer-philosopher of the early twentieth century. Craig might himself have been surprised, but it was he who, in 1906, decried the reliance of the theater on the playwright and wrote that the theater "must in time perform pieces of its own art," becoming "self-reliant" by using its own resources of "action, words, line, color, and rhythm." *Dreamgirls* is much more a "self-reliant" Craigian theater piece than it is a conventional musical.

Besides, which is a quite different fact, it's a smash hit. Whenever such a hit opens—not a common event—I get the feeling that the whole island of Manhattan relaxes and smiles. Garbage in the streets? Crime? High prices? All still there, of course, but New York seems to be saying: "See? This is what we're here *for*. No place else could do it." Believe in Broadway or not, smash hits make it more attractive.

Grownups

(Saturday Review, February 1982)

Jules Feiffer's new play *Grownups* is meant to be scathing—furiously, satirical-
ly scathing. It's not. When it isn't boring, which is much of the time, it's
repellent: not because Feiffer is succeeding in his "savagery" but because he
isn't. His play takes on a faint odor of smugness—the author who thinks he's
being daring when he's only being trite.

Mike Nichols and Elaine May used to do a sketch in which a world-famous
Jewish scientist telephones his mother who starts to complain about his neglect
of her, and within a minute this important man is reduced to a cringing child.
Feiffer's first act takes the first half of his play to do more or less the same thing.
This time the man is a reporter for the *New York Times* (though we're given no
hint of his qualifications or past experience that got him the job), and the act
takes place in the large kitchen of his sister's suburban home. Dramaturgy has
rarely been clumsier than Feiffer's as he keeps a party out on the back lawn and
contrives reasons for selected characters to meet in the kitchen for confronta-
tions. (The clumsiness is translated into Andrew Jackness's set. There's only
one entrance backstage center, so the only possible entrances and exits are in
the least effective manner—at right angles to the footlights.)

What we learn from Act One is that the reporter's parents have smothered
their two children with possessive love and with prodding for their own ego
satisfaction. (The reporter's wife dislikes her in-laws so much she won't attend
the party and keeps her child away.) These old folks are conventional middle-
class monsters, with their illnesses and recipes and resentments and iterated
phrases. Mother has never let her daughter finish a story; Mother and Father
never really recognized their son until he "made" the *Times*. Even this mustily
familiar set of tensions might have been made really tense again if Feiffer showed any gift for characterization; but these people, particularly the old folks, are
not even the cartoons with which Feiffer has sometimes peopled plays—they
are stock, from plays and films and TV. Just a few inches further and Feiffer
might have written an Ionesco comedy of platitudes, but he doesn't seem to
realize that it's all platitude; apparently he thinks he's tearing the disguise of
familial sentimentality from his people as he tears the scales from our eyes.
Along with the play's staleness of character and dialogue, it subscribes glibly to
diluted Freud. Everything that's wrong with us, it says, is our parents' fault.
Anything that's right with us is our conquest of our upbringing. Parents are
not only the great but the sole curse of Western civilization.

Act Two, in the home of the reporter and his wife and their small daughter,
is a bit better because it shows how a fierce marital quarrel can flare out of a trifle and can reveal buried ego infringements. But Feiffer has to drag in the old
folks again toward the end to establish some sort of conneciton between the
two halves of his play. For the final curtain, the reporter announces that he has

quit the *Times*. This move toward independence of his parents' regard is as unexplained as the way he first got the job.

Parts of Feiffer's past work, like the last scene of *Little Murders*, have had wickedly funny bite. *Grownups* is toothless. Many of the world's best plays, from Athens to O'Neill, have dealt with family troubles, but they are never assumptive, as Feiffer is; they always justify themselves; and they always move, as Feiffer does not, to themes deeper than the immediate family grievances.

When Frances Sternhagen (who plays the reporter's mother) disappoints, then a show really is in trouble. Bob Dishy underplays the reporter in his customary manner, which results in an uneasy blend of a Second City satirist being "sincere" and an Elliott Gould manqué. The only member of the cast worth a salute is Cheryl Giannini, who strikes some truth as the reporter's wife. The director, John Madden, seems to have spent most of his time wrestling with the stiffness of the script; and lost.

Torch Song Trilogy

(Saturday Review, March 1982)

Harvey Fierstein's *Torch Song Trilogy* consists of three one-act plays with two characters running through them, the principal one played by Fierstein himself. The three plays were produced separately Off-Broadway at La Mama E.T.C. during 1978-79; now they have been assembled into an evening that runs four hours. Thus grouped, Fierstein's three plays form the best theater work that I know on the subject of homosexuality.

In 1966, while, for a short period, I was the theater critic of the *New York Times*, I wrote two Sunday articles about the stupidity of a culture that forced homosexual playwrights to disguise their experience as heterosexual, then rebuked them for writing female characters who were merely transvestite men. The articles caused a storm. When I think how dated the articles have become in sixteen years, I feel a glimmer of belief in progress. Much of the frankly homosexual theater in New York during those years has been camp, gleefully welcomed by gays in the audience, doggedly applauded by "straights" as, in my view, penance for past injustices. Much of this gay theater was artistic trash and social vengeance. *Trilogy* is not the first valuable, nonvindictive gay work, but it takes first place in the field so far. It is seriously revealing, not just in the informational sense ("So *that's* what 'they' are really like!"), although that's true, too; Fierstein treats his characters as any serious author does, trying to dramatize as much as he can of their mystery.

Yet—and of course this is no contradiction—his mode as writer and performer is comic. He plays, with husky-voiced feeling and sparkle, a Brooklyn-Jewish gay named Arnold Beckoff, witty, bitchy-witty, bright, lonely. Apparently Arnold is a model and a drag night-club performer; his vocations are not quite clear. What's clear is that, without apology or bravado, he is gay; that is his being, not his affliction or complex or limitation.

In the first play, *The International Stud*, which is the least of the trilogy, Arnold takes us on a kaleidoscopic tour of the gay "singles" life, including a visit to the dark back room of the bar whose name names the play. There he meets Ed, a bisexual in his thirties (ten years older than Arnold) with whom he falls in love: but Ed leaves him because his own life is confused.

The second play, one year later, *Fugue in a Nursery*, is the cleverest of the three. It takes place almost entirely in an immense bed, eight feet by nine, which is occupied by Ed and his girlfriend Laurel, by Arnold and his boyfriend Alan. The conversations of the four, sometimes in separate pairs, sometimes interwoven, but never of four people in bed together, obey roughly the musical structure of a fugue and trace themes of selfhood and morality through a spectrum of desire.

Five years later comes the last and best play, *Widows and Children First*. Arnold now has a fifteen-year-old foster son, David (appealingly played by Matthew Broderick), whom he took in after Arnold's lover, Alan, had been murdered in a park by queer-hunting thugs. Ed, after a quarrel with Laurel, now his wife, is staying with Arnold. Arnold's widowed mother (the excellent Estelle Getty), who knows of her son's gayness but hates to acknowledge it, comes up from Florida to visit. Ed's presence is discomfiting enough to her; her discovery of David's permanent residence here brings a harrowing but funny clash with Arnold. (It's heightened when Arnold tells her that David was gay before he arrived: "The whole purpose of placing him here was for him to grow up with a positive attitude about his homosexuality.") The play—therefore the trilogy—ends with some measure of added understanding on both sides.

Sometimes Fierstein's writing is gag-tainted. Ed goes to the supermarket and returns nine hours later; when Arnold asks him where he's been, Ed says "Buying milk." "For nine hours?" asks Arnold, and Ed replies, "I was on the express line." After we laugh, we realize that Ed couldn't possibly have said it. It's a Neil Simon touch, converting everyone in the world into a stand-up comic. But on the whole I agree with James Leverett's introduction to the book of *Torch Song Trilogy*. (Published by The Gay Presses of New York.) Leverett writes:

[The trilogy's] radical accomplishment is to show gay sensibility in its true relation to the more general sexual upheaval in our society; that is, to accord homosexuality absolutely equal, undeniable status within the entire range of human experience; equal as a way of life, equal as a source of wisdom.

Othello

(Saturday Review, April 1982)

James Earl Jones has had two intertwined theatrical careers. The first, which is of continually growing beauty, has been in vernacular plays. The second, in

Shakespeare, has been disappointing—so lacking in growth as almost to seem the work of a dull twin. Career One has moved from the blandness of his early work through the agonies of *The Great White Hope* and *Boesman and Lena* and *Of Mice and Men* and *A Lesson from Aloes*. Career Two has been sadly different: Jones's Othello (which I first saw in 1964), Macbeth, Lear, Timon have shown no comparable increase in control and power. His Shakespearean acting has tended to be a plunge into capital-P Poetry, without much deep understanding or technical refinement, with easy reliance on his physical attributes, and with much roaring.

His latest *Othello* is a small step forward in Career Two. He is not yet nearly the actor of Shakespeare that he is of lesser dramatists. Much of the "presence" of this Othello is still in his size, rather than internal qualities. Jones's ability to sway us with the use of language is still less than his reliance on his organ-voice itself. He works harder here for phrase and point, but the great speeches—"Like to the Pontic sea," for instance—boom into blur. Still, he has his moving scenes, and oddly enough, they come in this big man's broken moments. Example: after he's convinced of his wife's falseness, he collapses on her bosom in tears, remembering what he thinks has been lost.

Christopher Plummer, the Iago, is so diametrically opposite an actor that comparison seems pat. He has long been fluent in what Jones still lacks—in verse, anyway—a fine-honed, subtle control of voice and movement that carves excitement out of sound and space. In 1962 I went to Stratford, Ontario, to see Plummer's Cyrano, which was marvelous, and his Macbeth, which triumphed over a loony production by Peter Coe (the credited director of this new *Othello*). I thought that this Canadian would go on to have a Gielgud or Olivier career. Plummer has done a lot of great plays since then, in Britain particularly, but the truly great actor has not arrived. What Plummer lacks is what, outside of Shakespeare, Jones has—engulfing humanity. So what Plummer has become is not a Gielgud or Olivier but a larger-scale John Wood: he's a dazzling virtuoso who is less interested in acting than in gobbling up roles as fodder for his breathtaking skills. To hear Plummer say that, out of Desdemona's goodness, he will make the net "that shall enmesh them all"—drawing out the "sh" of "enmesh," then dropping in the last two words like little stabs—is to be electrified, but by Plummer, not by Iago. I'm surely grateful to Plummer for giving the production most of the vitality that it has, but this is not the same as admiration for an artist serving his art.

Desdemona, like Ophelia, depends more on casting than on talent. Granted a minimal competence, what's essential is a young woman who is irresistibly touching, who can, in her very self, suggest a child being run over by a juggernaut of events she doesn't understand. Dianne Wiest plays the role with modest competence, but she just doesn't have the requisite personality.

Peter Coe is listed as director, but Zoe Caldwell took over his job during the pre-Broadway tour. Director Coe-well, then, encouraged Plummer, I'd guess, helped Jones somewhat, and managed to evoke a bit of maidenly daze from Wiest. Where Coe-well failed completely is in the visual. Whenever there are more than three characters on stage, the others are ranged around like a 1910 operetta chorus. The duke's throne in Act One and Desdemona's bed in the last scene are plunked upstage center, the most obvious position and the one most difficult to play *to*. When Desdemna dies, her feet stick up between us and her face.

Yet, whatever the production's faults, one element in the play itself is strengthened as I've never seen done before. Ever since that notorious seventeenth-century critic Thomas Rymer, *Othello* has been censured because the plot depends on the Moor's being so easily gulled by the trick about the handkerchief he gave his wife. Jones, by the very blackness of his being, makes the trick credible; he makes us feel that under his majesty is a gnaw of insecurity because he is the sole black in this white world. He cannot be entirely oblivious of the venom ("thick lips," "old black ram") spat out behind his back; even the loyal Emilia at the last calls his marriage a "most filthy bargain" right to his face. With Jones, I accepted that this man, surrounded by tacit but apprehensible contempt, might be vulnerable to that handkerchief trick, might be sick with fear that his wife secretly regretted her "betrayal" of her race, that she might have tried to regain white "status" with a white lover. I've seen other black Othellos, including Paul Robeson, but none answered Rymer's objection as Jones answers it for me. Doing it, he underscores Shakespeare's genius in understanding this facet, too, of human fallibility.

How I Got That Story

(Saturday Review, May 1982)

"Remarks," Gertrude Stein reportedly remarked, "are not literature." Well, ideas are not plays. Amlin Gray has an idea in *How I Got That Story*, a good one, but he lolls on it instead of developing it, and the result is retread instead of exploration and advance.

The cast consists of two actors and many characters, all of them written in sufficiently limber dialogue. One actor, Don Scardino, plays one character, an American reporter who comes to cover the war in Amboland (Vietnam), where the play is set. The other actor, Bob Gunton, does more than twenty characters, male and female, American and Ambolese. Gunton is listed in the program as playing the Historical Event.

That last is the good idea—to have the Vietnamese experience presented as a series of "turns" by one actor, to underscore its basic mendacity with arrant theatricality, to heighten the cruelties and futility, the corruption, the wasted courage and sacrifice by showing them as different faces presented by the one Historical Event. But that's where Gray's invention stopped. To this idea he added only one trite character, a naive American, a wet-behind-the-ears Midwest reporter who goes down the long slide in Amboland from eager beaver to cynic to heart-riven sympathizer with the enemy to a homeless wreck unwanted by either side—in short, who fulfills the pattern we expect when we see his bright dewiness at the start. Not many of us need to go over once again the making of the Vietnamese quagmire, not after all the plays and films, not after the spate of books (preeminently Michael Herr's *Dispatches*), not after the war itself was brought into our rumpus rooms by TV. But essentially Gray's play does no more than retell that story.

Scardino, not previously an impressive actor, has been helped by the director, Carole Rothman, to give the most authentic, least consciously wistful performance of his that I've seen. Gunton has shown in *Evita* (as Perón) and elsewhere that he is highly competent. Here he is equally competent and also over-praised. Ask any actor whether he would rather play one big part, as Scardino does, or twenty vignettes—ranging from a tough U.S. press chief to a villager to a dragon-lady dictator to a bar girl, etc., etc.—and if he's sane, he'll jump at the twenty; because a) sketching is easier than painting if you have any talent at all, and b) sharply contrasted bits—which are easy for a professional—always score big with the groundlings. (Among whom I'd include most critics.) I come not to bury Gunton but to appraise him.

If Gray had more political and human insight, if he had employed his good idea to something more than basically facile repetition, he might have got something pertinent out of it. The Reporter is surely a metaphor for America, and the increasingly apparent fact is that—apart from the sufferings of many individual Americans—the country as a whole, in terms of political and human wisdom, learned very little indeed from Vietnam. But suppose that Gray had used a wise-guy reporter who encountered the whirl of brutalities and "Oriental inscrutability" presented by the Historical Event and who (as some did) beat the experience of the Event into the mind-shape that he had brought with him and that he took home with him. At least this would have made the play less of a dip into used theatrical-cinematic-fictional materials and would certainly have made it more ironically relevant to our present and our seeming future. As is, Gray was overly pleased with his one good idea and, figuratively, quit work there; the result is just another piece of ritual American self-flagellation, with more masochistic pleasure in it than perception.

Eminent Domain

(Saturday Review, June 1982)

Here it is again—the old enemy, mediocrity. It has always been with us in the theater, of course, but lately there seems to be a growing crusade, mounted by playwrights' festivals and conferences and foundations, to promote it. Naturally they don't call it mediocrity; it's called encouragement of talent. But look carefully at the work that they produce and publish and circulate and hail, and you can infer the motivating principles. Anything that is Not Bad is Good; anything that treats an American subject with first-hand knowledge deserves lenient judgment; anything that is sincere is sound.

In art the enemy of the best has never been the worst, it's always been the mediocre. The worst is naked; the mediocre is often prettily disguised. To encourage the mediocre is to make the theater unattractive to the better talents that might be drawn to it, and it's corruptive of taste in general. Just because a play is written in recognizable English and attempts to deal seriously with serious characters and themes is not enough reason for tears of joy. Crusade or no crusade, I can't see that our theater drastically needs more A. R. Gurneys and Lanford Wilsons.

A recent instance is Percy Granger, not a dreadful writer and not a cheap trifler but not a dramatist whose work, as yet, is worth seeing. And what's particularly discouraging is that his first full-length play to be seen in New York, *Eminent Domain*, has reached us with more prenatal care and obstetrics than Princess Diana's offspring will get. Better luck to the royal child. *Eminent Domain* was "first presented as a staged reading" at a playwrights conference, then was "further developed" in two different productions. Presumably it was also "further developed" in its Circle in the Square production. I wonder what it could have been when it started if, quadruply developed, it comes out so flaccid.

The leading characters are a middle-aged professor of English and his artist wife, so we know before we see it or its reviews that it's going to be called "literate." No playwright would deal with such characters unless he could deliver at least some semblance of donnish rhetoric and coy epigram. Granger can do that adequately enough. What he has failed to do, however, is to disclose any real reason for the play's existence.

The professor and wife are mutually courteous but physically estranged; she's a reformed drunk, he's a secret drinker. (*Who's Afraid of Virginia Woolf?*, twenty years later and fuzzier.) Their son, an only child, ran away at sixteen and now, eight years after, is a noted poet. A doctoral candidate, about the son's age, arrives to do research for a dissertation on the professor's son. (But what faculty would have sanctioned a dissertation on a poet so early in his career?) The young scholar comes just when the professor is awaiting a call from Brandeis confirming his appointment to their staff. It's not quite the Harvard post he would have liked; still it will get him out of the Midwest provinces (as he thinks them) where he has been so long.

Now all the above are ingredients for a possible play. But, in Granger's mittened hands, they remain disparate ingredients. No strong connection is made between the couple's troubles and their son's flight; no insight illuminates the father's jealousy (he sidles away from what has been written of the dissertation on his son); no revealing drama is crystallized between the ambitious young scholar and the declining older one. Lurking beneath these ingredients, teasing us until we tire of disappointment, are themes of cultural ambition and cultural corruption, a marriage caught between, and a child who fled his parents in order to surpass them. But none of this is fused, fired. The play is a collection of moderately engaging ideas; it has no center, no drive, no kind of enlargement. There's no reason why any reasonably intelligent, cultivated person should bother to see it.

But, says the mediocrity crusade, Granger is not a bad writer and therefore is a good one; and if we want the American drama to prosper, we must applaud not-bad writers. Include me out, as Sam Goldwyn is said to have said. I'll wait for the not-mediocre writers; and will hope that Granger may someday be among them.

Paul Austin directed as fluently as possible in the domestic interiors racked across the grotesque, racetrack playing space of Circle in the Square. Betty Miller gives lovely, resonant quietness to the wife. But, sorry though I am to say it, the career of Philip Bosco, who plays the professor, is suffering from inflation analagous to that inflicted on some playwrights. I often admired Bosco in the old Beaumont Theater days when he contributed acutely drawn supporting roles to a wide variety of plays. Lately he has been elevated beyond his powers, like a reliable opera *comprimario* bumped into leading roles. He simply could not supply the Plutonian power and magisterial humor for Undershaft in Shaw's *Major Barbara* or Tarleton in Shaw's *Misalliance*. In *Eminent Domain*, the demands are very much less, but his role is even bigger. Some actors have the resident strength to engage us for a whole evening; Bosco, skilled and likable though he is—intelligent, too—is not one of them. For innate strength, he substitutes—consciously? fearfully?—mere push.

'Master Harold' . . . and the boys

(July 1982)

Athol Fugard is both an actor and director and, so far in a busy writing career, has used that experience to create at least one play apparently destined to last: *Boesman and Lena*. He has gone on writing with no less fire but with considerably less art to keep before us the torments of his homeland, South Africa. Last year *A Lesson From Aloes* forecast its didactic demonstration in its title. Now he presents 'Master Harold' . . . and the boys; since the play concerns a white boy named Harold and two black men, the title is somewhat more iron-handed than ironic.

But 'Master Harold' is a better play than *Aloes*. Even though we're told truly at the end that "there's been a hell of a lot of teaching here today," even though this eighty-five minute play is some sixty-five minutes of preparation and twenty minutes of drama, those twenty minutes are unforgettable.

On a rainy afternoon in 1950, in a dingy tea room in Port Elizabeth, the two black servants, Sam and Willie, are cleaning up, preparing to leave, while Sam advises the duller Willie about the dance competition his friend has entered. Hally, the owners' son of about fifteen, comes in from high school for his lunch; learns that his mother, who runs the shop, is at the hospital to get his crippled drunk of a father, a patient there, and bring him home. This news dismays Hally who, in one of the contradictions that are the play's best assets, loves his father but feels closer to Sam, the wise black waiter, and doesn't want the closeness disturbed. Sam has long understood Hally's love/shame about his father and (another contradiction) has tried to compensate for what the boy was missing.

But it's transition time for Hally. He is leaving the liberties of childhood for the restrictions of maturity, among which in his country is rigid race separation. For Hally the transition is especially painful because of his affectionate past with Sam, more than with his father. Hally is so ashamed of his dread about his father's return that (another contradiction) he vents the shame venomously; he repeats his father's crude joke about a black man's behind. Sam calmly lowers his trousers to show him, and us, a black man's behind so that in future Hally will know what he's joking about. The Moment is near-biblical in its strange dignity. It's much more affecting than the less credible moment soon after, that is supposedly climactic; after a last grasp at Sam's wrist like a last grasp at boyhood, Hally (contradictorily) spits in Sam's face. The action desolates both of them—and Willie, too.

Hally leaves as what he wanted to become, Master Harold, but he leaves forlorn. Willie desperately puts a record on the juke box, and Sam sadly teaches him the foxtrot as the lights dim.

It's greatly moving. (Despite a heavy Fugardian touch: the juke box tune is, of all songs, "Little Man, You've Had a Busy Day.") But we've had to wait a long time for it, for the play really to begin. As in *Aloes*, Fugard doesn't dramatize from the start; he recites, in preparation for the drama to come. In part, this may be because he is obsessed with casts of three characters, sometimes two. If Hally's mother had been present at the start, or had come in, this would not only have eliminated some telephone dramaturgy—phone calls at key moments—it could have helped Fugard to begin dramatic tensions much earlier. And those tensions, growing throughout, could have moved to fulfill the fundamental theme of the play, now left unfulfilled; not race but fatherhood. Millions of boys in racially undisturbed countries choose surrogate fathers, often socially inferior, whom they have to abandon in time as Prince Hal did Falstaff. If Fugard had seen his play as an instance of a world phenomenon—here sorely exacerbated because of racism—'*Master Harold*' would have, as *Boesman* has, the force of the particular bursting into the universal, instead of remaining a localized instance of cruelty.

In this production, which moved from the Yale Repertory Theater to Broadway, Fugard directed the two black actors excellently. Zakes Mokae, an old Fugard hand, plays Sam with lovely gravity and wit, and with accomplished technique. (Mokae knows how to elongate words for emotional flavor without letting them sound distorted.) Danny Glover, the Willie, has a very difficult part and does it superbly. He is on stage throughout, has much less to say than the others, but must be "present" without mugging or distracting. This calls for quiet truth in an actor, which Glover has.

As for the white boy, it's odd that, though Fugard misses no chance in interviews to call the role autobiographical, it's the one place where his direction is askew. Hally is supposed to be exceptionally bright, yet he sounds and behaves like Smike in the RSC *Nicholas Nickleby*—crabbed, whiny, mentally fogged. The trouble may be that Fugard cast a young man, Lonny Price, in the part instead of a youth, and Price spends much energy trying, clumsily, to seem adolescent.

The Hothouse

(July 1982)

All good dramatists write well for actors, but some do it better than others—usually those who have been actors themselves. Skimming over such early actor-dramatists as Aeschylus, Shakespeare, and Molière, we come to Harold Pinter; and Pinter, in that one aspect of writing for actors, takes a back seat to none of them. The acting style that he knows is, naturally, of his era: understatement, pause, incantation of the commonplace to frightening or funny effect, laconicism occasionally varied with jets of rhetoric. Pinter's writing style is composed, essentially, of what modern actors can *do*.

He wrote *The Hothouse* in 1958, following eight years' experience on the stage, after he had written some short plays and his first long play, *The Birthday Party*. He thought *The Hothouse* unsatisfactory and put it away; in 1979 he changed his mind—correctly, I think. If it's not top Pinter, still it's good luck to have it. He touched up a few lines and directed the play in London, where I saw it. This year Adrian Hall did it at his Trinity Square Repertory Company in Providence, and that production was brought to New York.

Let's note—really to get these matters out of the way—that *The Hothouse* is set in a government mental institution, that we see only the staff, the chief, and some assistants, and that their lives proceed in rivalries and desires unrelated to the patients' sufferings. Let's note, too, that the play can be viewed as a parable of concealed irrationality versus explicit irrationality, statism versus individualism, with plentiful et ceteras. What the play basically is about is a young theater animal showing how well he knows his magical habitat.

This is far from saying that the play is an empty exercise. Early Verdi isn't empty because what we remember from it is exuberant melodic line rather than the musicalized character of the later work. Yet sheer theatrical wizardry is what marks *The Hothouse* before it's two minutes along: we know we are in the hands of a writer who can set moods and evoke laughs simply by jeweler-like precision, done deadpan. (At one point a young man, strapped to a chair, is being questioned over a loudspeaker. A voice drones: "Are you virgo intacta?" The man says: "Yes. I am, actually. I'll make no secret of it." The voice drones on: "Have you always been virgo intacta?")

The play climaxes with an inmates' riot, and a last scene attributes it to the chief, for reasons not supported by earlier dialogue. That omission seems to me deliberate, already typical of the Pinter who later said, "I do so hate the becauses of drama." He is much more concerned with effects; and he makes those effects, sequentially but not consequentially, out of stage materials. Pinter has changed through the years; later plays, beginning with his masterpieces *The Homecoming* and *Old Times*, have dealt increasingly with the depth-bombs of erotics and with time. In *The Hothouse* he is still exulting in his newly realized abilities to conjure with theatrical powers more than he is probing theme or character.

Two elements in this production seemed to me superior to the London performance: George Martin's blustering but shrewd chief and Eugene Lee's metallic institutional set, full of wire-mesh partitions and clanging doors. Adrian Hall directed acutely and wittily.

Nine

(July 1982)

Soon after *Dreamgirls* arrives *Nine*, which is much closer to Michael Bennett's show than to Fellini's masterly *8½*, its remote source. This is to say that in *Nine*, as in *Dreamgirls*, what stands out is neither the book nor the score but the theatrical event made by the director, designers, and cast. The show's pleasures, which are almost all in the first of the two acts, come from the imagination of the director, Tommy Tune, from the pow performers, from the scene and lighting designs by Lawrence Miller and Marcia Madeira, who worked with Tune on *Cloud Nine*, and from the sensational costumes by William Ivey Long.

Anyone who doesn't know *8½* may have trouble figuring out what's happening in the story; anyone who does know *8½* will soon stop trying and will settle, or not settle, for the remnants that have been retained. Fellini grappled poetically with the problem of the contemporary artist's continuing nourishment, the struggle to sustain a creative career in our time (also the subject of Antonioni's *La Notte*); and Fellini put this (his?) mid-life crisis right in the middle of the different time-streams that all of us bear constantly within us—the present moment, the remembered past, dream, and daydream. These swirl around his film-director protagonist with a cinematic-theatrical virtuosity that, by its very brilliance, underscores the artist's desperate hunger for a core, a theme. The cast for a new film has been assembled; the producer is harassing the director, Guido; and Guido, for all his virtuosity, cannot come up with a usable story idea.

These complexities are not only missing from Arthur Kopit's book for *Nine*, the shreds of the film that he has retained—like a nine-year-old Guido who runs around his mature self—are only a sentimentalized mockery of a fine art work. Tune has apparently realized that Kopit couldn't reproduce the exquisite texture of Fellini, including its marvelously apt show-biz solution; so Tune has settled for just enough mock-Fellini to serve as scaffolding for an ingeniously presented program of songs and dances.

Miller's set is some tiers of large black-and-white cubes, possibly suggested by the tiles of Guido's immense bathroom in the film, plus a runway around the orchestra pit. On these cubes sit, at various times, some or all of the women in Guido's life. Even the producer is here made a woman. Guido, played by Raul Julia, is the one man in the cast; he is on stage throughout, "conducting" his women in song or wryly surrendering the stage to them. The source for this production idea is apparently the celebrated "harem" sequence in 8½ where Guido fantasizes that all the women of his life, those he has had and those he has only longed for, are living with him and competing for his favors. Tune cleverly exploits this harem-sultan situation, though he takes it out of Guido's fantasy and makes it relatively realistic, therefore ironic. In itself, considered quite separately from Fellini, it makes a good gimmick for a musical. The continuous presence of Guido and, as needed, his cavalcade of women provides chances for musical numbers, some of which are well-engineered showstoppers.

Tune's choreography is not innovative, it's the traditional *in excelsis*; he does little that we haven't seen before, he just does it with more brightness and excitement. The songs by Maury Yeston, predictably well orchestrated by Jonathan Tunick, are pleasant, though they are the traditional not quite in *in excelsis*. Outstanding among the gifted group of women are Liliane Montevecchi, Guido's producer (with the longest feather boa in captivity), Karen Akers, his wife, and Shelly Burch, his dream girl. Julia himself is not a show-stopper. He has ease but little command and less singing voice.

The first act is black and white, like 8½. Long's costumes, probably inspired by the miraculously baroque clothes that Piero Gherardi designed for the film, are fine enough to honor the art that inspired them. But when color enters the costumes in Act Two, the show begins to get colorless, the songs and production texture get thinner, and it all ends drab.

Present Laughter

(August 1982)

The last thing that George C. Scott needs to be told is that his role in Noel Coward's *Present Laughter* is "wrong" for him. That's precisely why he chose it —it's what actors call a "stretch." On balance he comes off much better than as Willy Loman in *Death of a Salesman*, which he did in 1975 at the same theater, Circle in the Square. Miller might seem closer to him than Coward, but Scott had a looser grip on Willy than on the slick London actor-idol of this fragile comedy.

Present Laughter, which was first done in 1942 with the author in the lead, is lesser Coward, therefore belongs with the greater portion of his output. What is admirable about Coward, and is obscured by his image as a butterfly, is that he was a prodigious worker—twenty-seven plays, almost 300 songs, some screenplays, some volumes of short stories and autobiography, a novel, all in addition to his numberless performances. Some of his plays in the early 1920s, like *The Vortex* and *Fallen Angels*, were thought wildly radical at the time and were showered with the sorts of abuse that had greeted Ibsen and Strindberg. ("Disgusting, "degrading," "obscene," and so on.) T. E. Lawrence, of all people, called him "a hasty kind of genius." Today, nine years after Coward's death but much longer than that since his career peaked, perspective lets us separate the wheat from the chaffing. Many of the songs still charm, and at least two of the plays, *Hay Fever* and *Blithe Spirit* seem destined to twinkle for an eon or two in the comic firmament.

Not *Present Laughter*. It's a faded patchwork, centering on the amorous traffic in the home of a middle-aged, highly successful "romantic comedian" just before he leaves on a tour of Africa. Coward is never not theatrical, but sometimes he's not anything else. Much of the characterization, structure, and dialogue here seems like paste-ups of carbon copies. The wit, some of which inevitably *is* witty, is mostly built on elaborate articulateness about trifles, and occasionally descends into revue-sketch parody of himself. When the actor returns a comb he has borrowed to a woman who insists on having it back, he says: "Here's your sordid little comb." Bankruptcy.

Scott, for his own reasons, decided to do just about the last sort of play one would expect of him, a Coward comedy. He chose a star vehicle, no real competition from any other role, and one that was a beat off the beaten Coward track. What's pleasantly surprising is that, gauzy though the play is, remote as it is from Scott's temperamental core, the evening holds up moderately well, because of his acting, despite his own direction of the play, and because of Marjorie Bradley Kellogg's set.

Kellogg has filled the Circle oval with chromium-glass-plush delight that seems to tinkle like the best Coward chit-chat even before the play begins. Then, after the usual ground-laying scene by others, in comes Scott in dressing gown, sounding like a hoarse basso with tenor ambitions, brimful of conviction about everything he does and says, a conviction that is genuinely comic. By taking the minor contretemps and the more discomfiting crises with equal gravity and poise, he makes them funny. His comic touch comes as no surprise to those who saw him on Broadway in *Sly Fox* or in such films as *Dr. Strangelove* and *The Flim Flam Man*, but they were different kettles of fish. *Present Laughter* is a cup of English high tea, and without pushing the Mayfair accent too far, Scott pushes his pot-bellied self in and out of tangles like a self-amused harmless egomaniac.

The rest of the cast is both supporting and non-supporting. Dana Ivey, the loyal secretary, and Elizabeth Hubbard, the equally loyal ex-wife, are neatly affecting. Christine Lahti, as a *femme fatale*, is voluptuously vapid. And Director Scott should (but won't) be ashamed of what he did with the roles of the Swedish housekeeper and the young aspiring playwright. Just to hear the labels is to know the roles, which is what Coward wanted, but Scott has put these two actors through a lot of incredible antics, trying to keep laughter present in *Present Laughter*.

Still, Scott's performance is good enough to make the occasion fundamentally sad. He energizes a stage so easily, he has such three-cushion-billiard skill with fine points, that he makes us wonder what in heaven's name he is doing with his life. Where are the theater and film careers that this gigantic talent-cum-ego ought to have? How happy we could be to see him in this rhinestone gem if we knew it was an interlude between, say, *King Lear* and a serious film.

Plenty

(Saturday Review, March 1983)

David Hare, the British dramatist, spoke at Cambridge University in March 1978, a month before his play *Plenty* opened in London. Said Hare: "I would suggest to you crudely that one of the reasons for the theater's possible authority, and for its recent general drift toward politics, is its unique suitability to displaying an age in which men's ideals and men's practice bear no relation to each other." *Plenty* then substantiated Hare's suggestion—and not "crudely" either. It was produced at the National, directed by the author with Kate Nelligan in the leading role, and both the play and the actress won praise and prizes. Four years later the play reached New York—at the Public Theater off Broadway, where I saw it—with Hare again directing, Nelligan again in the leading role, and the reception again warm. Now it has moved to Broadway.

A pleasant change: I can report that there's nothing puzzling about its reception. What a pungent, deft, engrossing play it is. If ultimately unsatisfying, still from the very first minutes it's highly intelligent and extraordinarily skillful. And from those first minutes it's clear that *Plenty* is about scarcity—scarcity of convictions in the midst of material plenty. I can't recall an age when, in Hare's terms above, men's ideals and men's practice *have* borne much relation to each other, but he has chosen an age in which the disparity between ideals and practice was particularly painful, and he has sliced to the center of it with a keen theatrical scalpel.

The protagonist is Susan Traherne who, at the age of seventeen, was in British Intelligence, serving in occupied France during the Second War. But we first meet her in 1962, in the first of the play's twelve scenes, after her mind and spirit have been battered by what has happened to her since the war. Thus Hare insures the acrid tone under Scene Two when we move back nineteen years to wartime France, where Susan is aiding a British agent who has just landed by parachute, a Susan who is clear-headed, courageously frightened, tensely radiant with the pleasure of being useful and used.

The rest of the play journeys ahead to 1962, dramatizing with bitterness and bitter wit how Susan came to be the disturbed, desperate woman that she is. The very last scene returns to France, Susan on a hilltop with a French farmer on the day of liberation in 1944. Joyfully she says, "There will be days and days and days like this," the last line of a play that has just blackly contradicted this last line.

We have seen Susan move on a descending pilgrimage, through an affair with a former Intelligence colleague which was apparently an attempt to keep in touch with a companion of the war days; through an affair with a Foreign Office attaché that turns into a strained marriage; through a cool (and unsuccessful) arrangement with another man to father a child; and, possibly trying to sublimate frustration about this failure, through a sorry attempt with a Foreign Office chief to improve her husband's career. (The theme of the Foreign Office runs through the play like the ghost of former British power; also, the very idea of service, bureaucratic though it may be, has a grip on Susan's sensibility. The one heroic character in the play is a former British ambassador who resigns in disgust over British behavior at Suez in 1956 and who dies soon after.)

Susan's own life, in advertising before marriage and in frustrating idleness afterward, unravels; brings her close to mental collapse. Because of her interference at the Foreign Office, her husband has been forced to leave the government; he has gone into insurance, is doing all right, is still devoted. But her postwar disappointments in herself and in the world finally boil up into quarrels between the pair. When she fulminates against the clutter and weight of their material possessions, their plenty, and turns on him, he fights back: "Which is the braver? To live as I do? Or never, ever to face life like you? . . . You claim to be protecting some personal ideal, always at a cost of almost infinite pain to everyone around you." The pain she causes, including her own, is very clear. Her lack of bravery is more complicated.

It's possible to see Susan's postwar disintegration as the penalty for facile idealism. It's also possible to see it as merely pettish, a childish demand that the world give her what she wants. (Hare counterpoises Susan with a friend named

Alice whose life wobbles a bit at the start but who rights herself with socially contributory work.) And it's also possible to see Susan as a congenital high-speed neurotic whose condition was camouflaged by the excitement of war, then revealed by the humdrum dailiness of peace. For me, the truth about Susan lies in a different complexity, intrinsic and extrinsic, a complexity that combines a view of Susan herself with a view of the play that she inhabits, along with a view of its author.

One conflict, the intrinsic one, is between Susan's expectations of change in her country, because of the capacity for sacrifice shown in the war, and what actually did happen there after the war: the quick slouch back into pre-war materialism. But, in longer view—which is where dissatisfaction with the play begins—there is also a conflict within the overall entity of *Plenty*: a conflict between Hare's writing and structure, which are astringent and precise and incisively unsentimental, and the sentimental assumption that life *would* be exalted by the war experience. When has that ever happened after a war? (The fabric of the play implies that Hare himself shares Susan's expectation and disappointment. The one small indication to the contrary is the French farmer's behavior on the day of liberation; he dourly expects no more from the future than the drudgery he has known in the past.)

And then, in even longer view, there's a stranger conflict, caused by what is left out of the play. What is missing, the lack that keeps *Plenty* from being first-rate, is political belief. In his Cambridge talk, Hare mentioned the [British] theater's "recent general drift toward politics." Hare, like many of the best British dramatists of his generation, is a political radical; *Plenty* is a political play with the politics left out. The audience has to do some heavy inferring to perceive that the lost chance for change through radical politics is central in the morass of Susan's disappointments. This implication is left much too faint in the play. Clausewitz said that war is the continuation of politics by other means; *Plenty* would be even better than it is, would be complete, if it showed Susan realizing the reverse of Clausewitz's dictum—that peace is a means of continuing the politics that were heightened by war. Even though her political struggle had failed, it would have taken her collapse deeper than self-centeredness and would have put the thematic base of the play more closely in key with the acerbic dialogue.

I offer this as dramatic criticism, not as argument for a politics that I don't support anyway. I'm not calling for propaganda, blatant or subtle. I suggest only that Hare, the radical artist, could have served his *art* better: not by giving us dogmatic answers but by embracing profounder questions. As *Plenty* is now, Susan's agon corrodes into neurosis. Too long after the play is over, we are left to deduce that Hare might have been saying: "Don't you see? If Susan had believed in social change through politics, had worked for it—whether or not the change had come about—she would have escaped the postwar letdown. Her life would have stayed at the 1944 pitch."

This is simply not dramatized for us. But what Hare does give us, he handles with feline grace, economy, hauteur. And he has directed with a discriminating eye and with a musician's ear for inflection and pause. The setting by John Gunter is excellent: a huge high room with shadowy murals—a hall in a Stately Home—within which various bits of mundane England are set and lighted.

Kate Nelligan is superb. I had seen her previously only in a silly suspense film, *Eye of the Needle*, and the *Thérèse Raquin* TV series shown on PBS, in which she was little more than luscious. Stature, fire, command, and irony—all these were wonderful surprises in her performance here. Futures are hard to calculate in our flaky theater/film world, but hers could be brilliant.

As her husband, Edward Herrmann does the best work of his that I've seen. His control of character, like his English accent, slips slightly, but he creates a man of understated strength and devotion. Ellen Parker as Alice, George Martin as the disgusted ambassador, Daniel Gerroll as the failed procreator, and Bill Moor as the Foreign Office chief, all do much to keep the performance springy, tight, electric. In fact they are all so good that they leave us with a final paradox: their vivid acting, made possible by the play's pithy writing and lithe structure, helps to reveal the play's basic thematic gap.

True West / The Tooth of Crime

(Saturday Review, April/May 1983)

Two recent New York productions of Sam Shepard plays were so good that they were not only gratifying in themselves, they illuminated elements in the whole Shepard career. Those elements compose his uniqueness. Now forty years old, he has written some forty plays since 1964, short and long, in differing forms and voices, with differing artistic success but always with fire and self; yet, though he is internationally known and is a Pulitzer laureate, he has never been produced on Broadway. This speaks to his maverick quality. He has acted on stage and screen—his latest picture is *Frances*—and his lean powerful presence would probably make him a film star if he had the time and interest. His acting talent helps explain his theatrical fluency. And he is an accomplished jazz and rock composer/performer, abilities that are almost always manifest in the diction and rhythms of his writing.

Shepard's *True West* had its first Manhattan production in 1981 at the Public Theater amidst a publicized dispute between the author and the producer, Joseph Papp. This later production is perceptibly better than the first. It was directed by Gary Sinise with fair competence, and Sinise also plays, somewhat threadily, one of the two leading roles, a screenwriter named Austin, in his early thirties, who is slogging away at a script for a producer. Austin is serious, married (though alone at the moment), and goal-targeted. His older brother, Lee, played with scary self-appreciated menace by John Malkovich, breaks in on his solitude. Lee is his brother's mirror-image, feral, shrewd, a petty thief and gambler. Austin is combining his work with house-sitting for his vacationing mother, in her home about forty miles east of Los Angeles, which is where Lee turns up unexpectedly. Thus these contrasting brothers meet, figuratively, within the mother's embrace, in her tidy kitchen and breakfast nook. Their father, never seen but often mentioned, is apparently her opposite, an unruly drunk much like the father who *is* seen in Shepard's *Curse of the Starving Class.*

Contrasting parents produced contrasting sons, but the play proceeds to dramatize the volatility of the difference between Austin and Lee, to suggest that they are opposing but matching components of one human nature. Lee's intrusion, sniffing out money possibilities and thievery possibilities, unsettles Austin's balanced life, and leads to their reversal of roles. Austin's producer, who comes in for a time, is persuaded, almost bullied, by Lee into taking on a Western story that Lee has cooked up, a true Western. (What, Shepard implies, would this producer of synthetics know of the true West?) Austin is now supposed to write the script of Lee's story, but in drunken disgust he goes out to steal while Lee is left to slam the typewriter.

The drama is brought to a head, but not resolved, by the sudden return of their mother. The play ends with the two brothers, stripped to primitivism by their conflict, tensely facing each other, with the next move—let alone the conclusion—in dangerous doubt. Through much of its being, *True West* is like a contemporary version of Tom Sawyer and Huck Finn, older of course and wised up, one from a neat life and the other from a disorderly world, except that this Tom and this Huck are locked in a tension of possible interchange, are imprisoned by brotherhood, rather than the edges of a raft, are barreling toward confrontation, not sailing to adventure.

Confrontation of the two men, linked but hostile, is also the essence of *The Tooth of Crime* (first produced in 1972). Vividly, violently, yet subtly directed by George Ferencz, this new production originated at the Syracuse Stage in upstate New York and was brought to the La Mama E.T.C. Off-Broadway. The two-tiered setting by Bill Stabile concealed a rock band in the shadows of the bottom half, while the action took place on a slanting platform above, furnished only with a small sofa and lighted with intense theatricalilty by Paul Mathiesen.

Ray Wise, one of America's as-yet unrecognized acting treasures, played and sang Hoss, an aging rock star, living in apprehensive and guarded isolation, fearful that his reign is on the wane. His challenger is a rock singer called Crow, played and sung by Stephen Mellor in a mode to match the name, except that his singing didn't croak. Hoss learns that Crow is coming to his stronghold, orders that the younger man be admitted, and challenges him to a "duel" to settle supremacy. The weapons are rock songs and tirades in rock language, but the contest is classical: Hector versus Ajax, two medieval knightly champions settling a war. And beneath these classical implications is the image of two king stags battling for a forest realm.

Shepard has never sensed better the rhetorical possibilites in the vernacular, has never written more pungently than in this play, that duel. Savagely, Hoss attacks the weakened Crow:

> You a blind minstrel with a phoney shuffle. You got a wound gapin' 'tween the chords and the pickin'. Chuck Berry can't even mend you up. You doin' a pantomime in the eye of a hurricane. Ain't even got the sense to signal for help. You lost the barrelhouse, you lost the honkey-tonk. You lost your feelings in a suburban country club the first time they ask you to play "Risin' River Blues" for the debutante ball. You ripped your own self off and now all you got is yo' poison to call yo' gift.

It's the modern counterpart of the frontiersman's invective, those wild furry arias that Mark Twain loved. Despite this outburst and more, Hoss finally loses his crown. Power is fickle: it moves from one man to another in Shepard plays. *The Tooth of Crime* (I've never understood the title) ends with the victorious Crow singing "Rollin' Down," one of the eight songs Shepard wrote for the play.

Shepard overflows with gifts, and the penalty—there's always a penalty—is that they sometimes sweep him along without permitting him to refine his work. Not all of his plays are as fulfilled as these two. Sometimes he can grasp so eagerly at myth that he fumbles it, as in *Buried Child*, his Pulitzer play. Sometimes he starts a play with a dam-burst of energy, like *Curse of the Starving Class*, then falters halfway along, and pulls out sweaty pop devices to see him through. These potentially fine plays, and some others, are waiting for Shepard really to finish them some day. But fundamentally his work never lies limp, never imitates, never does less than mock most contemporary playwriting just by showing what the theater can be.

Shepard's imagination feeds on the fast-food data of his America, the juke, the jive, the comic-book fantasies, the movie mystique, and, especially, the car mystique. Automobiles are like banners in his plays. (When Hoss hears that Crow is approaching, he asks, "What's he drivin'?" When his aide replies, "A '58 black Impala, fuel injected, bored and stroked, full blown Vet underneath," Hoss says, "I'm gonna like this dude. O.K. let him through.") But also Shepard hates that very same America because it is rolling over his "true West." With the language of his day raised to bardic heights, he does battle against it, on the oldest of our battlegrounds, the clash between innocence and use, the frontier and the city. The battle may be between farmers and real estate developers as in *Curse of the Starving Class*, between job-holding and instinctual life as in *True West*, but it is this mythical West, this sustaining West, that Shepard is struggling to preserve from the onward roll of the cement mixers.

This obsessive theme puts Shepard in a great American line. From Cooper's Natty Bumppo to Faulkner's Isaac McCaslin pursuing the bear—and since— our best writers have sought out whatever danger was left in their time and have cherished it. I don't equate Shepard with his predecessors, but I do see him clearly as their scion. Once (he says, as they said) this was a New World, a dream of horizons. Must it wither at the heart just because it is physically crowding up? Must it become like the Old World, just because so much of the Old World is becoming like us?

With imperfect artistry but with art nonetheless fierce, Shepard is refusing merely to mourn. He mourns, all right, but he also fights.

Sore Throats

(Saturday Review, July/August 1983)

Howard Brenton's Sore Throats, the strongest play about sex and marriage since Pinter's Old Times, had its American première in April at the Repertory Theater of St. Louis. I had seen its first production in 1979 at the Royal Shakespeare Company's smaller London theater, the Warehouse, and had been overwhelmed. Productions followed in Denmark and Australia and I waited impatiently for a production here, but in the intervening two years all that happened in this country was the publication of the play in the Spring 1981 issue of Theater, the magazine of the Yale School of Drama. Then, last December, Sore Throats was given a public reading by a professional cast at a SoHo café in New York. I went to that reading and was smitten again by the play's power. When the St. Louis production was announced, I hastened to see it. An exceptionally fine performance, in the Rep's Studio Theater, convinced me yet again of the importance of Brenton's small-scale, large-scope play.

The title comes from Brecht:

> I have heard that lovemaking can give you a swollen throat. I don't want one. But the swing-boats [amusement-park rides], I have heard, can give you a swollen throat, too. So I shan't be able to avoid it.

Yet Brecht, whose influence is marked in much of Brenton's work, is not his model here. Sore Throats is, as its subtitle says, "an intimate play," about the relations between a man and a woman. With only three characters and one simple set, it plunges into the remotest secrets that men and women try to keep from themselves, let alone one another. It grows directly from the line of venturous psychosexual plays that flourished in Europe in the nineteenth century and that was thrust into our century by Strindberg.

Sore Throats is thus an anomaly for Brenton. Most of his work has been fiercely political. Now forty, he is one of a coeval group of vigorously radical British playwrights that includes David Hare, the author of Plenty, with whom in fact Brenton once collaborated. Since his Cambridge days, he has been pouring out plays, short and long, that imaginatively dramatize his social concerns. He is the son of a policeman who, after twenty-five years in uniform, became a Methodist minister. Without neatly tagging Brenton genetically, one can see recurrent conflicts between force and spirit in his work. Many of his characters are policemen, including the man in *Sore Throats*, and he often opposes worldly authority to inner authority. His first long play, *Revenge*, done at the Royal Court in 1969, is about a criminal and detective who are sworn enemies, both of them played by the same actor: it ends in a quasi-mystical union. One of his most recent plays, *The Romans in Britain*, done at the National in 1980, interweaves scenes of Caesar's invasion (uniforms and force again) with scenes of present-day Ulster troubles (inseparable from religious connotations.) For the National, Brenton has also written new versions of Brecht's *Galileo* and Büchner's *Danton's Death*, two plays that center on the conflict between government and the individual will. *Sore Throats* is not such a play, not political except in the spacious sense that we are all affected by the political systems under which we live.

Yet it *is* about a conflict between world and spirit. I'll describe *Sore Throats* more fully than is usual in a review because a mere summary of the action could be uniquely misleading. Only a sampling of its texture can suggest the extraordinary quality of its characterization, structure, and vernacular imagery: and can show that, beneath the language and the action, both of which are often brutal, is a drama of exquisite compassion.

The play is in two acts. Jack, a London policeman of forty-five, has lately divorced Judy, thirty-nine, to live with a younger woman. Seized with remorse when he left his wife, he had written her a letter giving her full title to their house. He has since had more sober, pragmatic thoughts on the matter; he wants half the money from the sale of the house to help him start a new life with his new girl. Now, in Act One, he has come, in uniform, to the flat that Judy has just rented, to get her signature on an agreement granting him half the proceeds from the house. Judy, sitting on the floor with the bottle of wine that is the flat's only furnishing, starts to speak of what she remembers when she sees him, of the failed sex betweeen them, torments sparked by her imaginings about his sexual behavior with his new girl.

So, from the start, knives flash between Judy and Jack, as they slash at each other and even at themselves. What they cut loose are the demons that entangle love and sex with ego and money, that turn homes into smoldering battlefields. As those knives reveal, marriage may bring union but it also brings rivalries, along with stratagems to conceal the rivalries. Even a marriage begun in reason implies some expectation of male dominance, in the minds of women conditioned by centuries of dominance. Husbands, often the best of husbands, know of that expectation, resent it, then sometimes fulfill it; to a degree, they do so vindictively.

Money, the persistent nag of money needs, runs underneath all these rivalries and constrictions. Even before Judy learns why Jack has come, she fantasizes about what she will do with her windfall from the house, fantasies in which the money that she has "earned" by living with a man will bring her revenge on a man.

> I am thinking of using this money to have an operation. I would like bits of ferocious animals grafted onto me. Adders' heads for breasts? Nipples that suck, rather than get sucked? . . . A tiger's head for a womb? . . . Won't I be a nice surprise for middle-aged men, cruising in cars.

Jack, not naively and not slyly, still hopes for friendship between them. He has found some tenderness in life, and Judy's fantasies, her bitterness, touch him with concern. ("You can't live on pain all the time.") But he works around to what their marriage had become, why he had needed escape and a new woman, and how feeling had been deadened by the press of daily obligation:

> When all you want is a bit of tenderness . . . why, in marriage . . . do you end up talking about the insulation in the loft all the time? . . . In the last stages of my divorce, I had a bit of a fantasy. One night, driven mad by the mill of marriage and sex, I saw myself discovered by a fellow-officer, outside a Trustees Savings Bank, my trousers and my Y-fronts down . . . with my cock jammed in a twenty-four-hour cash dispensing machine.

This terrible nightmare, an epitome of the inevitable grittiness underlying even the warmest impulses to marriage, brings him to a plaintive coda:

> . . . You've got to feel free. That you do things freely. Or one thing, the best thing. ·Love. Even if you're a policeman, you've got to feel that!

But all Judy can remember at the moment is that she found the young woman's panties "in the trouser pocket of your second best uniform."

Jack moves to the point of his visit, the agreement about the money. Judy laughs. She says that he and the young woman can "live off each other." Then she cries. "Not for our marriage. I'm crying for me. Me! Me!" She recalls what *her* past was like, what the marriage had come to mean to her.

> You put me in that house. Or my mother put me in that house. Or I put me in that house. But put I was.

Sitting now on the floor of this bare flat, she says:

> I sat alone in the living-room every morning, having my coffee . . . Listening for something. But what? . . . There must be so many women in the city alone in rooms on afternoons. Listening, even beginning to count their own breaths.

Jack doesn't really hear her any more than she really hears him. In his mind is the vision that has brought him to her flat, "a big country. A lot of light."

Canada is where he wants to go with his girl. For that, he wants half the money from the house. Judy's refusal to sign the paper begins to drive him frantic. Then the drama of paradox bursts on him. Thinking of *tenderness*, of his new chance for tenderness, he hits Judy. In the mouth.

Contradictions continue to tear at him. With some wine dabbed on his handkerchief, he helps her wipe off the blood. Calmly, she remembers and re-counts every time he hit her in their married life. She ends, pointedly, with the blow we have just seen. He knows what she is telling him. "For Jesus' sake," he says, "for some fucking sake, I'm in hell. Give me the money."

He punches her, and she falls. He takes out the legal paper. She starts to crawl away. He grabs her ankle. He kicks her in the stomach. Again. She is still refusing. He steps on her head.

All the while, remember, he is in uniform. All the while, he is a visible figure of order roweled with buried disorder.

> Is it the money? [He mutters:] Can't be money. Money can't make me boot in a woman lying on the floor, pissing in my pants the while, hating myself.

In pain, groggy, virtually prone, Judy signs the paper, ceding him half the money. "Whoopee," says Jack. He leaves weeping.

Silence for a moment, as she catches her breath; indeed, as we catch ours. What we have seen is so naked, so ripped open, so disclosing of *our* possible buried connections to what we have just seen, that we need the moment—to sit and tremble.

After she can pull herself upright, after she can see again, Judy reads aloud a letter that Jack brought her from their son, who is in Africa. The letter describes a harsh punishment for theft that the boy has witnessed, a punishment on which the thief had insisted. Then Sally comes into the flat, twenty-three, presumably not much older than Judy's son. Sally is here in answer to Judy's advertisement for someone to share the place. The younger woman is sharp, experienced, alert; she quickly scents the trouble in the air. Soon she says, "You open a door, any door. And you find yourself in an abattoir."

Judy, stupefied into immediate confidence, responding to the mere presence of another woman, tells Sally what has just happened. Jack returns. He has left his penknife, with which, in their quarreling, he had taunted Judy to do herself injury. There's an altercation with this stranger, and Sally, angered by what she has already been told of him, hits him with her bag. A boil on the back of his neck bursts; he had been en route to a hospital to have it lanced. He faints with the pain. Judy finds the legal paper in his pocket. He recovers, dazed, sees the paper in Judy's hands, and watches her tear it up. Growling a foul word at both the women, he staggers out. Judy and Sally are left with each other. Sally decides to stay and share.

Scorchingly eruptive, seemingly at the mercy of characters' outbursts, Act

One is nonetheless consummately crafted. It achieves the optimum: it leaves us wanting to know what will happen with no idea of what that will be.

If Act One resembles the Strindberg of scathing marital antagonisms, Act Two, which takes place about a year later, is like the Strindberg of symbol and dream. The difference in tone between the two acts suggests cause and effect, launch and flight.

Act Two opens in darkness. We hear Judy and Sally come in, sounding a bit drunk, giggling about the boy they expect to be waiting in the dark: thief and lover. At last the lights come on; no one else is there. The room is not really furnished, it is strewn—with cushions, lamps, unwashed dishes, empty bottles, trash. The bare stage of Act One, fitting for the starkness of what happened there, is now littered with detritus of sloth and fantasy. Says Judy gleefully—defiantly?—"I wanted to get away from domesticity."

Sally soon begins what is almost a long aria, about the boy who might have been waiting for them there. Remembering the many boys who have been in the flat during the past year, she imagines this visitor in every detail; she finishes with a graphic description of how she and Judy will sexually drain this imaginary boy. That very description seems to expose the way they have been living, straining after pleasures, and she ends somewhat wearily, glimpsing futility. "Yes," she says, "it's very dodgy, the search for ecstasy. No wonder millions settle for a nice cup of tea."

Judy has withdrawn her remaining money from the bank, in cash. It's in a large plastic bag. Now she pours the banknotes on the floor. The two women, who have made a wild trip to America, who have been flinging wildly with boys and men, actually have been trying to discover what their freedom amounts to, after one is free of marriage, the other free both from work and the usual dating game. Now, as the money begins to dwindle, they wonder what is ahead. Will Sally go back to her phone-answering job? Perhaps. She pictures it vividly. But Judy will not go back, not "to that front room. In the back of my mind, like a ghost, I am still there. Drinking coffee, listening to the rain drip in the hedge." She contemplates destroying the banknotes, as if to prevent her return to safe torpor. She even plays with the idea of stealing to live.

Into this mélange of dream and desperation, this muzzy liberty, steps Jack, out of the rain. In civilian clothes, with a well-covered infant's carry cot. "The door was open," he says apologetically. Judy stares silently. Sally utters an obscenity.

Jack puts down the carry cot carefully, fusses to make sure it's out of any draft, then begins to speak: quietly, piteously. He tells the story of the child's birth after a car accident in a remote part of the Canadian countryside with no one but himself to assist his girlfriend. Balanced against Sally's aria about the frenetic quest for pleasure, Jack's aria is a testimony to change, to regeneration. As in the first act, Brenton gives the man an agony that accompanies the even greater agony he has caused a woman: in this case, the childbirth after the accident.

At the finish, Jack admits that his girl later went off with another man. Judy, not much moved, mocks his paternal tone. She asks to see the baby. He refuses. A tussle. The carry cot goes flying across the room. A sudden freeze of horror. Sally turns over the carry cot—and takes out two bricks wrapped in blankets. "No baby," she says.

Jack says defenselessly, "The birth was real." His girl took the baby when she left. Now, for the first time, Judy is touched. "Jack, what are you doing stumbling around the London streets, with a carry cot full of bricks?" He says that, since he couldn't have his daughter, he "nicked a few of her things." Bereft, broken, he wonders: "Why can't men have wombs, breasts, the works." Sally replies, "Want the whole world, do you, mister?"

He wants *something*—from Judy. Embarrassed, he whispers in her ear. She is hushed by what he says; then she repeats it to Sally. "He says he wants to come between my breasts." It is Peer Gynt returned, from his long wanderings, to Solveig ("My mother! My wife! . . . O hide me in your love!"), except that this present-day Peer wants the mother-wife in more than poetic phrase.

Still somewhat hushed by the frankness of Jack's appeal, by his condition, all Judy can do is suggest a cup of tea, at which they all laugh. Then she recovers and starts tearing up the banknotes. Her action parallels the tearing of the agreement at the end of Act One, the agreement that would have taken away half of that money.

Jack begs for a few pounds. She keeps tearing. Sally asks, laughing, "What are you going to do? Work?"

Judy strikes a match. She says, "I am going to be fucked, happy, and free." She looks from the match to the money. Blackout.

That last line, blunt though it is, expresses an almost Athenian ideal. The whole play surges forward, through its wrenchings and fantasies and disappointments, with that ideal implicit until, at the last, it is spoken. The play ends with a question fixed by that ideal, fixed for us as it is for these people: after we see the chasm between that ideal and the probabilities, how do we live our lives with "tenderness," with decency toward ourselves and toward others? Brenton's art gives the only possible answer: it clarifies the question, powerfully.

The whole production in St. Louis surged to that last line. The director, a young woman named Jan Eliasberg, understood the play well: she perceived it as the modern quintessence, sometimes vulgar and violent, of deep, old, prototypical agonies. In fire and flow, Eliasberg shaped the performance beautifully.

Joan MacIntosh, who has grown and grown through a career in Off-Broadway and regional theater, made Judy a near-titanic figure, magnificent in anger, enthralling in despair. The English-born Denise Stephenson, pert and true and quick, was perfect as Sally. Stephenson crystallized the seeming (*seeming*) nonchalance of Sally's generation that sees the snares in marriage but sees no good alternatives. David Little, if not quite rightly cast as Jack, is a gifted and honest actor who created the essentials: the agony in Act One that keeps the conflict from being sheer brutality about a man who kicks his wife into signing an agreement; the desolation in Act Two that completes Jack's pilgrimage.

In that small basement theater-in-the-round, Eliasberg and her actors realized the play as a rite of revelation. Congratulations to the Repertory Theater of St. Louis for giving Brenton's play its first American life—and in such sensitive hands. For me, this production confirmed that *Sore Throats* is a candidate for greatness.

'night, Mother

(Saturday Review, September/October 1983)

If the hoopla about Marsha Norman's new play were credible, the current state of American drama would be better than it is. *'night, Mother* has lately been garlanded with a Pulitzer after lusty cheering by many critics. Because the play has only two characters, is in one long act, and ends with a death, some of its admirers have called it classical and have invoked Aristotle. I envy their rapture; the play itself keeps me from sharing it. *'night, Mother* is certainly better written and constructed than Norman's last New York production, *Getting Out*, but like that earlier play, the new one is fundamentally a stunt. More: I think it has been misconstrued—by most who have written about it and apparently by the author herself.

Getting Out, done in 1979, dealt with an unruly Southern girl, her troubles with the law, and her struggle for rehabilitation after prison. The protagonist was shown at two ages, in her teens and in her twenties, and was played by two actresses. This tired ingenuity, which was embossed with tired candor, camouflaged the fact that the play was not much more than a rehash of a 1930s Girls in the Big House movie. Inarguably *'night, Mother* ad ' esses deeper themes, is less flashy, and has a number of sharp lines; nonetheless it, too, is a device, a stunt, not an authentic drama—and doesn't even fail at being the drama that it claims to be.

The play seems to be about a woman in her thirties for whom life has lost savor and point and who decides to make a quick exit with one bullet: it seems to be a drama of the courage to face nullity, to recognize and reject it. Jessie is a plump, divorced country woman who lives with her widowed mother in the family home. (The dead father/husband was a hardworking farmer. Norman never explains how he left enough money, insurance or otherwise, for these two women to live on without worries.) At the moment that the play begins,

Jessie comes into the parlor-and-kitchen set carrying a beach towel and asks her mother, who is in the kitchen, whether there's a sheet of plastic around. The question is matter-of-fact, as is her question about where Daddy's gun is. She climbs to the attic, gets the pistol, and announces, as she cleans it, that she is going to kill herself. At the end of an hour and a half—by the clock on the wall crammed with doodads—she goes into the bedroom, locks the door, and does it. (The play might have used the same title as the last Norman work.)

After Jessie's calm announcement of intent, Thelma, her mother, goes through recurring stages of disbelief, fright, panic, near-petulance, near-acceptance, and dismay. Jessie just plows ahead through the last ninety minutes of her life, occasionally pierced by stabs of feeling but mostly making careful preparations or informing Thelma of preparations already made, including much trivia about deliveries of groceries, milk, and candy.

The trivia are used as light background for the dark matters that are revealed. Jessie has been divorced by the husband she still loves; her teenage son is a thief and drug addict living on the loose; she has epilepsy as her father had before her. She has had a year's remission of the illness, which apparently is meant to underscore that she is not committing suicide to escape the illness. Neither is it because of any other circumstance that we learn about her life. Why, then, is she killing herself? She is empty. She has been waiting for herself all these years, and " 'I' never got here." Her life is so unvaryingly flavorless that, she says, death will only be like getting off a bus fifty blocks before the end of the line. She is quitting life fifty years before the end because she will be in the same "place" then as she is now.

Despite her mother's increasing terror, Jessie is obdurate. ("You are my child!" cries Thelma. "No," Jessie replies, "I am what became of your child.") At the last, a self-determined last, she tears herself from her mother's grasp, goes into the bedroom, locks the door (so that Thelma can't be suspected of murdering her), and, after a moment, shoots.

Ostensibly we have been watching the last moments of a present-day spiritual aristocrat, a woman who can look on life and death with a judicious eye and can choose courageously, a woman who recognizes desolation and declines to be humiliated by it even if her choice costs her life. But is that what we have really seen?

How can we accept Jessie's statements about herself, her condition of emancipated despair? If they were true, what possible reason would she have had to *announce* her decision, then put her mother through those ninety minutes? She says that she is doing it to spare Thelma the pain of discovery after the event. Is this a rational way to spare another person pain? To subject her mother to these ninety minutes and leave her with a memory of them in *addition* to the suicide? Could a nobly philosophic, privately resolved Jessie really have come in calmly with that blanket, calmly asked for a plastic sheet and a pistol, calmly sit there cleaning the pistol in front of her mother?

In reality what we are watching is an act of vengeance. Jessie is not, as implied, our vicar in a Slough of Despond that possibly threatens us all: Jessie is a case. She is a woman haunted by an illness that may recur, a woman parted from the husband she loves because, she says, he asked her to choose between him and smoking! As for her relationship to her mother, Thelma has said that she got tired of watching her and her father (whom Jessie loved) "going on and off [with their illness] like electric lights." This is the same Thelma who walked away from her husband's deathbed to watch *Gunsmoke* because he wouldn't talk to her.

Add up these elements, and Jessie stands clear as a vengeful neurotic, not a tragic heroine. It's a commonplace that suicides are committed *at* someone, and this play, intentionally or not, dramatizes it. Jessie's last utterance, which is the title of the work, is the last twist of the knife. Instead of a woman quietly exalted by ultra-rational choice and the will to carry it out, we see a woman deceptively serene (as serenity often is) whose life has been made impossible by ill luck and warped values, whose buried hatred for her mother has italicized her despair, who is bent on suicide and who comes in to torture her mother for ninety minutes before doing it. That grim, twisted Jessie is latent in the script, of course, or she couldn't be perceived, but Norman, deliberately or unwittingly, has chosen to present her as a rustic female samurai who speaks implicitly to the residual nobility in us all.

Thelma, too, is contradictorily drawn. From Moment One she is almost a caricature of a self-centered old baby, with no more brain than she needs to make hot chocolate and watch TV. And what does this silly old woman do when she hears her daughter's suicide plan? She plunges into deterrent chat with her, in domestic light-comedy style. Instead of the hysteria we might expect from this dodo, instead of the screaming or fainting or struggle or even a transparent ruse to get the gun, she casts herself as a partner in a "clever" cat-and-mouse duet, as if she were accustomed to such crises and were competent in them. When she sees deterrence failing, she thinks more of the threat to herself than to Jessie, the disturbance of her cozy life, and in childish pique, she makes a mess—she throws pots on the floor. Thelma's actions result not from the complexities of character but from the traffic-management of a character by an author to make the play possible.

That is the pervasive flaw of the whole play: manipulation. To put it another way, if the play were true—to Norman's characters as she wants us to think of them—it wouldn't exist. Either Jessie would shoot herself before it begins or as soon as she discloses her plans, Thelma would collapse. Thus, though 'night, Mother is more subtle than Getting Out, it is at bottom equally a stunt, a contrivance, the author's tyrannical governance of characters in order to flesh out a gimmicky framework: the suicide announcement at the start and the pistol shot at the finish.

Thelma's one impeccable line comes right after the shot. Against the locked bedroom door she sobs: "Forgive me. I thought you were mine." The drama that really leads to that line—of a clawing Electra complex, of the mother's mirror-image hatreds, and of pity overarching both—has not been written.

Books

Memoirs*

(Saturday Review, November 1, 1975)

"This book is a sort of catharsis of puritanical guilt feelings, I suppose." That may be the statement least expected in a memoir by Tennessee Williams. He is the first dramatist in American history whose work is closely associated with the theme of sexuality—not love or marital problems, but the musk of sexuality. It is strange to remember now, in the light of the last decade's rapid changes, how hot and scandalous his earlier plays seemed to many in this country and around the world. Yet their author now tells us that he has puritanical guilts that need to be purged. From our point of view, looking at the man through the works, this purge mostly consists of confirmation that, until quite recently, his plays were heterosexual metaphors for homosexual experience. A good deal of the book reads something like the memoir that, say, Proust might have written about the young men on whom he based Albertine.

To put it more ironically, more bitterly, the book suggests to one reader that if the present freedoms both in America generally and in the American theater had existed when Williams was beginning, his life and his career could have been very different. If the frankness of his recent Small Craft Warnings had been possible when he was writing A Streetcar Named Desire and Sweet Bird of Youth, those plays would probably have been other than what they are. I don't assume they would have been better: metaphor is not necessarily falsification, and it's not smug to point out that anguish is where some artists need to live. Nevertheless many of Williams's plays would have been different, and not only would this book have been different—it might not have been necessary.

I must not imply that the only way to read these memoirs is as a key to his works. There is a great deal in them besides that, and anyway Williams often tells us explicitly in the book how he transformed some of his experiences, sexual and otherwise, into his plays and other writings. Some of his fiction was un-

*Published by Doubleday.

disguised from the beginning, like his lovely allegory "One Arm," about a kind of homosexual martyr, which was published in 1948. But, as he says, the center of his career has been the theater, and his plays did have to be disguised; the truth behind those disguises, the truth of his life in a society that enforced those disguises, is the primary substance of this book.

It is the story of an agonized life, though it is not a complete story and is not agonized in any neatly pathetic way. Williams tells us that this "thing," which is what he calls the book, was undertaken for money and was written in "something like the process of 'free association' which I learned to practice in my several periods of psychoanalysis." His recollections are interwoven with interludes from the "present," when he has passed his self-styled "stoned age" of the Sixties, during which his aggravated drinking and drugging almost killed him. Those latter-day passages, with their anxieties and exhibitionism and vapidities, only heighten the pathos, the sense that we are reading the remembrances of a wounded and exhausted artist, frightened of sterility and critical judgment yet needing to keep risking both.

As chronicle, the book is irregular, capricious, and occasionally inaccurate, even about details of his own career. (You Touched Me! was produced in 1945, not 1946.) But there is a lot of detail, personal and professional, and most of it fascinating. (And there is a fine gallery of 144 photographs, personal and professional.)

His relations with his family—his father, who lost part of his ear in a poker game fight, his mother ("a little Prussian officer in drag"), and his beloved sister, who had a lobotomy in the Thirties—will doubtless provide rich lodes for psychoanalysts, especially amateurs. Much more rewarding than such analysis, which, ex post facto, can do little more than prove that Williams ought to have had different parents in a different world, is our perception of his life with these people and with others as bruises and embraces through which he tried to make his way toward self and possibility.

The professional life began early: he sold his first story (to Weird Tales!) when he was sixteen. Even before his college years he began to think of himself as a writer. And that is the most compelling, the most affecting element in the book: the totality with which he committed himself to writing, the complete subscription to art, the willingness to take risks—within himself and in the world—for an artist's life, the complete absence of cagey self-protection or of careerism in anything like a crass, maneuvering way. Through several kinds of hell, some of them made by himself, all he has really wanted to do is to write well; and, under some present patches of calm, he is desperately afraid that he has badly harmed his gifts. After the première of In the Bar of a Tokyo Hotel, in 1969, his mother said to him, "Tom, it's time for you to find another occupation now." But he insists: "If there are stop signs ahead, they are not yet visible enough for me to stop going on. . . ." (Incidentally, he tells us how he chose the name Tennessee—his family antecedents—but not why he changed his given name, Thomas.)

The story of his sexual life, of which there is plenty, is much like what we would expect an account of homosexuality to be now: boastful, scheming, ecstatic, cruel, gleeful, and defiant. He had one heterosexual affair in college; after that, males only. He had one affair that lasted fourteen years, but for the most part it has been the "conventional" busy gay life. Rightly he puts quotation marks around *gay*, too. He has had his beatings and violent quarrels; he has had the heartbreak, and he has the grinning exhibitionism. (". . . I no sooner had him in my arms for the ostensible motive of dancing than I began to kiss him and paste my pelvis to his.")

The sexual history is relevant to his work in more than the substantive factual way, in at least one conceptual way. Williams is vulnerable to the inflation of vocabulary that sometimes afflicts the homosexual writer, and this inflation can be seen even through the heterosexual disguises in his plays. The sheer itch for sex is occasionally poeticized into "loneliness" and "love" at various pseudo-spiritual levels. Writing about the love poems of Cavafy, the great Greek homosexual poet, Walter Kaiser said: "The one emotion most conspicuously absent from them is precisely that of love. . . . His subject is pure sexual longing and fulfillment in a world of *louches* cafés and sordid beds. . . ." Emphasizing that my intent is clarity, not censure, I think the same can often be said of Williams. This aggrandizement is less likely with heterosexual writers because their conduct, however libertine, is more generally accepted.

Winding through the book, and obviously connected psychosomatically with his sexual and professional lives, is the astonishingly miserable story of Williams's health. As a small boy he had "diptheria with complications. It lasted a year, was nearly fatal, and changed my nature as drastically as it did my physical health." All his life he has had cardiovascular trouble. He had three operations for cataracts between the ages of twenty-nine and thirty-four. He had a dangerously delayed intestinal operation. He has often been hospitalized, for everything from sheer fatigue to suspicion of hepatitis. He has even had an operation for suspected cancer of the breast—in Bangkok, of all places. And, inevitably, his chaotic drinking and drugging led him to the violent ward of a hospital, an incident he describes like an episode out of Poe. Of course, since he is now sixty-one, this is the story of a man of tremendous vitality.

A life like his must include paradoxes and laughs and horrors. After his first play closed out of town, he had to get a job; he was working as an usher at the Strand in New York during the run there of *Casablanca* when his agent called him in and told him she had got him a writing job at MGM. He once had an extensive meeting with Fidel Castro, thanks to an introduction from Hemingway. He finished *The Glass Menagerie* in a Harvard Law School dormitory where he was having an affair with one of the students. Between the time he signed a contract for the production of *A Streetcar Named Desire* and its première he spent a night in the revolting "tank" of the Jacksonville jail.

He describes people vividly—Carson McCullers, the young Brando who came to see him on Cape Cod to read Stanley in *Streetcar*. He tells us how he rejected Margaret Sullavan twice—mistakenly, I would say—for the role of Blanche. He takes a hard view of the cloying Helen Hayes, who was in the London production of *The Glass Menagerie*. Despite his much-publicized differences with Elia Kazan, he writes glowingly of the director's sympathy and courage.

His critical judgments are more valuable as insights into him than as criticism. Twice he tells us that Jane Bowles, whose special interest was the survival of the estranged and weak, was "the finest writer of fiction that we have had in the States." About his own work he is sometimes less than clear-eyed. He says that *Camino Real* "freed so much of contemporary American theater from realistic constrictions." I would doubt that *Camino Real* has had any kind of large effect, but in any event it was preceded by a number of American plays that tried to fracture realism, including works by Cummings, Pollock, Rice, Saroyan, Anderson—even Kaufman and Connelly.

The style of the book ranges from chit-chat ("the whole bit" and "immortal oldie") to the coy (Cupid is called "that little kewpie-type god") to lines that sound like a middling Williams play ("You know how love bursts back into your heart when you hear of the loved one's dying") to the noble ("What is it like being a writer? I would say it is like being free"). In this aspect of ranging around in style—as well as in views of terror—the book reminds me of the last journals of Strindberg.

Has Williams written a good book? Perhaps not by standards of cohesion, consistent high level of writing, and strictness of selectivity. But his memoirs are much more satisfactory as literature than his recent novel *Moise and the World of Reason*, which tried to transmute the experience of a homosexual writer into fiction. And the memoirs are important: they are the confession of a man who, although a giggling, silly, bitchy voluptuary, is the second most important dramatist this country has produced. No American save O'Neill has been so widely performed throughout the world; no American save O'Neill has touched the tragic as Williams did in *Streetcar*; no American *including* O'Neill has consistently written so wonderfully for actors. In theatrical terms this volume of William's memoirs slips down behind his dramas like a backdrop, imperfect certainly, but providing a perspective against which they must from now on be seen.

*Theater Design**

(August 6 & 13, 1977)

This magnificent book is, first of all, a bargain. I don't understand how this volume is priced at only $49.50 in today's market.** A few details: 631 pages, double-columned; page size 11¼" high by 12" wide; more than 900 illustrations, most of them exquisite drawings made for this book, with five fold-out pages (the author collaborated on the layout); four-color end papers; full cloth binding; heavy coated paper. It's designed for desks and tables, not laps: it weighs twelve pounds. It's a bargain.

Second, it's not about design of scenery but of theater buildings—specifically, the insides where the performances take place. Students of theater history will know that, after Vitruvius whose *De Architectura* was written in the first century BC, the three big works in the field are Dumont (1774), Constant and De Filippi (1860), and Sachs and Woodrow (1896-98). These books are beautiful and invaluable, but they are in effect atlases: collections of drawings and plans of outstanding theaters of the day, with minimal comment, if any. *Theater Design* is a *text*: the many drawings, as fine as any in the above and meticulously accurate, illustrate that text and also are used in themselves as instruments of argument. This book is not a clothbound gallery: it's a history, an analysis, a philosophy, an esthetics, a technical guide. It does not replace the earlier works, but it surpasses them.

George Izenour (pronounced Eisenhower without the "h") has just retired as Professor of Theater Design and Technology at the Yale School of Drama where he taught for thirty years. During that time he worked as a theater consultant (still works as one), and advised on 120 theater-building projects, eighty of which were realized all around the U.S., in Venezuela and in Israel. His inventions—he holds nineteen patents—have greatly affected theater lighting and other theater technologies. To say that he is world-famous in his field is only precise. I've been hearing about this book for years: it was a decade in coming, and a friend of mine was one of the artists who prepared the drawings under Izenour's exacting scrutiny. I expected the result to be authoritative, which it is: I didn't dare to hope that it would be as splendid, as exciting, as it is, with much to reward anyone who cares about the theater or about the cultural past and present of the West and a salient aspect of its future.

The history of theater design in one way parallels the history of the drama itself: it began great and very soon got worse. Like many a tourist, I have stood in the last row of the theater at Epidaurus for the match-box trick. My guide, in the middle of the orchestra 200 feet away (the measurement from the scale of Izenour's drawing), struck a match, and I heard it as if it were next to me. On

---

*Published by McGraw-Hill.

**By 1983 the price had risen to $195. Still something of a bargain.

the other hand, I was at the first night of Peter Brook's *King Lear* at the then-new State Theater of Lincoln Center in 1964 and, sitting in the fifth row, knew that the sound was dying as it reached me. In the first intermission a man got up in the first row of the first balcony to protest the rotten acoustics—and no one could hear him!

This leads to a recurrent polemic in this book, Izenour's war with architects, the contest of the theater consultant concerned with the realization of performance for artist and audience versus the architect interested in the beauty of buildings and in self-expression.

> Theater history shows the essential theater design reforms of the past century have been brought about mostly in spite of architecture. . . . The basic functional aspects of theater design (seeing, hearing and seating), by tradition rarely understood in any age, are even less understood today.

Izenour's first chapter deals with these "basic functional aspects," makes matters vivid with diagrams and photographs, and makes us wonder how such seemingly obvious essentials could have been and still are so abused.

Then come two of the three long chapters that are, to the non-technical reader, most important: a history of theater design, replete with drawings, plans, and photographs; and the superlative chapter, a book in itself, "Chronological and Graphical Development of Theater Design," in which Izenour analyzes carefully, stringently, illuminatingly the design of forty-five theaters from the Colosseum in Rome to the Loeb Drama Center at Harvard. The plans are pellucid, the drawings superb, the result is cultural enlightenment. All the drawings are done to the same scale—1/8" to the foot. They are reduced differently to fit the book page, but the constant scale (a measure on every page) helps us to see what happened and, sometimes, why. For instance, Shakespeare's Theater, conjecturally restored, is followed by the Guthrie in Minneapolis: the juxtaposition is itself a lucidity. (Some of the drawings have their whimsies. For instance, under the Colosseum, rats frisk. Drawn to scale.)

> The intent [says Izenour] is to enrich the total heritage of theater history by recounting failures of design, engineering, and architecture as well as successes. . . . It is only . . . in the context of performance before an audience that they succeed or fail, which is a thing quite apart from architectural design. . . .

Exploding popular myth, Izenour makes clear that the theaters of the past are a quite mixed bag: the bad ones didn't begin in our time. La Scala in Milan has sound and sight traps; Symphony Hall in Boston, acoustically supervised by Wallace Sabine, is a gem. Exploding another myth, Izenour emphasizes that the sciences of acoustics and seating geometries are not newfangled. The myth of their newness was probably fed by the disasters at Philharmonic Hall in New York. I won't quote Izenour's comments on Lincoln Center—other paper may be more flammable than his book's paper—but I'll risk what he says about

Kennedy Center. He indicts the commission in charge for "rushing headlong into architecture" without adequate theater advice, and says:

> What they have now to justify is an architecturally archaic, unrealistically sized, and badly sited performing arts center which the city of Washington, DC, cannot properly support and, because design of individual facilities reflects the past century and not the present one, the nation at large cannot be proud of owning.

He makes his case.

For Izenour, "the Bayreuth Festspielhaus . . . marks the beginning of contemporary theater design." Built in 1876, it embodies the then-revolutionary ideas of that multifarious genius and horrible man, Richard Wagner, who was helped by the architect Otto Bruckwald (Izenour is quick to credit architects where due) but especially by Carl Brandt, the first theater consultant of modern times. The transverse secton shown here makes clear how Wagner concealed the orchestra; how he gave a simple sweeping rise to the audience floor to provide full view and intimacy (for over 1700 people); how the dome on the roof is *not* echoed in the ceiling of the hall, thus avoiding an acoustical snare. Izenour notes that the radius of the first row at Bayreuth and the steep rake for the succeeding rows are about equal to those at Epidaurus, plus the astonishing fact that the whole auditorium is almost a duplicate of a theater building in the Athenian Agora that was not excavated until sixty years after the Festspielhaus opened. This is especially interesting in light of the relation that Wagner (and the young Nietzsche) saw between his music-dramas and Greek tragedy.

Wagner is at the head of Izenour's list of innovators who changed theater design in the last one hundred yers, along with Carl Brandt. The others are the American engineer Dankmar Adler (the Chicago Auditorium-Theater); the German architect Max Littmann (the Weimar Hoftheater); the American acoustical scientist, Sabine; and three stage directors, Max Reinhardt, Jacques Copeau, and Sir Tyrone Guthrie. In the matter of theater design Izenour might want to apply to these men an arresting statement he makes elsewhere:

> . . . in the end, it is only technique in the hands of a genius that effects change. The mutations of genius *change* history—technique *becomes* history.

The third outstanding chapter is on the multiple use of theaters where, with more drawings and plans, Izenour discusses twenty-five such theaters on which he has worked since 1955. He concedes that a few singular performing groups need buildings of their own. Otherwise, multiple use is indicated. Economics dictates it. ("In the United States it is already evident that even the largest and richest privately owned and operated metropolitan cultural institutions are in serious trouble . . . and will eventually become publicly owned and operated. . . .") Technology enables it: electrically movable wall units and ceiling units, lights, seats are available to change the opera house into the chamber theater, even to vary shapes during performance. Izenour believes that the multiple-use theater will be the base of the Western Hemisphere's "own tradition in theater design."

He includes chapters on building codes—the history of theater fires and panics is a subject in itself—on financing, on engineering systems. Two scientific collaborators provide chapters on acoustics. There are chronological charts, an immense bibliography, and three indexes. To keep my critical franchise, I'd better point out that the captions on p. 243 are mixed and that there are some minor errors in the historical charts. But I must also make clear, if it's not already obvious, that I haven't done anything like justice to this fascinating and monumental book, surely a permanent addition to many kinds of libraries and, I hope, to many private bookshelves, too.

Several passions burn in this book. First, not to be easily assumed, a passion for accuracy: Izenour got the dimensions of most of the extant theater buildings, new and old, by measuring them himself. Then there is a passion for his profession, theater design. But beneath that is a root passion: he sees the encounter between live performer and audience—possibly in modes not yet predictable—as integral to civilization; and he sees the task of housing that encounter in a fitting and beautiful way as a challenge to the best that science and art can afford. Izenour is talking about an art *for* artists, and his faith in it, rational and iconoclastic, is strong.

Wilhelm Meister's Apprenticeship*

(August 26 & September 2, 1978)

"Apprenticeship" is concise but not exact: *Lehrjahre* literally means "years that teach." Georg Lukács said that the theme of Goethe's novel "is the reconciliation of the problematic individual, guided by his lived experience of the ideal, with concrete social reality . . . a reconciliation between interiority and reality . . . sought in hard struggles and dangerous adventures. . . ." The word "apprenticeship" doesn't fully convey "lived experience." And it's also important to note that the hero is called William Master—that's what a German sees when he reads the name, and it ought to be in our minds too when we read this story of a young man seeking various kinds of mastery.

I first read the book when I was a drama student because I had heard that it was about a young man who goes into the theater. (Since then, I've kept in touch with it only through occasional snatches of Thomas's *Mignon*, which is based on the book.) I've now reread it for precisely my original reason and want to discuss it only from that aspect: the theater. Its structure, which combines strategical plan with tactical patchiness; its characterization , which is superficial except for the coquette Philina; the English of Carlyle's translation—

*Published by Dutton: Everyman's Library.

someone once said that Carlyle's style is like hearing a load of coal being delivered next door—all these are not my business.* What fascinates is what Goethe has to say about the theater, its practice and its possiblilites.

Goethe wrote a first version, *Wilhelm Meister's Theatrical Mission*, in 1777, when he was twenty-eight; a manuscript was discovered early in this century. He published the present book in 1795, four years after he had been made director of the Court Theater in Weimar. He published a sequel, *Wilhelm Meister's Travels*, thirty-four years later—a gap that is greater than the one between the two parts of *Faust*.

The *Apprenticeship*, our subject here, begins with the young Wilhelm having an affair with an actress in his home town. It's Germany but we don't know where—there are no place names in the book. He discovers that his beloved is having an affair with another man. Two things are important about this discovery. First, it's accomplished by a device that is theatrical in the most vernacular sense, as if Goethe meant to weave the stuff of popular theater into the texture of his novel about the theater. Second, very much later, Wilhelm learns that he was mistaken about the betrayal: this is one of the many presentations of "fact" that are subsequently shown in other lights, like glimpses backstage to show us the reality behind the appearance.

Disconsolate, Wilhelm goes on a journey to collect debts for his merchant father. In another town he meets a company of actors and eventually joins them. In time he plays nothing less than Hamlet. (Much has been made of Goethe's infatuation with Shakespeare, particularly with *Hamlet*: we often see the quotation about Hamlet as "an oaktree planted in a costly jar." What is not often noted is that Wilhelm revises the play for his company.) When the novel is about two-thirds through, Wilhelm fairly suddenly leaves the company. The change, like many of the sharp turns in the mazy plot, is thinly motivated. Goethe strategically needs his hero to move on, so tactically he more or less wills it. "On looking back upon the period which I passed in their society," says Wilhelm of the actors, "it seems as if I looked into an endless void; nothing of it has remained with me." This in a novel from an author who was then running a theater, writing plays, and devising new methods of production!

But before Wilhelm's change of heart, Goethe, through him, sheds some light on what he thought about and experienced in the theater. He gives us veristic details of actors' chat, along with technical details of contemporary stage machinery. He voices what we may have thought a recent opinion that "it was easier to write or represent a tragedy than to attain proficiency in comedy." He asserts the primacy of the actor over production: "A good actor makes us very soon forget the awkwardness and meanness of paltry decorations; but a splendid theater is the very thing which first makes us truly feel the want of proper actors." And more than a century before Stanislavsky wrote, he says that not

---

*A recently published translation by H. M. Waidson (Riverrun Press) is more fluent.

many actors know

> [how] to seize with vivacity what the author's feeling was in writing; what portion of your individual qualities you must cast off in order to do justice to a part; how by your own conviction you are to become another man.

And he pleads with actors for "that internal strength of soul, by which alone deception can be brought about; that lying truth, without which nothing will affect us rightly."

Equally astounding are the ideas about directing that run through the theater episodes. Directing was then hardly a profession in the theater—it wasn't fully established even in 1824 when Carlyle did the translation, yet he uses the word "director." Some of Goethe's ideas are usually thought to have come into theatrical theory much later. For instance, the use of improvisation in rehearsal. The actors do an extempore play while traveling on a boat, just for fun; then one of the group says, "It should be a custom with every troop of players to practise in this manner." Wilhelm, when he becomes a director, put forth principles, still fresh in that era, of careful rehearsal and balanced interpretation: "What advances we should make if . . . we ceased to confine our attention to mere learning by heart . . . Can anything be more shocking than to slur over our rehearsal, and in our acting to depend on good luck or the capricious chance of the moment?" And: "A common error is to form a judgment of a drama from a single part in it . . . not in its connection with the whole."

Goethe doesn't mention Lessing's *Hamburg Dramaturgy*, which had been written almost thirty years before. (Lessing's *Emilia Galotti*, however, is the last play in which Wilhelm appears.) But it seems reasonable to infer that Lessing's central themes were in Goethe's mind: the need for a true and truly German theater, both for its intrinsic benefits and as a unifying, elevating national force. The many references to a feeling of high occasion make an American reader think, despite the fact that Goethe is writing about a comparatively ancient country, of Walt Whitman's call, in *Democratic Vistas*, for a new drama that would fit the new America.

This sense of a new age, new choices, is heightened by the recurrent counterpointing of commerce with the hero's idealistic-spiritual quest. Wilhelm's father is a rich merchant, and Wilhelm's prospective brother-in-law Werner, of whom he is fond, will have a business career. Werner is contrasted throughout to Wilhelm but with no facile mockery, with the feeling that it is a new age for the bourgeoisie as well. "Where then," says Werner early in the story, "will you find more honest acquisitions, juster conquests, than those of trade? . . . May we not embrace with joy the opportunity of levying tax and toll, by *our* activity, on those commodities which the real or imaginary wants of men have rendered indispensable? I can promise you, if you would rightly apply your poetic view, my goddess might be represented as an invincible, victorious queen, and boldly opposed to yours." There is never any possibility that Wilhelm will share Werner's (historically important) enthusiasm, yet he starts his journey into the world on a commercial assignment, and when he has to do business, he does it well. In reply to a report of his, Werner writes: "Highly as I thought of thy powers, I did not reckon such attention and diligence among the number. Thy journal shows us with what profit thou art traveling. The description of the iron and copper forges is exquisite; it evinces a complete knowledge of the subject."

The praise is counterproductive. Wilhelm turns his back on this business talent, on a career that his brother-in-law finds inspiring, to become an actor. It has long been in his mind. An earlier passage: "He beheld in himself the embryo of a great actor: the future founder of that national theater for which he heard so much and various sighing on every side."

Eventually this dream fades for him; he must seek a different "reconciliation between interiority and reality." Nevertheless most of the book and its strongest strokes are about the theater. Wilhelm's avowals ring clearer than his disavowals. Even when he later rails against the theater, a friend of his laughs and says, "Do you know, my friend, that you have been describing, not the playhouse, but the world. . . ?" The theater has prefigured the world for Wilhelm, has been the chief instrumentality in his "apprenticeship" to life.

But, in this revulsion of Wilhelm's against what had attracted him, Goethe conveys, I think, something other than that the theater is one step in a life's journey. Put Wilhelm's rejection of the theater against the fact that this book is by a man whom Gordon Craig called "in many ways one of the greatest of stage-directors," and we can envision that Goethe is giving us one point in a *cycle* of feeling about the theater, a still-recurrent cycle. He is very possibly making us privy to the recurring doubts that he himself had to, and did, deal with. On the threshold of the modern age he sees the theater as what, in our culture, it has become: an art so marvelous with promise and so ridden with debasement that disillusion must always attack, but whose attraction persists because, for one reason (as Wilhelm's friend says), it epitomizes the world.

Because the world itself persists, we continue, despite our knowledges, to hope in the world. Because the theater persists—the world intensified in dream and dross—we continue, despite our knowledges, to hope in the theater. Seeing Theater-Director Goethe in the act of writing this novel, we can take him to be saying that the theater, with its "lying truth," is at last no worse than the world; that "lying truth" is better—much better—than none at all.

Themes

The Theater in New York*

(New York Affairs Vol. 4 No. 4 1978;
Theatre Quarterly [London] No. 32 Winter 1979)

New York has been the theater capital of the United States since about 1825. At that time the population of New York began to exceed the population of Philadelphia, which had been the theater capital until then; and because the theater center of a country is always the place with the largest potential audience, New York forged ahead, where it has remained. But both Philadelphia until then and New York for about fifty years thereafter were capitals in a way different from the present situation. They were the biggest of a number of theater centers, they were not overwhelmingly dominant. From independence until about a decade after the Civil War, theater enterprise was decentralized. There were touring circuits but, more important, most American cities had at least one resident theater company and many of them had local playwrights writing for them—Boston, Baltimore, Washington, Richmond, Charleston, among others, and as the nation spread west and south, St. Louis and New Orleans.

This situation—New York as *primus inter* (something like) *pares*—began to change in the 1870s with the extension of the railroads. Paradoxically, as the farther reaches of the country became more accessible, New York became more and more monarchical. It became cheaper and easier for a local manager to book successive touring companies, complete with scenery (which they had not been able to bring with them before), than to maintain a resident company on a seasonal basis in a repertoire of plays with much less impressive scenery. Most of those new complete touring companies—in 1900 they averaged 339 throughout the country every week—came from New York because most new plays were done in New York, most important revivals originated there. By the early

---

*Some facts and figures in this essay are, inevitably, out of date. To correct them would mean only that some of them would be differently out of date by the time this book appears. I offer the essay as a historical statement—of fact and atmosphere at the time it was written.

twentieth century New York had become much more than a supplier of tours: it was effectively where the American theater was. All the creative minds of the theater worked in New York. What the rest of the country got most of the time were spin-offs of New York successes or tours of New York stars or of European stars certified by New York.

Through this century the number of touring companies dwindled as quickly as films and radio and television ate up leisure time, but—and it's no occasion for joy—the basic situation has remained the same. New York is the theatrical mother on whose dugs the rest of the country suckles. When one talks about the health of the theater in New York, to a still considerable degree one is talking about the health of the theater throughout the country. A great deal has happened in the last twenty years to affect that situation and one hopes that more will happen, but a real and fundamental change has not yet occurred.

Nowadays, however, there is no such thing as *the* New York theater: there are several New York theaters. To examine this influential complex, which is the purpose of this essay, I propose to identify them typologically, then to offer some value judgments, even some speculation.

Places and Kinds

Broadway: It happens that, at this writing, I have been going to the theater in New York for fifty years. My first show was an all-black revue called *Blackbirds of 1927*, incredible though the title may seem today. It was a Broadway show, of course. There was, consequentially, no theater other than Broadway in New York at the time.

By coincidence the record shows that the season of 1927-28 was the (now-celebrated) highpoint of Broadway production: 183 new plays, fifty-three musicals, and twenty-eight revivals for a total of 264 productions. America lived, theatrically speaking, by that Broadway power. Although there were a few other theaters elsewhere in New York and a good deal of so-called Little Theater around the country, Broadway was lodestar and king. The most serious actors and directors and designers aspired to Broadway. So did every play-carpenter. So did Eugene O'Neill. And though Hollywood had long outstripped it as a gold mine, many Hollywood persons of note, who had not gone there from Broadway success, wanted to come east and have such a success to prove that they were not mere movie people. The professional finish of Broadway was then the highest level of American theater performance. Broadway success was proof of that finish.

Ticket prices were a $3.30 top for plays, a $4.40 top for musicals.

The epitomic New York theatergoer was dubbed the Tired Business Man, but even when it was the active clubwoman or the acclimatized immigrant or the tourist, their relations to the theater were generally subscriptive and self-congratulatory. Broadway was the theater of the middle class, and in that day the middle class was usually taken as the emblem of all kinds of good.

Nevertheless, though these people were the majority of the audience, the range of Broadway was much wider than it is today. For one basic reason, this *was* the theater, more or less: if a play was going to be produced at all in New York—in other words, if it was going to be professionally recognized in America—it had, almost without exception, to be done on Broadway. So the widest extant spectrum of tastes in theater artists and, to some degree, in the audience had to find satisfaction on Broadway: and *could* find it to a remarkable extent because expenses were lower and adventurousness was higher. Of those 264 productions in 1927-28 many were doubtless very middling fare and some, to judge by such titles as *That French Lady* and *Immoral Isabella*, were even more trifling than would be ventured at today's cost level. But there were also productions of *Electra* with Margaret Anglin, *An Enemy of the People* with Walter Hampden, *The Taming of the Shrew* with Basil Sydney and Mary Ellis, and *The Doctor's Dilemma* with Alfred Lunt and Lynn Fontanne. Max Reinhardt brought over his company from Germany in productions of *A Midsummer Night's Dream, Everyman,* and *Danton's Death. Show Boat* had its first production, and the Pulitzer Prize went to O'Neill for *Strange Interlude.*

One index of the flexibility of Broadway is the production of Shakespeare. Through most of the intervening seasons since 1927, it was a rare year that included no Shakespeare; often there were several productions. In recent years there has been none.

Another important and frequently overlooked aspect of the earlier Broadway was the place itself. No other city in the world, with the possible exception of London, had such a showy theater district. One can't say that Broadway was ever truly elegant, but it certainly had sparkle and excitement. (G. K. Chesterton, it's said, walked down Broadway one night in the 1920s amidst all the twinkling signs and remarked: "What a wonderful experience this must be for someone who can't read.") The mere act of going to Broadway had an effect on its public, quite apart from its shows, that was profanely analogous to the effect of the shrines at ancient Epidaurus before that audience entered its theater.

Fifty years later Broadway is still the American theater capital but in a changed situation. First of all, Broadway is down in number of productions and up in costs and grosses. This puts it in a less decisive position esthetically but increases the potential for success of the shows that do get produced.

Annual totals of productions declined rapidly after 1927. By 1938 the annual total sank below one hundred, and it has never again got near that figure. The low point was the season of 1970-71 when there were only forty-six productions. By 1976-77 the total had risen to sixty-six.

The graph of box-office receipts has zigged and zagged dramatically in the last few years. In 1974 the situation was so bad that *Variety,* the weekly trade paper, had the front-page headline: "Theater Is Now A National Invalid" (June 5,

1974). Just one year later (June 4, 1975) the *Variety* front-page headline was "Legit Season Hits Historic High." In 1977 the League of New York Theaters and Producers, a Broadway group, issued a report showing that in 1975 the public had spent $57 million on Broadway admissions and that in the middle of the 1977-78 season ticket sales were twelve percent ahead of 1976-77.

Clearly this rapid rise does not reflect the general economic situation. The drop in 1973 was surely connected with the recession of that year, but there has been no rise in the stock market or employment corresponding to the Broadway boom. Top ticket prices are now $15 for plays and $20 for musicals—one musical charges $25 on weekends—and the hits "go clean" (sell out). The League's report says that the real, adjusted-to-inflation price of a musical ticket is down eleven percent compared to 1972-73, but things in general are not eleven percent better.

I cannot guess at the reasons for this Broadway surge—it's most certainly not due to a substantive improvement in the plays and musicals themselves—and I know of no comment by an economist that helps. But I can cite three contributory factors. First, TV and radio advertising, a relatively new idea, has greatly helped shows capable of appealing to TV and radio publics. (So the electronic media are returning, or lending, some of the audience they took away.) Second, the Theater Development Fund, a body established in 1967 by a group of theater people with funds from foundations and the National Endowment for the Arts, has helped Broadway plays that it deemed worthwhile by buying up blocks of seats for resale at cheaper prices to students, teachers, union members, and other groups. Third, the TDF set up ticket booths on William Street and in Times Square that sell tickets at half-price plus a small service charge on the day of performance—a good way to move unsold seats. (The basement of Gray's Drugstore at 43rd St. and Broadway did the same thing until the Second War—we used to go there to shop for a show to see that night, often for 50¢.) These ticket booths not only make bargain seats for Broadway houses centrally available, they restore, at least partly, the element of impulse to theatergoing.

But the bulk of the audience does not come from these ticket booths: most of it is the same middle class as fifty years ago, allowing for three important changes. First, there are now some middle-class blacks in the group. And of course there are now big Broadway shows with all-black casts that attract predominantly black audiences. (Is the title *Bubbling Brown Sugar* much of a step upward from *Blackbirds of 1927*? The show certainly wasn't.)

Second, that middle-class audience no longer lolls securely on convictions of its rightness. After at least thirty years of various anti-bourgeois attacks, from gentle spoofing to slashing hate, the middle class has not lowered its estimate of itself but is considerably more defensive than it used to be, less reflexively reliant on the approval of the world around.

Third, most of that audience now are college graduates, a much greater proportion than in its antecedent fifty years ago; and they are, or feel an obligation to be, more open-minded on matters that would have been restricted before. Authentic intellectual exploration and esthetic innovation are not among those matters: but liberality of language, of sexual reference and behavior are à la mode.

In the past fifty years that middle-class ritual, the theater party, has blossomed. Such parties existed fifty years ago—my parents were sometimes in them; but they were not nearly as organized and influential as they are today. Now there are businesses set up to organize block sales of tickets to groups in the metropolitan areas, which the groups can then resell at a mark-up for philanthropic purposes. These theater parties are now so profitable that occasionally there is a "Broadway Theater Preview" to allow party organizers to see bits of upcoming shows so that they can advise their subscribers. One hears, and can readily believe, that some shows are designed with the party-public in mind. Pre-première subscriptions are money in the bank—sometimes a good deal of it.

Against all this good news about Broadway must be set some darker news. The expense of production is, as noted, higher, astronomically higher than it was. Fifty years ago a one-set, small-cast play could, with some scrimping, open on Broadway for an investment of $10,000. In 1977 The Gin Game, a one-set, two-character play, cost $250,000. This means that hits are more necessary than ever. Fifty years ago there were occasional productions of plays that were not expected to be smash hits, were just expected to find "their" audiences (as the phrase went) and to run for five or six weeks. No one today would produce a new play with that intent. The play that comes to Broadway without long-run ambition is almost always either at the end of a long tour in which the investment has been recouped or else is a pre-tested British play with famous actors and with its possible deficit in the charge of some foundation.

And the place itself has deteriorated. In 1927 there were eighty Broadway theaters; today, after three recent additions, there are thirty-nine. But that reduction is the least of it. Broadway has become, if we don't want to mince words, a high-crime area. Apart from the porno flicks and sex-act palaces that festoon the neighborhood, prostitution, drug-peddling, and mugging flourish in the sidestreets and adjacent avenues and are not eliminated by publicity handouts to the contrary.

Most of the traffic on Broadway proper these nights is created by the remaining giant film theaters, and most of them cater to young black audiences. These people, whose forbears were unwelcome in the past, are now determined to have their Broadway, and they could not be less interested in maintaining its historical chic.

There was always a touch of the midway in Broadway's brightest glamour: now the glamour is gone and the midway rules. Where Broadway theater-going was once a double experience, of place and play, now it is only the play. Attendance booms: the League reports that in the four years to 1976-77, attendance went from 5.4 million to 8.8 million. But whether they know it or not, it's a changed Broadway experience that those people are having.

Off-Broadway, Off-Off-Broadway: Neither of these theaters existed fifty years ago. There were productions away from Broadway. Downtown were the Provincetown Playhouse and the Neighborhood Playhouse, in East 54th Street was the American Laboratory Theater, and there were others. But the *Village Voice* of January 9, 1978, lists, in addition to twenty-nine Broadway shows, twenty-one Off-Broadway shows, and sixty-nine Off-Off-Broadway shows, as well as two productions in other boroughs. Fifty years ago, even proportionate to the population, such activity away from Broadway would have been unimaginable.

The difference between Broadway and the two other types of New York theater is easy to state. Broadway, by rule of Actors' Equity Association, is the area "bounded by Fifth Avenue and Ninth Avenue from 34th Street to 56th Street and by Fifth Avenue and the Hudson River from 56th Street to 72nd Street." Within that area, or in any theater anywhere seating more than 499 persons, any professional production must operate under full-scale Broadway contracts unless Equity consents otherwise in writing.

But the differences between Off-Broadway and Off-Off-Broadway have become almost impossible to define, least of all geographically. The two terms do not define relative distance from the prime area outlined above nor, though they started as distinctions from each other, are they reliably clear in any other way by now.

Off-Broadway (OB) is generally said to have begun under that name in 1952 with the Circle in the Square production of *Summer and Smoke* in Sheridan Square. The movement was apparently the result of the postwar influx, into both theater work and the audience, of more educated and artistically ambitious people. OB was a mode of production that was fully or mostly professional, that cost less money than zooming Broadway was already beginning to cost, and that would therefore permit productions of new plays and of revivals too risky for full-scale budgets. For about ten years OB flourished: then Broadway producers began to use it to produce shows that were on the Broadway border-line—"almost" commercial. The character of OB began to change from a locus of some daring to a pocket-size Broadway or a place for Broadway tryouts. Partly in consequence of this change and partly because of general rises, OB costs began to skyrocket. In December 1977 an OB musical, *The Misanthrope*, closed soon after it opened at a reputed loss of $400,000. This is only about half of what the loss would have been uptown, still it is very far from the limberness of 1952.

The OB audience is, if one may indulge in sociology by observation, now substantially the same as the Broadway audience. Joseph Papp likes to say that he gave up the Beaumont Theater because of the uptown audience's reaction to his daring choices of new plays. I am unable to note a difference in look or conversation between the Lincoln Center audience and the Public Theater audience or between the bulk of the Broadway audience and the OB audience in general. Most of the people at *The Act* seemed to be the same sorts of people who were at *The Club*.

OB has become so variegated in modes of operation in order to deal with rising costs that some knowledgeable people maintain that, in the 1952 sense, there is no OB any more. Contractually, many productions operate under special letters of concession from Equity, but basically Equity has devised an OB contract with wage scales pegged to capacities and receipts of theaters, from 499 seats and $13,000 (over which salaries must be at least the Broadway minimum) down to fifty seats and $1,500. Theaters with fewer than 350 seats may use non-Equity actors in specified proportion to the total cast. To complicate things further, some OB theaters operate under LORT (League of Resident Theaters) contracts. For example, the Negro Ensemble Theater in Manhattan uses the same basic contract as the Arena Stage in Washington.

Off-Off-Broadway (OOB) inhabits the same geographical territory as OB with the same excluded middle of Manhattan, but it is very much more free in organization and intent. It began recognizably around the end of the 1950s as a reaction against the increasing sleekness and expense of OB, in order to safeguard experiment and reach and to go further with both. OOB operates in many different kinds of places: a few relatively conventional theaters but mostly in lofts, backs of bars, cafés, church basements, converted garages— sometimes the place is simply called a "space." (Henny Youngman has a joke on the subject, of course. Man, getting into a taxi: "Take me to one of those Off-Off-Broadway theaters." Driver: "You're in one.")

Much OOB work is done from scripted plays, new or revived, often highly unconventional. Some of the work is group effort: theater pieces worked out by an ensemble, with or without a director, with or without script or even a scenario, sometimes with a writer to provide words for a sequence that the group has devised, sometimes with improvised words that are recorded and fixed, sometimes with improvisation at every performance.

The audience for OOB is noticeably different, on the whole, from that of Broadway and Off-Broadway. The age level tends to be younger than elsewhere, and the look is generally more (to use an archaic word) bohemian. As far as one can tell from observation, most of the audience at the Ontological-Hysteric Theater would not only not be interested in Broadway hits, they would not be much interested in Off-Broadway hits.

Contractually Equity tries to cope with the OOB situation by providing a showcase contract devised to protect its members who want the chance to display their talents in minimally financed productions. The working conditions are stipulated, and there may not be more than twelve performances over a three-week period, the theater may not seat more than one hundred nor charge more than $2.50. In these cases Equity members may work merely for expenses. One might say that the showcase contract reaches a little upward from the financial floor while the OB contract reaches far downward as the two theater forms intermingle and the union wants to cover all contingencies. But many OOB productions, probably most, have nothing to do with Equity or any other union. The personnel are non-union, sometimes frankly non-professional, and the working conditions are often, one may say mildly, idiosyncratic. Costs of OOB productions are often well under $500.

Institutions and Subsidy: The most neglected fact about the New York theater is that, if it is taken as a whole, most of the work in it is done by institutional groups, not by a management set up for one play and then disbanded but by established and continuing theaters. This fact is overlooked, particularly in the clamor about establishing a permanent theater in New York because: a) very few of these theaters are interested in classical repertory along the lines of the Comédie Française; b) the few classical companies are not very good; c) none of these established theaters is on Broadway, some of them are OB, and the overwhelming majority are OOB. But the statistical fact remains: there is an ignored and staggering number of established theaters in New York. The OOB Calendar, published by the Theater Development Fund, in its issue of Jan. 6-Feb. 16, 1978, lists sixty-one established OOB theaters performing in that period—out of a total of about 200 such theaters.

Almost all of them are built around organizing principles: a theatrical theory or classical repertory or new plays or non-plays or the modern repertory or a particular social perspective: black, Hispanic, homosexual, feminist.

It is common knowledge that one strong reason for the formation of these groups is the rule that only fixed institutions may be funded by the National Endowment for the Arts and the New York State Council on the Arts. (To get the funding they must also be officially non-profit theaters.) All these theaters, as well as the OB ensembles and those under LORT contracts, need and often get such funding. This is not to "expose" either side in the matter. The funders are right not to support one-shot projects; the theater people, many of whom would want ensemble work anyway, are sensible to react to this added impetus to institutional continuance.

In 1976-77 there were sixty such theaters in Greater New York that received subsidy from the National Endowment for the Arts—out of a national total of 181 theater grants. There were eighty-two state grants in Manhattan and nine in other boroughs—out of a statewide total of 138 theater grants.

Judgments and Speculations

The (compressed) taxonomy above outlines a situation that is widely sensed but is infrequently articulated: no city in the world is more theatrically active than New York. Since New York is one of the world's theater capitals, it is still the theater capital of the United States. I do not slight the fifty or so American resident theaters nor the increased activity in such cities as Boston and San Francisco and Los Angeles nor the indisputable national fervor for theater work. I served on the Theater Advisory Panel of the National Endowment for the Arts from 1972 to 1976 and saw plenty of evidence of enthusiasm and commitment from all over the United States. But I can't find reason to change my view that New York is not only the largest American theater center, which no one would dispute, but also the most influential, the greatest source of plays, people, and ideas. I genuinely regret this centralization: the theater in this country would be healthier if it were as truly rooted in many places, as locally responsive, as it was before the Civil War. Despite the hard and often good work in many places, that has not happened.

Why has theater activity increased so astronomically and so variedly in New York in the last twenty-five years? First, obviously, the population has increased and altered: there are not only more people, there is greater ferment. Second, education is more general, and, despite much that can and must be said against its quality, it has had at least some minimal effect on ambitions and taste. Particularly in people educated for the theater, there is increased reluctance to accept the old forms and values. Third, social dynamics of the last twenty years, national and international, stratal and sexual and racial, have found at least part of their outlet in the theater. Fourth, in the aftermath of the huge 1960s enthusiasm for film, which is still strong, some people who were perhaps originally kindled by film have found work in the theater much less expensive, much more flexible.

But statistics are only the groundwork of discussion in the arts. We must move now to qualitative matters. When the lay person asks about the state of the theater, he almost invariably means, "Are there any good new plays and playwrights?" Let us begin with the subject of new plays and then look at other intrinsic factors—in each of our three types.

Broadway: This is the area where, for reasons made clear, the lowest expectations about new plays would apply. Those expectations are well fulfilled. The last new American play of substantial merit and lasting consequence to be produced on Broadway was, in my view, Edward Albee's *Who's Afraid of Virginia Woolf?* done in 1962. Albee himself has written nothing since then of comparable interest, and the American record on Broadway has been—to be generous—spotty. Not all the plays have been meant as mere entertainment: lately, in fact, there has been a rash of plays about dying people, possibly suggested by Albee with his vacuous *All Over*. However intended, the results have been patchy and poor. There have been some American plays by writers who command further interest: David Mamet (*American Buffalo*), Milan Stitt (*The Runner Stumbles*), Ntozake Shange (*For Colored Girls Who Have Considered*

Suicide/When the Rainbow is Enuf). But the only new plays of whole, achieved quality that I have seen on Broadway in that period have been foreign—and not many of them.

Of course this is opinion as is much that follows, but I will not say that is is "only" opinion. It is not glib. Pulitzer Prizes in drama cannot be taken as warranties of anything—*Virginia Woolf* didn't get one, and some of the choices have been ludicrous. But just because the judges apparently often struggle to honor *something*, I note that in the fifteen seasons from 1963 to 1977, only nine Pulitzers in drama have been awarded.

It's possibly even more pungent to observe that the genre which has always been the particular joy of Broadway, the musical, has been dismal in recent years. What show has there been that compares remotely with *Pal Joey* or *Guys and Dolls* or even *The Music Man?* There was some taking, old-fashioned brassiness in *Funny Girl*, there were Zero Mostel's performance and Jerome Robbins's staging in *Fiddler on the Roof*, both done in 1964. But what since of comparable quality even among the gold-plated hits? Surely the score is the chief criterion of a musical. Who can hum a tune from *Pippin?* Or more than one from *Annie* or *A Little Night Music? A Chorus Line* is a biological sport, conceived as an almost anti-Broadway exercise for an Off-Broadway theater and so successful that Broadway co-opted it. It has its pleasures, but a) it is out of—really against—the tradition we're discussing; b) can you hum one tune?

Broadway will survive. When business slumps, some of the biggest producers cry for government subsidy, but boom makes them cocky again. Business sinks in response to stock-market recessions, but it always recovers ahead of the market and employment. One reason for this, I think, is a syndrome engraved in the New York metabolism more deeply than in any other American city. Every night of the week, boom or bust, there is a certain amount of money, *x* thousands of dollars, depending on the economic cycle—that *must be spent*. Some of it goes to restaurants and night clubs and discotheques, and some of it must go to Broadway because that is one of the things that New York is *for*. The hits may not be very good by any intrinsic standard, they need only be the best available baskets for catching some of those nightly dollars, but there is never a time with absolutely no hits.

The press, one can say without any imputation of venality or any need for it, is on the suportive side. The press feels a civic obligation to keep Broadway going. There are always more failures than successes, but this is a long way from saying that the successes have much genuine merit or that they closely resemble what has been said about them. Try the game of circling the adjectives in the theater ads of the *New York Times* on any Sunday. Had you known previously that you were living at the apex of Western culture? Could the figurative Sunday papers of olden Athens have printed such adjectives about the Theater of Dionysus?

As for the Broadway district itself, committees and commissions exist to clean it up. What can one wish them but luck? But what can one believe? Renovation of some small theaters on 42nd Street west of Ninth Avenue goes forward at a cost of $1 million. Manhattan Plaza, across the street from them, provides low-cost housing for 1,700 performing artists, according to the plan. Will these moves measurably improve the area? Did other theater renovations improve it, did the new apartment houses on Eighth Avenue?

It's possible that porno and prostitution and drug trade can be driven to other parts of the city if enough pressure and money are applied and if that is what is meant by cleaning up. The reasons for the increase in those trades are not our subject here. They flourish in all the boroughs, and they flow where the money flows. They gravitate toward the area where there are the most people —O ancient and depressing phrase—out for a good time. And where else is that but Broadway?

I can imagine one treatment, not a solution, of the situation: a Broadway of the future that has the attributes, architecturally and communally, of a shopping mall. (With, of course, underground parking, like Lincoln Center. The municipal garage is now as essential to a city as a major church or cathedral used to be.) Imagine it. A wide pedestrian thoroughfare, building to building, with big film theaters for those to whom moviegoing still entails spatial ecstasy, with large show-shops for musicals, medium show-shops for Neil Simon and his brethren, and a few smaller show-shops for the occasional relative risk; with carefully supervised porno nests and sex shops in the sidestreets, like Hamburg and Amsterdam; and with little nooks and crannies, imaginatively planned, where pushers can murmur as one passes (as they now do out of grimy alleys) "Nickle bags. Joints." Possibly the pushers will be overtly licensed instead of, as they now incontrovertibly must be, covertly licensed by collusion or bribery. All this would at least make a convenience, if not a virtue, of necessity. The shopping mall is already there, fuzzily seen; it just awaits clarification.

Off-Broadway, Off-Off-Broadway: The qualitative situation is very different because, as noted, costs are lower and will remain lower, relative to Broadway, even if they rise. Or else someone will devise an Off-Off-Off-Broadway to regain some flexibility.

A paramount fact about American playwriting is that, because of increased Broadway constriction, the ambitions of the best American writers have shifted to these two other areas. If we compare them merely as fields of activity, OB and OOB are today what Broadway was until shortly after the Second War. Instead of the prolific Philip Barry and George S. Kaufman and Maxwell Anderson and Rachel Crothers, among others, we now have the prolific Lanford Wilson and John Guare and John Ford Noonan and Maria Irene Fornes, among others. These latter people write what they want to write, and though I assume they have no objection to making money if their plays move to Broadway, they have little interest in trimming what they write specifically for the

Broadway market. It is surmisable that some of them, named and unnamed, might be writing for Broadway if its requirements were only as broad as they were fifty years ago, that their virtue is enforced; but whatever the reason, it seems to me indisputable that most American playwriting is now much more free, personal, and serious than it was in the past.

Having said that, I have to add more grim opinion. None of these writers, none of many other writers I could name whose work I have seen—some of them much more than once—has yet written one play of whole, achieved quality and lasting consequence. Play after play, year after year, they "show talent." That is something, surely, but in the long run it is not enough. I am grateful to whatever muse is on duty that they exist, that new ones keep arriving. I have the most genuine respect for their devotion. But, for me, the hard judgment is as I have put it. Only one playwright in the OB and OOB world seems to me to rise somewhat above that judgment, and the irony is that he is the writer I would have named ten years ago: Sam Shepard. His work doesn't conform to any neat line of progress, but in some of his plays there is the electric shock of indispensability. This is what is lacking in the others.

A factor that may help the playwriting situation away from Broadway is the gradual growth in established theaters of the profession of the dramaturg: a profession that is two centuries old in Europe but relatively unknown in this country because, until lately, we have had so few permanent theaters. Among the functions of the dramaturg, who is much more than a play-reader, is the job of finding and guiding writers, new and older. (Often one sees playwrights in their fifth plays as stagnant in their shortcomings as they were in their first.) A talented dramaturg is a boon to a theater. The New York State Council on the Arts, through its Theater Program, has lately made the first grants in this field, providing half the salaries for dramaturgs in six theaters. This program will not "solve" the play problem—there will always be more inferior plays than good ones, even among the sincere—but with continuance, with the right appointments, it can help in a field that has been plagued with wind and waste.

The brighter side of the OB and OOB situation, relatively, is performance. One has more chance there than on Broadway of seeing intelligent risks taken in casting and directon, of seeing more than machine-made productions; and of course one can see theater pieces, unavailable on Broadway, many of which are mind-boggling but some of which are mind-stretching. The worst aspect of OB and OOB is the revival of older plays, most of which are usually outside the stylistic competence of the theaters attempting them. The Broadway slack in Shakespeare, for instance, has not been well taken up in these other theaters. But the general performance level is higher than the writing level.

Admittedly this has been true in almost every period and place of the post-Renaissance theater. And admittedly I don't know of one theater group in New York that approaches greatness with the exception of the La Mama Repertory Company under Andrei Serban, which did stunning versions of some Greek tragedies in the mid-1970s. (This company is now in—I hope—temporary disarray.) Still there are many actors and directors of respectable ability or better working on OB and OOB.

The answer to the lay question about the state of the theater these days is: "If you mean playwriting, overrated. Not often worth the time of a cultivated person. If you mean performance, fairly often rewarding, particularly away from Broadway. If you mean commitment and enthusiasm, wonderful, particularly in the institutional theaters."

General Estimate

Ever since the Industrial Revolution, the history of the Western theater has been the history of schism. Until around the end the eighteenth century, no matter how many groundlings attended, the theater had been the province of the noble and/or wealthy. Though there were plentiful exceptions, this group included the best educated and most tasteful people of the day. From the theater's endeavors to please them, we get most of the so-called classic repertory. Through the eighteenth century an elevated bourgeois taste had taken over, which in itself had dismayed Goldsmith and Goethe, and as the century turned, the audience was further transformed by petit bourgeois and working-class taste. The schism deepened. The minority who knew what the theater had been and, even more painfully, what it could be, a minority working in the theater and attending it, had to fight for those occasional moments that made the long, drab, or merely entertaining stretches tolerable—in retrospect, anyway.

The reason that New York is important to the theater is that there are more of those dissatisfied people in this city than elsewhere in the United States, more in the theater and attending it. But it is not a sheerly numerical matter: it is a chemical one. Many American cities are big—Philadelphia didn't shrink to a village after 1825—and most of them have some theatrical activity; but the absolutely fundamental reason that the American theater is not yet truly decentralized is that there are more of the chemical catalysts in New York than elsewhere. What operates is a kind of irritation, of anger about the theater, even a certain oxymoronically motivating hopelessness. (Beckett: "I can't go on, I'll go on.") The very horrors of New York, its broiling dirty dangerous horrors, discharge some of their animus into theater channels. The very lack of an ethos in anything like an Athenian or Parisian or Madrilenian sense has created a kind of rude ugly center, strong, multifarious, stimulating. The ternary New York theater, as I have outlined it, with its shabbiness and sleekness, its smugness and its sincerity, its crudeness and its hype, and its unswervable minority desperately gritting their teeth for excellence, is a profile of the place. I don't offer the New York situation as a prescription for getting a lively theater; but given the situation, one can see that the theater has burst and slithered out of it.

One should not look at the present-day theater as necessarily an interim situation, a profane John-the-Baptist theater preparing the way for savior-geniuses. It is not past belief that there may never be another titanic genius in any art; the spread of education and the enablement of many capable people may, by occupying figurative space and absorbing ideas, preclude it. It may be that playwriting will continue to "show talent," that the level of performance will give some satisfaction and will only rarely be of brilliance, that our theater will give up the traditional romance of the genius-quest and will exist as a focus for the most honorable theatrical energies of the time. Far from discouraging the discriminating minority, this gives them a possibly stronger reason to keep our theater—our various theaters—at their achievable best, since they at their best are the best we can have and no thaumaturge genius is going to reach down into the useful coal and make diamonds of it.

There is a last paradox. I have argued that New York is important to the theater, but the reverse is also true: the theater is important to New York, important even for those who don't go to it or care about it. Everyone who lives in the New York vicinity feels, shares, the city's atmosphere of power. Its arts are prime signets of that power, and the theater, since it is of all arts the most dependent on place, especially signifies New York's pulse and brawling challenge. All New Yorkers, those who go to the theater or don't, live in a city with a heated theater life, and the force which makes that life helps to make their city great.

Goodbye to Great Careers?

(Saturday Review, September 1980)

What do we want of an actor's career? We often say of a talented actor that he isn't fulfilling himself, but what actually do we expect of him? (Or her, of course.) Because of Richard Burton, I thought about the question during *Camelot*—even with Burton, there's plenty of time to think during *Camelot*—and I'm not as sure about the answer as I used to be.

All of our criteria for an actor's career, which are not quite the same as those for acting itself, derive from an increasingly remote past theater. We remember the adage that great actors are made by the great roles they undertake; we remember some towering figures; and we sigh. But we overlook two facts. First, the great careers of the past include lots of dubious plays and, especially up to 1900, even more dubious conditions of performance. (Famous story about Edwin Booth: he was guest-starring as Hamlet with a local troupe somewhere, and the Ophelia asked him where he wanted her during the "nunnery" scene. Reply: "My dear, just stay downstage of me and six feet away.") Second, old-time virtue is to some degree negative. Until about fifty years ago, there were no lasting temptations for a serious actor outside the theater; until about one hundred years ago, theater itself was practically synonymous with repertory.

Another way to put it: what would Booth's career be like if he had been born in 1933 instead of 1833? How could he have worked almost continuously in repertory in a society whose economics tries to strangle repertory? How could he nurture a national theater audience, as he did by touring so much of his life, in a country saturated with film and TV? What resident company that we have today would be worth the lifelong devotion of his genius? How could—I'd say "why should"—he resist offers to do good films or, if there should ever be such a thing, a good TV play?

The usual examples of modern great careers come from England: Gielgud, Richardson, Olivier. But their lives were shaped before 1945 when repertory work was easier even in England, and they too have since had to pick their way carefully through a society culturally inimical to the highest acting standards. If Gielgud and Richardson now do tiny parts sometimes at the National in London, if all three appear in trashy films, they are secure in the knowledge that they are already classically great and famous. That combination is not so accessible any more, even to extraordinary talent. What lesser known member of the National or the Royal Shakespeare Company, apparently devoted, would refuse the chance of big commercial success elsewhere, even if it narrowed his career? Does this mean that outstanding careers, historically tied to repertory and/or classic roles, are doomed? That only minor actors will stay in worthy companies? That the better people, who go into the glitzier world, can never fulfill their talents?

Most of the American actors who, in recent years, have opted for long-range company commitment, for lives as artists, have been members of unconventional groups like Mabou Mines or the Other Theater. Those ensembles are not concerned with traditional acting: rarely does one see in them a talent that could flourish elsewhere, valuable though they may be as contributors where they are. Outside such groups, for "mainstream" actors, gifted and serious, our culture is fundamentally so full of obstacles, so unconsonant with their seriousness, so seductive commercially, that human pride and ego cannot long withstand the tugging. (Most of us critics who berate actors for "selling out" get *our* ego satisfactions from the berating.)

I do not begin to suggest that acting be judged less rigorously. (That's a laugh. It could hardly be less rigorous most of the time in most places.) What an actor chooses to do, he's responsible for. It's the context of his choices that has changed, and it's this change that I'm trying to understand. In our world, an actor has to fight very hard to work and grow as an artist. I'm thrilled by every actor who puts up such a fight—Christopher Walken and James Earl Jones are two fine examples—but am I arbitrarily to condemn every actor who doesn't? What a lot of good performances, scattered through haphazard careers, I'd be losing.

So when I see the magically gifted Richard Burton in *Camelot*, when I think of what he has done in the twenty years since he was last in the same show, I want to understand how I am judging his career. He could have done fewer cheap films (though two of his worst were classics, *The Taming of the Shrew* and *Dr. Faustus*). But what first-class films do we know that he turned down to do the cheap ones? He could theoretically have returned to the rep company in London with which he once played and could have spent the twenty years there. But then most of us would have missed his work, and a few of the things he has done elsewhere have been spendid: Burton suffers from the facts of his profession. We don't compliment a ballerina for sticking to ballet or a pianist for playing the best piano literature; they don't have much alternative. Where would Suzanne Farrell dance if not with a ballet company? On *The Big Show*? What music would Horowitz play other than his repertoire? Hard rock? In our world, virtue is easier for other performing artists than for actors. And the idea of virtue for actors needs reassessment, unflabby but realistic.

Still, without viewing the matter through nineteenth-century perspectives, I can't feel that Burton had to wander back, after two decades, to this really dreadful musical. (I'm not considering his personal problems because a) they're not my business and b) some actors have had great careers with similar problems.) The sadness I feel in seeing his talent spilled in this enterprise is not because he didn't found and run a Lyceum Theater like Henry Irving, but because I can't believe he ever faced the questions I've sketched above.

About *Camelot* itself, I have no nostalgia; I had not seen it before, on stage or screen. To see it now without nostalgia is, quite apart from Burton, depressing. The score by Lerner and Loewe has two modestly memorable songs, the title piece and "If Ever I Would Leave You"; the rest is failed music box, especially the numbers with two-note themes like "Follow Me" and "The Lusty Month of May." The book isn't good enough even to make a mockery of noble Arthurian legend. Sample line: "He'll stop at nothing to destroy you." Desmond Heeley's sloppily sentimental sets and costumes look like a 1935 Metropolitan Opera revival of one of its 1920 productions. The only other interesting member of the cast is Paxton Whitehead, who is funny as the quirky, club-grouch King Pellinore. The role of Arthur, as written for Burton, doesn't call on him to be much more than rueful, tender, weakly hopeful. It never comes close to straining him; he does it all with simple command, though a shade too abstractedly.

I wish an obvious wish: that Burton had made a great career. When I first saw him in *The Lady's Not for Burning*, 1950, I thought he might do it. I wish, too, I were more certain about how to reprove him for not doing it. But perhaps the abstraction I sense in him is because he's thinking about the future. "*Camelot* is a tryout," he has said. "I figure if I can do a year of *Camelot*" [after New York, the show will play Chicago, Dallas, Miami Beach, New Orleans, San Francisco, and Los Angeles] "I can do six months of *King Lear*." Allow for the inflation of interview talk; allow, too, that six straight months of *Lear* is not the happiest idea artistically; and still we can let ourselves have a hope for the 1981-82 season.

Postscript: The hope was futile.

The Worker—Seen in Plays and Films

(The Dial, April 1982)

The history of drama can be divided in two by its attitude toward people who work for a living. Up to a startlingly recent time, such characters in plays were usually figures of ridicule or pathos or sheer servility. Only in about the last 250 years, which is much nearer to the present than to the beginnings of the theater, have working people been treated as seriously as any others, have they begun to move to the center of the stage.

From Athens until well into the eighteenth century, the great majority of plays concentrated on protagonists who did not need money or who, if they did need it, were prevented by their code from earning it. In tragic drama, only such people were thought to live at an ethical height that made possible a true catastrophe; as for high comedy, it was possible only to characters with time on their hands, time that they had to fill with protocol and intrigue, amorous and otherwise. True, those high comedies about the highborn are almost all about money, but that's a quite different subject from work. From *The Merchant of Venice* to *The School for Scandal*, high comedy is frequently about getting money—usually through marriage—*without* having to work.

This concentration by the theater on higher social levels was the direct result of a social fact. The power center in the audience was the aristocracy and the highborn, who were chiefly interested in plays about their kind. But by the eighteenth century, people of sufficient wealth, whatever their backgrounds, had become as powerful as the highborn; and the rising bourgeoisie, as it grew in numbers, grew in influence. Inevitably, the theater mirrored this change. One key index is a once noted, now obscure English play, *The London Merchant, or the History of George Barnwell*, by George Lillo (1731). This was a tragedy about a young businessman. Seduced by a femme fatale, he steals from his employer, sinks to murder, and ends on the gallows. It had a big effect, at home and abroad. Lessing wrote his play *Miss Sara Sampson* under its example; Diderot saw it as an extension of the drama's territory.

With the Industrial Revolution, social colors altered even further. The big money-earners were, in population terms, out-numbered by the small money-earners. People left farms and cottages to seek work in factories and businesses. The bourgeoisie consisted largely of tradesmen who controlled their trades, whether factories or shops; the new working people controlled nothing except their physical ability to labor, which they rented out when and where they could. As these new earners swelled in number and moved to towns and cities, they became a money bloc important to the theater, and their wishes were reflected in what the theater performed.

In London, for instance, the population nearly trebled between 1811 and 1851. When the major theaters, Drury Lane and Covent Garden, had to be rebuilt because of fire, they were enlarged; and additional theaters were built during the late eighteenth century and the first decades of the next century. The playwrights of the day, especially at the minor theaters, were out to please this new working-class audience.

Their efforts took an interesting new dramatic form. Farce of course continued; farce with lower-class characters was an ancient form. Now came a new type of drama, which, among other uses, was well suited to plots employing working-class characters: melodrama. Credit for the invention of melodrama is usually ascribed to a Frenchman, René-Charles Guilbert de Pixerécourt, who, beginning just after the French Revolution, wrote fifty-nine melodramas (the once best-known of which, Coelina, is now forgotten along with all the rest), was immensely successful, and asserted: "I write for those who cannot read."

Melodramatists like Pixerécourt and his enormous progeny wrote frequently about common people but almost always in a manner that flattered the audience and reconciled them to their hard lot. All through nineteenth-century Europe and America, melodramas were popular with people who knew firsthand that they were not being shown the truth about their lives. Just one instance: Way Down East, an American melodrama by Lottie Blair Parker, was a big hit at the end of the century and was filmed by D. W. Griffith as late as 1920; it was seen by many thousands of farm people, not one of whom could have failed to note that it glossed over the harshness of farm labor. The situation was paradoxical: working people wanted to see people like themselves on stage, yet they wanted their environments made roseate, and they wanted to see their travails rewarded with ultimate justice. This fabricating process apparently reconciled them to their lives, which were nominally being presented ("poor but honest" became their boast), and this reconciliation did not displease the rich and powerful.

But nineteenth-century working-class drama wasn't all melodrama. There were discontents in the world, and they, too, found their way to the stage, though not in anything like the melodrama flood. The Factory Lad (1832), by the otherwise unknown John Walker, is a surprisingly bitter English protest against the unemployment caused by new machines. Friedrich Hebbel's Maria Magdalena (1844), a German milestone in realism, dealt with the agonies of a cabinetmaker and his family. In his preface Hebbel wrote: "One need only be human to have a fate, and in certain circumstances a terrible fate. . . "

This "new" truth forged onward through the forest of melodrama all through the century. Curiously enough, the two giants of the age, Ibsen and Strindberg, never wrote much about working-class people, but many dramatists—Zola and Hauptmann and Gorky among them—took realism and naturalism as a mandate to speak bluntly about the impoverished and the oppressed and the bamboozled.

American drama lagged far behind. It took the experience of the First World War to crack the American theater's resistance to realism on *any* subject. As for working-class characters, Eugene O'Neill led the way with his seamen and farmers. Today, in America and the rest of the West, we have reached the point where the occupations or the wealth of characters is of no significance one way or another. No audience would accept or reject a play just because it did or did not deal with working people.

A force, new in this century, concurrent and overwhelming, accelerated the arrival of our present view: the film. Certainly many films have, from the start, been adapted from reigning melodramas of the day. But also from the start film people have realized that their new medium could make the commonplace fascinating. In 1895 the brothers Auguste and Louis Lumière presented in Paris a program of film bits that included workers busy at various jobs, apparently on the premise that the actions of workers are vivid. And also from the start film people have understood that the new medium would have a much wider and less affluent audience than even the popular theater's public. In the (New York) *Moving Picture World* of April 9, 1910, Jane Elliott Snow wrote an article called "The Workingman's Theater." She said: "The reason why the motion picture show is the workingman's theater is because it comes within the limits of his time and means."

No sane person would contend that films have always dealt faithfully with the lives of working people (Paul Muni's *Black Fury*, for instance, in which coal miners' troubles were simplified and sweetened). But few would deny that, much more than in the theater, the verism of jobs and working conditions has increasingly been part of films. Truck drivers (*White Line Fever*), longshoremen (*On the Waterfront*), car washers (*Car Wash*), textile-mill hands (*Norma Rae*)—one can't begin to sample the occupations that have been rendered faithfully on film. It has long reached the point where jobs as jobs are accepted so readily that they can be used for farce (from *Modern Times* to *Nine to Five*, for instance). And television is now doing the same (*Laverne & Shirley*, for instance).

The result, the grave and momentous result, of the history sketched above is that now the *interior* state of the worker—the person doing work in which he has no ownership nor possible interest beyond his small contributory function—has become a locus for drama. Karl Marx foresaw, in 1843, that the human being thus employed would become what he called "alienated labor." He discerned four components of this alienation: the worker's feeling of distance from the thing he produced; the worker's alienation from the act of work he was performing; his alienation from "species-life," his social essence;

his alienation from his fellow beings. (Obviously, read "he/she" and "his/her" throughout.)

One need not begin to believe in Marx's remedies for this condition to recognize the psychological and spiritual validity of his analysis. Many, many plays and films have dealt with this condition in one way or another. Two examples only: Willy Loman, in Miller's play *Death of a Salesman*, has to plant a few things in his garden before he kills himself just to do something that's *his*; in Paul Schrader's film *Blue Collar* the very boredom of black and white auto workers lessens tensions between them as they join to find some kind of diversion, of escape.

This alienation, this disparity between the inner man and what he does eight hours a day, is what Studs Terkel talks about in the introduction to his book *Working*: "This book, being about work, is, by its very nature, about violence—to the spirit as well as to the body. . . . It is about a search, too, for daily meaning as well as daily bread . . . in short, for a sort of life rather than a Monday through Friday sort of dying." In our culture there is a crushing irony: people are defined by their jobs, and most people don't like their jobs. This irony is now widespread in the Western world; it applies to people in all kinds of jobs, not laborers only.

"Violence," says Terkel. Violence is the seed of drama—and, by natural extension, of film and television. We can see this violence being recognized and used, at different levels, in many countries. The torments of the New York advertising man (in Robert Benton's film *Kramer vs. Kramer*), of the London policeman's domestic life (in Howard Brenton's play *Sore Throats*), of the Bavarian factory employee's desperate emptiness (in Franz Xaver Kroetz's play *Request Concert*)—all grow from that basic violence.

The fertility of that growth has barely begun. The tension between worker and work, which promises to continue no matter what the government or the economic system, opens a dramatic terrain of almost frightening range, of true mystery. The drama, which for many centuries saw working people only as buffoons or instruments, which then for a few centuries exploited them through flattery and indoctrination, has come to recognize Hebbel's percept: "One need only be human to have a fate."

Letter to an Actor

(Theater Communications, March 1982;
Theater International, Number 7   3/1982)

Dear X,

I'm writing to you because I think that you're talented and that you want to make the most of your talent. I don't expect you to return the compliment; I'm not so dreamy as to imagine any actor, pleased though he may occasionally be by reviews, conceding talent and commitment to a critic. Let me concede them to myself: because the basis of this letter, or else there's no point in it, is that it's from one sort of gifted person who cares about the best exercise of his profession to another such person. We both know many actors, and I know many critics, who fall outside that description; they are not my concern. This letter is between you and me.

My subject is injustice—by critics to actors. What's more, it's an injustice that must continue, because it's ingrained in the circumstances of the theater. What's even more, the critic, in the true exercise of his profession, can't let the injustice deter him.

Begin with another art—say, poetry. A literary critic reads a poet's new book and thinks the poet is concentrating too much on pastoral subjects when his real strength is confessional; the critic hopes that the poet will develop that strength. Or a fine arts critic, reviewing a painter's new exhibition, deplores the change in the painter's style and hopes he will return to an earlier mode or find a new one.

Then a theater critic, myself in this case, afer seeing you in a new production, writes about your work in complete analogy with those other critics, as if you could control your career the way a poet or painter does. I write (let's say) that you are appearing in a play much inferior to or too much like or too different from the last one you did, and I make those comments as if you had chosen from a range of possibilites, just as a poet and painter can select subjects and styles. Of course you may indeed have had a choice among several offers or, if not, may still have taken the role eagerly, but we both know that this is far from the flat rule. You may have taken the part for the most human and usual reason that you need money; or because you don't want to refuse an influential director or author or producer; or because you are a member of an ensemble and want to support the ensemble enterprise; or simply because you hadn't done a play in some time and wanted to be visible again; or any one or several of other extrinsic reasons.

I rarely have any real knowledge about any of these extrinsic pressures, but even if I had hard facts in hand, what use could I make of them? "Gifted X is wasted in this wretched farce, but it's the only script he was offered this season." Or: "While I watched X cheapen his emotional power by lavishing it on this squalid melodrama, I reminded myself that his children's school bills must be paid next month." (For "he" and "his," read "he or she" and "his or her" throughout.) What use would such comments be to either of us? When you appear in a play, all a critic can do—must do—is judge your work in that play, bitterly though you may resent the seeming airiness with which he dismisses the stringencies of your personal and professional life.

And it's even more complicated than that, more unjust. You may get a good part in a good play and perform it well, and I can never know exactly how much of what you do is your own creation and how much was evoked and shaped by the director—or suggested by the dramaturg, if there is one, or by the producer's cousin who attended a rehearsal and thought it would be nice if you spoke that last line in a whisper. Conversely, if you are unsatisfactory in a part, how can I possibly know whether or not you wanted to play it differently, in a way that I might have admired, and that you are doing it this way only because of the director's insistence?

Occasionally, in both these contingencies, a kind of triangulation can help, based on the rest of the production and on a knowledge of the actor's past work. Here's an example. One: I thought that a recent New York revival of a great play distorted and bungled the author's intentions. Two: I know from experience that the leading woman is a good actress. Three: I felt justified in inferring that her disappointing performance was attributable to the director. Still, such triangulation is not always possible; and in every case, some of the good or bad things in an actor's performance are not his ideas. I know this, yet must write about the performance as the actor's whole work. Anything else would turn a competent critic's writing into the mess of blather and speculation that most criticism is already.

Often I've subsequently learned a "backstage story" about a production that must have made some comment of mine seem silly to those involved in the show. I can't help it, and can't cure it in the future. There has been a "backstage story" about every production since Thespis, and it has never been the critic's responsibility—or right—to know it. He has to deal with what is presented. Any other procedure would lead to chaos.

You, X, are not a star—not yet, anyway. There are at least a few reasons not to wish you stardom, and one of them is that, as you know, it doesn't automatically solve all the personal and professional problems that I've noted. Only ostensibly do stars have greater range of choice. Their pressures may vary but can be more intense. (Agents' avarice, for instance.) My withers are not drastically wrung by stars with tax problems, but such problems do exist; and so does a desperation to do a new show, so aggravated that it can lead to ridiculous decisions. And probably more than with other actors, the performances by stars that we see and for which we hold them accountable may be the result of committee work. With the star, personal managers, private coaches, and assorted gurus enter the already fuzzy picture. (The word "picture" reminds me of films—and TV. Everything I've said above applies to them at least equally keenly, but there are additional factors, also susceptible of unjust treatment by critics, that don't apply in a theater discussion.)

Thus there's injustice. The actor is blamed or praised for choices that may not have been freely made and for performances that may not be of his own design and may even be contrary to his taste. And nothing can be done about the injustice.

History, said Voltaire, is "no more than accepted fiction." So is the convention that a performance is the freely chosen and personally achieved work of the actors in it. But Voltaire's remark doesn't relieve the historian of the need for integrity and competence, and the fiction about performance doesn't relieve the critic of the obligation to treat the fiction as truth. We must deal with what is before us, not with the reasons, or rumors of reasons, that led to it. The first principle of Wittgenstein's philosophy is: "The world is all that is the case." For the critic, the production is all that is the case.

In the long view, if the critic is conscientious and qualified, justice is done according to his standards. Certainly not all the time. How could theater criticism—of all occupations!—possibly be an exception to the rule of human frailty?

Still, this is not a letter of apology. Those quotations from Voltaire and Wittgenstein, among other reasons, make apology quite inappropriate. I just want you to know that I know I'm only trying to make the best of a far from completely rational situation in my profession, just as you are trying in yours.

Index